Japan's Contested Constitu

From the beginning of the year 2000, Constitutional Research Councils have been set up in both Houses of the National Diet in Japan. The constitution, adopted when Japan was defeated and occupied, defines the nature of the Japanese polity and constrains Japan's military role in the world. The opening of the debate on constitutional reform is set to play a crucial role in shaping the realignment of domestic political forces and defining the international roles Japan may pursue in the new millennium.

As the Constitutional Research Councils begin their deliberations, this timely book brings together for the first time, in English translation, four of the major proposals on constitutional reform. These are the proposals of the Yomiuri and Asahi newspaper groups, one of Japan's major publishing houses, Iwanami, and Ozawa Ichirō, president of the Liberal Party of Japan and a key player in Japanese politics. Hook and McCormack place these documents in their historical and contemporary context, providing a thorough analysis of their significance in the development of thought on the constitution. Subjects covered include:

- the no war, 'pacifist' clause
- the tension between the constitution and the US-Japan security treaty
- the political import of the constitution for Japanese political parties
- the significance of the constitution for civil society in Japan.

Japan's Contested Constitution: Documents and Analysis presents extensive analysis of the evolution of constitutional government in Japan and examines differing interpretations of key clauses in the constitution. It is an indispensable resource for anyone with an interest in modern Japan, its politics, law and its international role.

Glenn D. Hook is Professor of Japanese Studies at the University of Sheffield.
Gavan McCormack is Research Professor of East Asian History at the Australian National University.

Sheffield Centre for Japanese Studies / Routledge Series

Series Editor: Glenn D. Hook
Professor of Japanese Studies, University of Sheffield

This series, published by Routledge in association with the Centre for Japanese Studies at the University of Sheffield, both makes available original research on a wide range of subjects dealing with Japan and provides introductory overviews of key topics in Japanese Studies.

The Internationalization of Japan
Edited by Glenn D. Hook and Michael Weiner

Race and Migration in Imperial Japan
Michael Weiner

Japan and the Pacific Free Trade Area
Pekka Korhonen

Greater China and Japan
Prospects for an economic partnership?
Robert Taylor

The Steel Industry in Japan
A comparison with the UK
Hasegawa Harukiyo

Race, Resistance and the Ainu of Japan
Richard Siddle

Japan's Minorities
The illusion of homogeneity
Edited by Michael Weiner

Japanese Business Management
Restructuring for low growth and globalization
Edited by Hasegawa Harukiyo and Glenn D. Hook

Japan and Asia-Pacific Integration
Pacific romances 1968–1996
Pekka Korhonen

Japan's Economic Power and Security
Japan and North Korea
Christopher W. Hughes

Japan's International Relations
Politics, economics and security
Glenn D. Hook, Julie Gilson, Christopher W. Hughes and Hugo Dobson

Japan's Contested Constitution
Documents and analysis
Glenn D. Hook and Gavan McCormack

Japanese Education Reform
Nakasone's legacy
Christopher P. Hood

The Political Economy of Japanese Globalization
Edited by Glenn D. Hook and Hasegawa Harukiyo

Japan's Contested Constitution
Documents and analysis

Glenn D. Hook
and Gavan McCormack

London and New York

First published 2001
by Routledge
11 New Fetter Lane, London EC4P 4EE

Simultaneously published in the USA and Canada
by Routledge
29 West 35th Street, New York, NY 10001

Routledge is an imprint of the Taylor & Francis Group

© 2001 Glenn D. Hook and Gavan McCormack except for 'A Proposal for the Revision of the Text of the Constitution of Japan' © Yomiuri Shimbun; 'International Cooperation and the Constitution' © Asahi Shimbun; 'Nihonkoku Kenpou Kaisei-shian' ('A Proposal for Reforming the Japanese Constitution') © 1999 Ozawa Ichirō, all rights reserved. Original Japanese edition published by 'Bungei Shunju' 1999. English translation rights reserved by Routledge, London, UK, licensed by Ozawa Ichirō arranged with Bungei Shunju Ltd, Japan.

Typeset in Times by
Curran Publishing Services Ltd, Norwich
Printed and bound in Great Britain by
Biddles Ltd, Guildford and King's Lynn

All rights reserved. No part of this book may be reprinted or reproduced or utilised in any form or by any electronic, mechanical, or other means, now known or hereafter invented, including photocopying and recording, or in any information storage or retrieval system, without permission in writing from the publishers.

British Library Cataloguing in Publication Data
A catalogue record for this book is available from the British Library.

Library of Congress Cataloging in Publication Data
Japan's Contested Constitution: documents and analysis / Glenn D. Hook and Gavan McCormack.
       p.cm.
    "Simultaneously published in the USA and Canada" – T.p. verso.
    Includes bibliographical references and index.
    1. Constitutional history–Japan. 2. Constitutional law–Japan. I Hook, Glenn D. II. McCormack, Gavan.

KNX2101 .J37 2000
342.52'02–dc21

00-062797

ISBN 0–415–24099–9 (hbk)
ISBN 0–415–24100–6 (pbk)

Contents

Acknowledgments ix
Conventions x
Abbreviations xi

PART 1
Analysis 1

Parchment and politics: Japan's living constitution 3

Introduction 3
Origins 4
Contested constitutionalism: the Cold War decades 9
Normative implications of the constitution 20
Okinawa 23
Anti-constitutional radicalism 26
Post-Cold War: searching for new arrangements 29
Revision 34
Conclusion 40

PART 2
Documents 53

Yomiuri Shimbun, 'A proposal for the revision of the text of the Constitution of Japan' (1994) 55

Sekai, 'Peace and regional security in the Asia-Pacific: a Japanese proposal' (1993–4) 92

Asahi Shimbun, 'International cooperation and the constitution' (1995) 129

viii *Contents*

Ozawa Ichirō, 'A proposal for reforming the Japanese
Constitution' (1999): breaking a post-war Japanese taboo,
a current Japanese politician rewrites its provisions   161

PART 3
Constitution texts   **177**

The Constitution of the Empire of Japan (Meiji Constitution,   179
1889)

The Constitution of Japan (1947)   189

Index   204

Acknowledgments

The authors would like to thank the *Asahi Shimbun*, the *Yomiuri Shimbun*, Iwanami Publishing Company and Liberal Party leader Ozawa Ichirō for permission to reproduce the documents included in this book. We are indebted to Chūma Kiyofuku, Llewelyn Hughes, Mizuno Kōji, Nakano Kunimi, Okamoto Atsushi, and Sakamoto Yoshikazu for acting as facilitators in this regard. Finally, Verena Blechinger deserves special thanks for providing up-to-date material on the issues addressed in Part 1.

The proposal 'Peace and regional security in the Asia-Pacific: a Japanese proposal' was first published in *Sekai*, April 1993 and December 1994.

Every effort has been made to contact copyright holders for their permission to reprint material in this book. The publishers would be grateful to hear from any copyright holder who is not here acknowledged and will undertake to rectify any errors or omissions in future editions of this book.

Conventions

The convention in Japan is for the family name to be followed by the given name. This convention is followed for all Japanese persons referred to in the text and for works published in Japanese. Those published in English appear in the same order as the original. With the exception of the place names Tokyo, Kyoto and Kitakyushu, macrons are used to indicate a long vowel, as in Satō, except in the case of Japanese authors whose work is published in English. Since some Japanese authors now publish under their names in the Japanese order, and others use the Western order, confusion may be resolved by reference to the index.

Abbreviations

ANZUS	Australia New Zealand United States
ARF	ASEAN Regional Forum
ASDF	Air Self-Defense Force
ASEAN	Association of Southeast Asian Nations
CFE	European Conventional Force Reduction Treaty
CIA	Central Intelligence Agency
CSCE	Common Security Conference for Europe
EC	European Community
EU	European Union
GSDF	Ground Self-Defense Force
JCP	Japan Communist Party
JDA	Japan Defense Agency
JVC	Japan International Volunteers
KGB	(Soviet) Committee for State Security
LDP	Liberal-Democratic Party
MSDF	Maritime Self-Defense Force
NATO	North Atlantic Treaty Organization
NGO	Non-governmental organization
ODA	Overseas Development Assistance
PARC	Pacific-Asia Resource Center
PKO	Peace Keeping Operation
RIMPAC	Rim of the Pacific
ROK	Republic of Korea
SCAP	Supreme Commander for the Allied Powers
SDF	Self-Defense Forces
SDPJ	Social Democratic Party of Japan – until 1991 known as Japan Socialist Party
UK	United Kingdom
UN	United Nations
UNSC	United Nations Security Council
US	United States of America
USSR	Union of Soviet Socialist Republics
WEU	Western European Union
WTO	Warsaw Treaty Organization

Part 1
Analysis

1 Parchment and politics
Japan's living constitution

INTRODUCTION

Japan enters the twenty-first century with the world's oldest unrevised constitution (*Kempō*). The words of Japan's supreme law remain as when first drafted, despite over fifty years of change through political interpretation.[1] The circumstances in which it was drawn up and adopted are now plain. References in the Preamble to the 'We, the Japanese people' as the progenitors notwithstanding, its key principles were actually dictates from the office of the Supreme Commander for the Allied Powers (SCAP), General Douglas MacArthur's allied high command, presented as a virtual ultimatum to the Government of Japan just half a year after it had surrendered to the Allies in August 1945.[2] In the early months of 1946, Japan was a defeated, exhausted, occupied country, still at that time without any representative institutions. The constitution's three central features – the 'symbolic emperor' system, popular sovereignty, and state pacifism – were non-negotiable demands imposed by the war's victors.

In January 2000, fifty-three years after it was promulgated, Constitutional Research Councils were set up in both the Upper House of Councillors and the Lower House of Representatives of the Japanese Diet. Their purpose is to consider, debate, and in due course make appropriate recommendations in regard to the constitution. The process is almost certain to lead eventually to revision of one kind or another. In view of the inauspicious circumstances in which the Constitution of Japan was born and came into force in 1947, and the hugely different circumstances of today, it is perhaps more remarkable that the constitution has survived intact as long as it has, than that its revision is now being seriously contemplated.

The opening of deliberations in the Constitutional Research Councils brings to a head a process of reconsideration of post-war Japanese history, identity and place in the world that has been building over a long period, but developed with growing momentum during the decade of the 1990s. The momentum to reconsider Japan in this way followed the ending of the Cold War and the Gulf crisis and war of 1990–1. Unlike the dramatic and sudden changes in Eastern Europe and the Soviet Union symbolized by the collapse of the Berlin Wall and the break-up of the West's nuclear antagonist throughout the Cold War period, in

4   *Japan's contested constitution*

Japan change only began to gather momentum after a prolonged period of unravelling, fatigue and uncertainty, during which the framework and direction imposed by Cold War politics and the growth economy dissolved slowly. The call on Japan to make a military contribution to the resolution of the Gulf War made the search for a new way forward all the more imperative, but it was only when it was clear that old ways no longer worked that the national debate slowly turned to focus on the options available for Japan in the emerging new world order.

Constitutions are statements of the *raison d'être* of states and nations. Written or unwritten, they define the balance of powers and duties between states, their parliaments, courts, governments, bureaucracies and armies, on the one hand, and their subjects, citizens, peoples or civil societies, on the other. Inevitably, they reflect the time of their conception and, so long as no absolute statement of the ideal mode of government is forthcoming, constitutions are bound to change.

The Japanese constitutional debate involves the three issues which may be described as 'classic' in constitutional theory – location of sovereignty, division of powers, and definition of the rights and duties of citizens and state. What is distinctive if not unique about the Constitution of Japan, however, is that it also involves a fourth issue, the declaration of state orientation (as pacifist or, more precisely, antimilitarist), as stated in Article 9. Much of the debate has revolved, and still revolves, on this matter.

Parties to the debate include those who insist on strict and literal interpretation, especially of Article 9 (constitutionalists, or advocates of *goken*), those who favor outright revision, commonly with Article 9 most prominently in their sights (revisionists, or advocates of *kaiken*), those who resile from the strict literal interpretation but prefer continuing the practice of the past half-century rather than actual revision, believing that it is enough to change the interpretation, not the words (advocates of k*aishaku kaiken*), as well as those who would retain the words and their literal meaning, but resolve the many problems surrounding them by passing various supplementary legislation (creative constitutionalists, or proponents of *sōken*). While the line between *kaishaku kaiken* and *sōken* may be blurred in practice, now many, but not all of these, have come together in a new category – those who, irrespective of their position, favor constitutional debate (*ronken*).

ORIGINS

Before the present constitution was promulgated in November 1946 and then came into force in May 1947, Japan was governed under the Imperial Constitution of 1889, often known as the 'Meiji Constitution' after the era (1868–1912) of its birth. Sovereignty then was plainly in the hands of the Emperor, who claimed to rule by divine right. He held supreme power, while all popular rights were circumscribed and the duty of people to serve and obey him was absolute, despite periods when in practice a government responsible to a Diet elected on a limited franchise managed most of the affairs of state. In sharp contrast, the post-war constitution of 1947 proclaimed the sovereignty of the people, defined a set of unequivocal rights, established formal separation of powers and also a strict separation of state and religion, and declared pacifism to be a central policy of the Japanese state.

The constitution was born of a week's intensive brainstorming by a specially appointed panel at the direction of General MacArthur. Not one Japanese was on this committee. The guidelines under which it operated were clear: the Emperor must be retained – he had been assigned an especially important role in United States planning and therefore was to be given immunity from prosecution as a war criminal; Japan must not be allowed to possess any armed forces; and 'feudalism' had to be abolished.[3] Once drafted, the document was handed to the Japanese Cabinet of Prime Minister Shidehara Kijūrō and published in March 1946. Paradoxically for a document which was to establish democracy in Japan, it came accompanied by a special Rescript from the Emperor *ordering* change, commanding that 'the constitution of our empire be revised drastically upon the basis of the general will of the people and the principle of respect for fundamental human rights.'[4] Significantly, the Meiji Constitution was therefore not rejected, but revised. The process was characterized by continuity rather than rupture, something that would have been inconceivable in post-war Germany or Italy. The responsibility for passing the Constitution Bill into legislation was assumed by Prime Minister Shidehara in the unreformed wartime (militarist) Diet. The bill was subsequently in some respects revised, and then, after the first post-war, that is, democratic, elections in April 1946, adopted in the Diet in June. Certain territories remained outside the purview of the constitution, however, most notably Okinawa, which was only returned to Japanese administration in 1972. Because of the special problems to which this has given rise, Okinawa is analyzed separately.

Symbolic emperor and popular sovereignty

Under the new dispensation, the Emperor was the 'symbol of the state and of the unity of the people, deriving his position from the will of the people with whom resides sovereign power' (Article 1). If the people were 'sovereign,' however, what then was the Emperor? At least he was a human being, as on New Year's Day 1946 he renounced all claims to being divine, a disavowal of the position of the Emperor of Japan as *arahitogami* (god who appears in human form). However, the concession was qualified. MacArthur's stipulation that 'feudalism' be abolished was mocked by the Imperial House Law (1947) under which imperial succession was confined to male heirs, contrary to the constitution's Article 24 (2) on the 'essential equality of the sexes' in all matters of family and inheritance. The 1947 law also exempted the Emperor and his family from any burden of taxation or right to vote, as well as providing immunity from the provisions of both civil and criminal law. Imperial humanity was further qualified by his continuing role as intermediary to the gods through the performance of arcane religious rites and through the preservation of the pre-democratic symbols of his authority, the 'Three Sacred Treasures' (mirror, sword, and jewel) preserved at Ise Shrine.[5] The difficulty of reconciling all this with the constitutional role of an Emperor whose position was 'derived from the will of the people with whom resides sovereign power' (Article 1), under a constitution which forbade state involvement in any religious activity (Article 20), was plain.

One eminent Japanese constitutional specialist believes that the English word 'emperor' has been inappropriate to Japan ever since its empire was liquidated in 1945: 'Without the empire of Japan, there is no basis for calling the *tennō* emperor.'[6] Neither monarch nor head of state nor sovereign (*genshu*), his role is constitutionally confined (Article 4) to precise and limited matters of state defined in the constitution. The matter is complicated, however, by the impossibility of knowing what it could mean to be a 'symbolic' rather than any other kind of emperor, and by his continued performance of the quasi-religious role of Shinto high priest, for which no constitutional warrant exists. Furthermore, this religious role is crucial to the production and reproduction of the privileged notions of Japanese identity central to nationalist discourse, for he is also the ultimate source of racial and cultural purity, the quintessence of 'Japaneseness.' The line between his constitutional and extra-constitutional role is unclear, and his prestige stems at least as much from the one as from the other.

Scholarly accounts such as those of Koseki and Dower make clear that Japanese interventions significantly modified the American draft of February 1946 before it was finally adopted, 'enriching the democratic content of the final text' in Koseki's words.[7] Yet the record is in certain cases ambiguous. There was actually little maneuver on the central points and some of it served to dilute, rather than enrich, democratic content. Thus the substitution in the Japanese text of the phrase '*subete no kokumin*' ('all Japanese') for the English 'all people' (literally all natural persons '*issai no shizenjin*'), which Koseki recounts, served to deprive all non-Japanese citizens of constitutional rights, including those of Korean or Chinese descent who found themselves living in Japan because they, their parents or grandparents, had earlier been mobilized one way or another to serve the Japanese Empire.[8]

On the central question of the locus of sovereign power, the 1947 Constitution's formula was somewhat paradoxical. The strange and unique system which evolved out of the formula has recently been dubbed by Dower 'imperial democracy.'[9] Although the sovereignty of the people was declared, the 1889 Constitution, rooted in imperial absolutism, was not rejected but inherited. Contrary to the idea of fundamental human rights being the 'fruits of the age-old struggle of man to be free' (Article 97), the new constitution was presented as though it were a gift from the Emperor, a revision of the constitution earlier 'presented' to the nation by *his* grandfather; its first eight articles concerned his position and role, and the date of promulgation was November 3 1946, the birthday of his grandfather the Meiji Emperor. Having been granted immunity from prosecution as a war criminal, the Emperor was installed as the center, albeit the symbolic center, of the constitutional system (Chapter 1, Articles 1 to 8), and imperial succession was determined by 'household' rules beyond political scrutiny and in accord with patriarchal lines of descent.

The decision to foreclose the question of war responsibility by granting the Emperor immunity from prosecution laid the foundation for a system of obfuscated responsibility which sent out tendrils throughout the emerging state system, blocking as much as it promoted democracy. The failure of the Japanese state to consider the question of war crimes, once independence was restored to it in 1952 on the coming into force of the San Francisco Peace Treaty, in stark contrast with its German counterpart, followed naturally from the earlier decisions and has bedevilled relations with Japan's neighbors ever since.

Historical hypotheticals are never more than suggestive, but had Japan been allowed or encouraged to deal itself with the issue of war responsibility, the process would certainly have been less orderly, but it would most likely have led to one or other of two possibilities. On the one hand, opposition political forces would have sought the abolition of the emperor system and contributed to a process of attributing responsibility for the catastrophes of war, and to Japan thereby becoming an ordinary state.[10] On the other, however, the strength of support for the emperor system on the mass as well as elite level could well have led to a royalist backlash against democracy and other elements of the 'American imposed' constitution. As it was, the imperial institution survived, because it was central to American planning. This was the first point on which MacArthur insisted. It was long thought that he was swayed by his first meeting with Hirohito on September 27 1945, but the record now seems clear 'that MacArthur had decided to retain the throne – and Hirohito on it – long before the war ended.'[11] In Washington the issue of what to do about the Emperor was debated from 1942.[12] Opinion there was divided, but that later doyen of American Japanologists, Edwin O. Reischauer, urged that the Emperor be given a central role in a post-war Japanese 'puppet state,' as a 'puppet who not only could be won over to our side but who would carry with him a tremendous weight of authority.'[13] The Emperor, for his part, deeply impressed MacArthur at least in part because of his view that the 'Japanese people's cultural level is still low,' they were too 'willing to be led,' and inclined to 'selfishly concentrating their attention on their rights and not thinking about their duties and obligations,' which led the Emperor to think that 'the Occupation should last for a long time.'[14] To MacArthur, such views must have been evidence of his perspicacity and cooperative character, proof of the wisdom of retaining him in office, and either confirmation, or perhaps the original source of, MacArthur's own assessment that the Japanese people were 'twelve-years-old,' as compared to the Anglo-Saxon or German adult who was 'forty-five years of age in development in the sciences, the arts, divinity, culture.'[15]

The insistence on the retention and centrality of the Emperor was the core of the *oshitsuke* or American imposition of the Constitution. So strong was this determination, that repeated moves from within the Japanese establishment to have Hirohito abdicate were rebuffed and resisted.[16]

State pacifism

Immediately after the series of provisions for the symbolic emperor institution follows the most famous clause, Article 9, which declares:

> Aspiring sincerely to an international peace based on justice and order, the Japanese people forever renounce war as a sovereign right of the nation and the threat or use of force as means of settling international disputes.
>
> In order to accomplish the aim of the preceding paragraph, land, sea, and air forces, as well as other war potential, will never be maintained. The right of belligerency of the state will not be recognized.

It is this clause which provides the basis for state pacifism. It is this clause, too, which has long been the subject of greatest controversy, public debate and legal challenge, and around which sharpest debate is bound to focus in the Constitutional Research Councils. Other constitutions, from that adopted by the French republic in 1791, and international agreements, such as the Kellogg-Briand Pact (1928), have outlawed 'aggressive' war, but this one, by outlawing war itself and the possession of armed forces capable of waging it, went much further. Only in the Costa Rica Constitution of 1948 (Article 12) can any real parallel be found, although there it was coupled with its natural corollary, the commitment to state neutrality. By the understanding of Yoshida Shigeru, who was Prime Minister when the constitution was adopted, any war, defensive or aggressive, was forbidden.[17] Japan's is therefore virtually unique among world constitutions in that it enshrines the principle of state pacifism; for many of those who would revise it, that is precisely the problem.

It is hard to gainsay the criticism that the 1947 constitution was originally an instrument designed to serve and suit American purposes. The Emperor was necessary as a bulwark against feared social upheaval or revolution: after all, as the American occupation forces strove to ensure Japan's integration into the western, capitalist camp in the Cold War confrontation with communism, the possibility of revolution was anathema. At the same time, Article 9 was the guarantee that Japan would never again challenge US interests in East Asia or the Western Pacific. As Theodore McNelly later wrote, 'I incline to the view that a principal purpose of Article 9 was the preservation of the monarchy.'[18] These two basic and non-negotiable demands together made up the 'imperial democracy' package.

There is therefore reason to doubt whether such a constitution met either the fundamental criteria of international law or the specific conditions of the Potsdam Treaty: that it be a free and unhindered expression of popular will.[19] That said, however, the level of debate was not insignificant, various revisions were incorporated to reflect Japanese sentiment, and despite resistance on the part of the Japanese elite, the broad outlines of the constitution were widely supported from the start.[20] Whatever its mixed origins, it became a Japanese charter, Japan's '*Magna Carta*,' indigenized during the half century that followed.

Human rights

The legacy of the human rights clauses, in which the dissolution of 'feudalism' was accomplished to meet the third of MacArthur's conditions, has been less ambiguous and more unequivocal. The difficulty in this area has been the doubt over whether all the rights formally recognized have been implemented in practice. People in positions of power in Japanese society have commonly been unenthusiastic about these elements of the constitution, and that lack of respect has inevitably permeated many of the structures of the state. From its inception in 1955, the Liberal-Democratic Party (LDP) platform has included a plank calling for revision of the constitution, and many prominent figures within it have led the movement for revision, being constrained only by insuperable political odds: on the one hand, it was widely supported; on the other, constitutional revision as spelled out in Article 96 required a two-thirds majority in both Houses of the Diet and a majority in a national referendum. On a strict interpretation of the constitution, LDP members should probably have been excluded from holding any public office so long as their party platform was in conflict with Article 99 under which public officials are obliged to respect and uphold the constitution.

Still, the idea of fundamental human rights was clearly included in the constitution, where Japanese nationals are to be 'equal under the law' and not subject to discrimination 'in political, economic or social relations because of race, creed, sex, social status or family origin' (Article 14). A range of freedoms also are guaranteed, such as those of expression (Articles 19–21, 24), residence and occupation (Article 22), and marriage (Article 24). At the same time, the people have certain responsibilities, such as to maintain the constitution's rights and freedoms by 'constant endeavor,' not to 'abuse' them, and always to 'be responsible for utilizing them for the public welfare' (Article 12).[21]

CONTESTED CONSTITUTIONALISM: THE COLD WAR DECADES

It is one thing to declare the Emperor symbolic and the people to be sovereign, ban the possession of war potential, and to enunciate a range of rights and freedoms, but quite another for the working principles of state and society to be recast accordingly. The Meiji state system was clearly authoritarian and the power of state officials subject to few restraints, so that in the new order set in place during and after the Occupation the stipulations and guarantees of the constitution were often contested.

Implementing the 'symbolic emperor' system

In the early post-war decades, constitutional specialists tended to assume that the popular sovereignty declared in the constitution, the limitations on the state powers of the symbolic emperor (and the absolute elimination of any state role) meant that the office was unproblematic. While attention focussed on the encroachments that were being made under Article 9, however, the Emperor's symbolic, extra-constitutional functions were steadily reinforced, and his cultural and religious roles grew to a point where doubts began to be expressed as to their compatibility with popular sovereignty.

Japan is fundamentally different from its wartime allies, Germany and Italy, in that 1945 was an interruption rather than a rupture in the Japanese state. After defeat, and a period of two quiet decades in which the imperial institution consolidated its survival and made a series of concessions to the new order, a process of re-centring the imperial institution in the national life developed. The imperial myths that celebrated the divine origins of Japan were revived. In 1966, the pre-war *Kigensetsu* (commemorating the founding of Japan by the gods) was reinstated in only slightly modified name as National Foundation Day (on the same day, February 11). In 1979, a law was adopted declaring that years should be known formally in accordance with the chronology of the reigning emperor (*Gengōhō*).[22] In 1989–90, various Shinto rituals were conducted on the occasion of the death of the Showa Emperor (Hirohito), and the subsequent accession of his son, despite the proscription in Article 20 of the constitution on any connection between the state and religion.[23] In the words of one prominent Japanese scholar, 'we can see evidence of a union between religion and the state everywhere.'[24] During the 1990s, the Ministry of Education steadily stepped up its administrative pressure to force all schools to incorporate the *Hinomaru* flag and *Kimigayo* anthem at the center of all school ceremonies. Then, in 1999, a new law declared that these were actually national flag and national anthem.[25] Japan had never had either before, although both had been symbols of the pre-war state, inextricably associated with the imperial cult.[26] Also, in 1999, an unprecedented state-sponsored public 'celebration' of the first ten years of the Heisei Emperor's reign was held on the anniversary of his accession.[27] Diplomatically, the tendency to accord the Emperor a role equivalent to king or head of state, and to employ him on various diplomatic missions (seven overseas trips by the Heisei Emperor in his first ten years) strengthened his political function through 'emperor diplomacy' (*tennō gaikō*).[28]

The flag and anthem law, though a very simple one on the face of it, merely bringing Japan into line with common international practice and giving legal sanction to common practice, was not so simple, for several reasons. Among Japan's neighbors the *Hinomaru* and *Kimigayo* are seen as symbols of imperialism, war, and aggression, much as the swastika and *Deutschland Uber Alles* are seen in Europe. Within Japan itself grave doubts were expressed about the propriety of the legislation. The bill was accompanied by a Prime Ministerial statement on how the *Kimigayo* anthem was to be interpreted.[29] The *Kimi* – whose eternal glory the song beseeches – was to be understood not in the sense of emperor as supreme ruler (as the official interpretation had fixed it from the late nineteenth century), or simply as 'you' as it had most likely been known through the long pre-modern history of the poem, but as emperor. The title of the song therefore came to mean 'the flourishing for ages eternal of the Japan which has a symbolic emperor.'[30] Complex matters of history and identity were thus resolved by a sudden piece of legislation, following the briefest of debates, plus a kind of 'papal' edict declaring a new 'orthodox' interpretation. The attempt to resolve things in this tortuous and yet peremptory way was scarcely consistent with popular sovereignty or with the constitutional guarantees of freedom of thought and expression. Both symbols had close links with the imperial institution, though they are not conterminous. The result is that Japan now has dual, and possibly divergent, sets of official symbols, the emperor on the one hand and the flag and anthem on the other. In a country in which the people were constitutionally sovereign, such a law, if interpreted in the common-sense meaning as establishing a hymn of praise to the emperor as national anthem, has been viewed by some as unconstitutional.[31]

The constitutional implications of the new legislation will be contested in the courts. The insistence that teachers and students in all the country's schools be now compelled to take part in prescribed rituals is described as a modern version of '*fumie*,' the ritual wherein suspected Japanese Christians in the seventeenth century were ordered to stamp on 'holy' pictures of those sacred to them.[32] In 1996, a group of seventeen teachers in the city of Kitakyushu launched an action under the constitution's Article 19 (on freedom of thought and conscience) against the forced participation in such rituals. From 1989 (in other words a decade before the passage of the flag and anthem law) the Ministry of Education's 'Outline Educational Directives' (*Gakushū shidō yōryō*) already compelled participation in the flag and anthem rituals under pain of various penalties (including substantial pay cuts). The directives from the Kitakyushu City Department of Education further specified that, not only must all staff and students stand, but that they must sing 'sincerely' ('*tadashiku kokoro o komete*'). This was precisely the same formula used in the 1930s to specify the way students under the Meiji Constitution had to sing the very same anthem as part of their state Shinto, emperor-worshipping education.[33] The Kitakyushu action joined a number of others launched during the 1990s and now pending in other courts around Japan on the constitutionality of one or other aspect of the strengthening of the 'symbolic emperor' system.[34] The actions will run for years, perhaps decades, but the traditional judicial timidity, especially at the highest levels, on such matters gives little ground for anticipating that they might be successful.

As the post-war symbolic emperor system was slowly constructed, the emperor's sacral character was downplayed, but it was not forgotten. The imperial family steadily withdrew from the public gaze save for certain, highly regulated occasions: appearances at New Year audiences and cultural and sporting events, or the issuance of imperial statements ('*o-kotoba*'). The media unanimously employed archaic and exaggerated respect language to refer to the emperor and his family, which continued to feed the slow process of shift from 'symbolic emperor' of a state in which the people were sovereign, to *genshu* (a sovereign in the traditional sense). The more the 'symbol' has been given substance, in other words, the more the emperor becomes 'head of state' and assumes an ambiguous role, floating above the body politic and its constitutionally sovereign citizens.

Moreover, the constitutional right to freedom of speech is in practice of little avail to protect not only the rights of the Kitakyushu teachers and students to their moral autonomy but also the rights of those expressing unpopular views, especially any concerning the imperial institution. Open discussion of such issues is effectively constrained by a combination of intimidation and terror that is known as the 'chrysanthemum taboo.'[35] Given the special position of the emperor in the 1947 constitution, the death of the Showa Emperor in January 1989 had the potential to engender a constitutional crisis. Its symbolic significance was flagged from the start by the use of 'X Day,' the term adopted for the day of the Emperor's death. When the *Mainichi Daily News* inadvertently ran the Emperor's obituary before he actually died, the journalist responsible was fired, his immediate superior was demoted, and a front-page apology was run on two consecutive days. The disciplinary action was published 'in the unambiguous hope that such sacrifices would ward off social censure – and discourage right-wing violence.'[36] The ability of the government to modify private behavior in domestic society through the use of 'mourning' for the Emperor, such that 'inappropriate' or boisterous enjoyment was subjected to 'voluntary restraint' (*jishuku*), testifies to the way that the imperial institution can still be employed in the creation of a 'subject mentality.' In this sense, the Emperor as symbol of 'the unity of the people' can be exploited to stifle citizen democracy, such that the Japanese community appears still to be one in which 'one hundred million hearts beat as one.'

The link between the violence of the right and the emperor has lain below the surface of the postwar political settlement and constitution. The *Asahi Shimbun*, one of the staunchest defenders of the constitution, has repeatedly been subject to attacks by right-wing groups, the bombing of its offices, or violent attacks on its reporters. Similarly, at the time of the Emperor's death, Christian universities such as Ferris were targetted by the right-wing, and the Christian president of Meiji Gakuin University was subject to threats due to the university's decision not to carry out any special events on the passing of the Emperor.[37] In the case of the Mayor of Nagasaki, his public enunciation that some responsibility for the war could be attributed to the Emperor led to a right-wing attack, which came close to ending his life.[38] Finally, the 'chrysanthemum taboo' operates in indirect as well as direct ways, as illustrated by the decision in the summer of 1999 by Polidor K. K, a record company, to block the release of a record album by the singer Imawano Kiyoshirō. The reason: he refused their request to delete his punk rock version of the *Kimigayo* anthem.[39]

At the same time, the workings of Japanese democracy were shaped by the same political force that had introduced the constitution: the US. In order to ensure the continued US military presence in Japan, the election of a pro-US government giving priority internationally to a pro-American, anti-communist policy was essential. After all, it was fear of the socialists gaining power following the 1955 reuniting of the left and right wings of the party, which had split in 1951, that led Japanese big business to put pressure on the liberal and democratic parties to merge as the LDP. It is this party which, except for a brief period of support by the New Liberal Club in the 1970s, governed Japan single-handedly until the election of the Hosokawa Morihiro coalition government in 1993. The LDP soon returned to power in 1994, albeit as part of a coalition government, following the collapse of the Hosokawa and the subsequent Hata Tsutomu coalition governments, and as of early 2000 it was still governing Japan under Prime Minister Mori Yoshirō. The dominance of the LDP from 1955–93, along with the weakness of the Social Democratic Party of Japan (SDPJ, known in English as the Japan Socialist Party until 1991) which as a permanent opposition party, was never able to gain more than about one-third of Diet seats, led to the use of the term '1955 system' to characterize the essential feature of Japanese democracy during these four decades.

While the LDP was kept in power by Japanese voters, US interventions also played a role. Already, during the Occupation, General MacArthur sought funding from the US government to help anti-communists in electioneering. Covert financing of anti-communist, pro-American politicians became established as part of the Central Intelligence Agency's (CIA) work in Japan from the mid-1950s onwards. In the 1950s, up to US$10 million annually was funneled primarily into the coffers of the LDP or handed over to individual politicians. The funds were designed to bolster the political fortunes of the LDP after the creation of the 1955 system. One of the recipients of US financing was a key member of the pre-war political élite, Class 'A' accused war criminal, and future Prime Minister (1957–60), Kishi Nobusuke.[40] Other political parties and media groups willing to peddle a soft line on the US's war in Vietnam also received funding. These interventions continued for at least a decade.[41] On the other side of the domestic Cold War political divide, the USSR similarly is suspected of providing covert financial support to the Japan Communist Party (JCP) and the SDPJ.[42] Given that these parties were confined to opposition, the Soviet funds naturally had less potential to influence the Japanese policy-making process. In the case of the US, the scale of the funding and the CIA's penetration to the very heart of the Japanese political system testifies to the potential influence exerted on Japanese democracy by the dominant power in the bilateral relationship.

State pacifism compromised

Despite the radical simplicity of Article 9, scarcely had the ink on the document dried and the constitution come into force than its contents were regretted, both by Japanese nationalists for its constrictions on sovereignty and by the US for its curtailment of a full Japanese role in the Cold War (or the anticipated Third World War). As the Cold War intensified and the Korean War raged between 1950 and 1953, successive US administrations applied pressure on Japan to circumvent, if not subvert, the constitution by establishing, upgrading and expanding its military.[43] Already in the third year of the constitution, Japan was called upon to mobilize a 300,000-man army to support the US effort in Korea (and a top-secret Japanese coastguard unit was assigned the crucial mine-sweeping operation preparatory to the landings by the US forces at Inchon that turned the tide of the war in Korea);[44] Richard Nixon, visiting Tokyo as US vice-president in 1953, referred to Article 9 as a 'mistake.'[45]

The words of Article 9 notwithstanding, a 'national police reserve' was established in 1950, which in 1954 became the 'Self-Defense Forces' (SDF).[46] Their role and functions were slowly upgraded and expanded, till by the end of the 1990s Japan possessed the world's fourth largest defence budget and the Ground Self-Defence Force (GSDF), Maritime Self-Defence Force (MSDF) and Air Self-Defence Force (ASDF) were of a size and technological sophistication to compare with the defence force of the United Kingdom, although Japan does not possess nuclear weapons or deploy aircraft carriers or nuclear-powered submarines.[47] Throughout the decades of the Cold War, Japan was incorporated within global military (including nuclear) superpower strategy under the US-Japan Security Treaty. If Article 9 was consistent with all of these things, one could reasonably wonder what it might forbid; the answer, at one extreme, seemed to be only aggressive war. In this way, the US-Japan Security Treaty, which was signed alongside the peace treaty in 1951, came to take precedence over the stipulations of Article 9. As we will see below, however, the Article still served powerfully to shape the norms of both policy-makers and domestic society.

Despite constitutional doubts, the existence of the SDF was gradually accepted, especially as its forces came to constitute primarily a national disaster relief force, prominent in the aftermath of floods, typhoons, and other natural catastrophes, and rarely thought of in the context of war. Yet popular support for Article 9 did not waver, and successive opinion polls continued to record overwhelming support for it.

Thus, opponents of constitutional revision were in a majority throughout the Cold War decades from 1955, by as much as 80 percent in the 1980s.[48] Each stage of SDF expansion was undertaken by governments in the face of negative public opinion.[49] Constitutional pacifism was therefore combined with the nuclear umbrella and the US strategy of 'Mutual Assured Destruction.' Public opinion resigned itself time and again to the *fait accompli* of each successive shift, from creation to expansion and widening of the role of the SDF, but at the same time it continued to record support for Article 9. Herein lies the contradiction: the people supported *both* the absolute pacifism of Article 9 and the high and rising levels of military preparedness *and* positive cooperation with the global military superpower.

Throughout the Cold War, the so-called 'radical' or 'progressive' forces, in particular the Japan Communist Party and the SDPJ, were committed to the preservation of key elements of the constitution, while opposition, including but not confined to Article 9, was a cornerstone of conservative politics. This can be seen in the role of Kishi Nobusuke, who was for long head of the Dietmen's Association for Establishment of an Autonomous Constitution (set up in 1955), and of the 'Assembly for the Establishment of a Sovereign Constitution' (established 1970). Likewise, Nakasone Yasuhiro (Prime Minister 1982–7) was critical of the constitution as not reflecting 'the history, tradition, and culture of the

Japanese people,' in other words, as not being 'Japanese.' As a young politician, in 1955, he authored a draft revised constitution and worked assiduously to spread the revision movement. In April 1956 he organized a 'Song Festival for Constitutional Revision' at the Takarazuka Theatre in Tokyo, where the famous Takarazuka all-women acting and dancing troupes perform. The concert, which sold out, included a rendition of the 'Constitution Song,' his own composition. It was later released as the B-side of 'Songs for National Independence':[50]

> Ah, defeated in war and occupied by enemy soldiers,
> Coerced by an Occupation constitution on the pretext of pacifist democracy,
> The plan was to enervate our native land,
> The war had been over for half a year.
>
> Ten long years drag by, but now freedom returns.
> We must make our own constitution to build the foundations of our country.
> If we fulfil our historic duty
> The decision will swell our hearts.

His tactical approach, though not his fundamental position, towards constitutional reform changed in the wake of the anti-*Ampo* demonstrations of 1960 (see later), and he preferred thereafter to focus on incremental change.[51] Inaba Osamu, when Minister of Justice in 1975, declared in the Diet that the constitution was flawed and should be revised. He too participated openly in the revision movement, as did various successors as Minister of Justice,[52] down to the Minister of Justice who in January 1999 devoted part of a New Year speech to attacking the constitution as American-imposed.[53]

The persistence of the gap between government and people on the issue of the constitution was a highly unusual feature of Japanese constitutional arrangements throughout the Cold War. Japan was also unusual in that the government party was the seat of pressure for radical change to the constitution, while the socialist and communist opposition was constitutionally conservative. The position taken by successive LDP governments was fundamentally contradictory: all were committed to revision as part of the party platform, although only some politicians were personally committed to it and even they knew that an actual revision of words was politically impossible. As a result, *de facto* interpretation reigned supreme and they persistently interpreted their way around Article 9. Prime Ministers Kishi and Nakasone were in this sense constitutional 'hawks,' but others were 'doves.' Prime Ministers from Yoshida Shigeru (Prime Minister five times between 1946 and 1954) to Miyazawa Ki'ichi (Prime Minister 1991–3) believed in sticking fast to the constitution, concentrating on economic management, and withstanding US defense and military pressures by gradual and minimum concessions. As the post-Cold War debate gathered force, Miyazawa issued a book opposing constitutional reform and calling for steps to give more practical implementation to the peace clause that existed.[54]

Thinking on both the SDF, and the relationship with the US under the original

16 *Japan's contested constitution*

US-Japan Security Treaty and the revised 1960 US-Japan Mutual Security Treaty (*Ampo*) – which authorized the continued presence of substantial US forces in Japan – was predicated on the existence of a fundamental, extra-constitutional state right. As the constitution could not be interpreted as denying the right of self-defense which was inherent in all states under international law (and therefore both superior and anterior to the constitution), the forces necessary to exercise such a right could not be described as 'war potential.' 'War potential' was defined as meaning only military capacity beyond the necessary minimum requirement for self-defense,[55] and self-defense itself remained flexible and undefined. It was a subtle, if not casuistical, doctrine, whose justification in constitutional theory was dubious. The Japanese state, in other words, was insisting that matters without constitutional warrant could still be legitimate under 'higher' law.

Even as the peculiar combination of 'peace' constitution, SDF military forces, and close *Ampo* security relationship with the US was being installed – a process that, adapting Dower's 'imperial democracy,' might be called 'war pacifism' – its constitutionality was naturally being called into question in the courts. In a famous judgement the Chief Justice of the Tokyo District Court, Date Akio, held in March 1959 that the US-Japan Security Treaty was unconstitutional, and therefore the presence of US troops in Japan under the treaty was also unconstitutional. It was a momentous judgement, challenging the international as well as the domestic Cold War order. However, on review, the Supreme Court held that the constitutionality of acts of government would not be questioned unless there was 'clearly obvious unconstitutionality or invalidity,' and that, although Article 9 banned the possession or use of 'war potential,' US forces in Japan were not *Japanese* war potential and were therefore not banned.[56] In 1976 (the Naganuma Case) the court went further. The judiciary, although empowered under Article 81 to 'determine the constitutionality of any law, order, regulation or official act' took the view that the Japanese division of powers was one in which the will of the legislature took precedence, and declined to intervene, holding that the question of constitutionality of the SDF was a political matter, involving legislative judgement, in which it would therefore not intervene.[57] Judicial challenges, both to the SDF and the Security Treaty, failed. The gap between the pacifist principle of the constitution and the reality, once established, grew and widened, although lawyers specializing in constitutional matters persisted in the view that the government was acting in breach of the constitution.[58]

Once constitutional questions were resolved to the satisfaction of governments, if not of constitutional lawyers, even nuclear weapons were stored and transported throughout Japan under the Security Treaty. In so far as any further constitutional question was posed by the presence of nuclear weapons in Japan, the Japanese government adopted the device of saying it would not ask (and the US would not specify) what weapons were carried on US warships or stored in US bases. 'Pacifist' and 'unarmed,' Japan became a core nuclear war plan country, welcoming while concealing the ultimate 'war potential.'[59] At least one

Prime Minister, Kishi Nobusuke in 1957, took the view that it would not be unconstitutional even for Japan to possess its own nuclear weapons, although this is not a view that commanded much support either then or subsequently.[60] In June 1994, the Japanese government also took the stance that the use of nuclear weapons was 'not necessarily forbidden under International law.'[61]

The revision of the Security Treaty in 1960 proved a watershed in pitting the Security Treaty against Article 9, *Ampo* against *Kempō*, and in highlighting the link between peace and democracy for many on the mass level. Although popular voices were raised in favor of giving life to Article 9 by pursuing a policy of unarmed neutrality – or, more precisely, unarmed nonalignment – the Kishi government forced the passage of the revision through the Diet, albeit amid unprecedented scenes of social and political protest and disorder. The Prime Minister's tactics engendered fears about the future of Japanese democracy. Thereafter, under a 'prior consultation' agreement, the US was committed to consulting the Japanese government before making major changes in the deployment of US forces, but strong doubts remain as to whether the US would consult Japan, and whether the Japanese government would say 'no.' With the treaty still in place, the US was able to utilize military bases in Japan in prosecuting the war in Vietnam and enjoyed the use of bases in Okinawa, which remained under virtually unfettered US authority even after its return to Japan in 1972.

The strictly 'self-defensive' role defined for the SDF when it was established in 1954 was gradually modified. From the beginning of the 1980s they began to participate in what were in all but name collective security maneuvers, to extend their defense line from territorial waters to a 1,000-mile sea-lane perimeter, and to deepen their integration within a US-commanded, regional, and global force structure. In 1983 Prime Minister Nakasone, one of the most committed proponents of revision, declared Japan an 'unsinkable aircraft carrier' for the western alliance. In due course, the 1968 Three Non-Nuclear Principles of non-production, non-possession, and non-introduction into the country of nuclear weapons, and the 1976 ceiling of 1 percent of GNP military expenditure were both lifted, and, by the late 1980s, Japan was emerging as a military power in the region.[62]

Thus, by incremental concessions, courts, governments, and bureaucrats swept aside constitutional objections and declared legitimate and proper the chain of military bases, the nuclear 'umbrella,' and the domestic force known as the 'Self-Defense Forces.' The idea that Japan, still basing its defense policy on the nuclear umbrella, might claim a unique status in global forums as a 'peace state,' or that it might join with its constitutional peer state, Costa Rica, in spearheading a call for global nuclear and general disarmament, was beyond the pale for a conservative policy-making elite committed wholeheartedly to the US-Japan Security Treaty. While efforts were made to behave as though it did not exist, Article 9 was seen by many in the bureaucratic and political elite as a continuing impediment on the military role Japan could play either independently or in the US-Japan alliance.

Human rights

Although the texts of Japan's nineteenth and twentieth century constitutions belonged to different traditions, the ethos underlying them was continuous. The legitimacy and propriety of the Meiji Constitution (1889–1946) and all acts under it was implicit in the way the 1947 constitution was adopted as its revision and extension, and despite the assumed radical discontinuity, actual practice of government and administration was often little-changed. Although expressed in unambiguous language, the rights of citizens were sandwiched in fact between the still sublime and unchallengeable imperial institution, on the one hand, and the precise and detailed regulations of policemen and bureaucrats, on the other. If asked, 'who runs the country?' most Japanese would be inclined to reply, first bureaucrats, second politicians and big business, with 'public opinion' coming a distant last.[63] Despite the last fifty-odd years, the abstract constitutional formula of popular sovereignty would seem not yet to have sunk deep roots in popular consciousness.

The character of Japan's post-war democracy was irrevocably stamped by the fact that the country was governed for four decades by a *de facto* one party government, the conservative LDP; and the bureaucratic-corporate nexus it became enmeshed in has been shown to be inclusive, collusive, and corrupt.[64] Because of this political context, certain fundamental principles built into the constitution, especially those of 'separation of powers' and an independent judiciary, may be seen in retrospect to have been only partially realized.

Although the constitutional statement of human rights seemed unequivocal, in practice the shadow of imperial absolutism and the associated feudal notions of 'loyalty,' service, and bureaucratic right, defined as quintessentially 'Japanese' in contrast with the 'imposed' post-war system, remained strong. The worthy sentiments of the constitution about non-discrimination in political, economic or social relations 'because of race, creed, sex, social status or family origin,' were heavily constrained in practice as a result of the rendering of the 'all people' of the original draft as 'all Japanese citizens' in the document adopted.[65]

Minorities, especially aboriginal (Ainu) and foreign residents, still struggle for the attainment of various fundamental rights. The Ainu people of the Saru River region in Hokkaidō were unable to assert their property rights against the state when the authorities decided to dam and flood their sacred sites against their wishes.[66] Foreign residents make up 1.20 percent of the population of 126 million, or 1.51 million, of whom about one-third are Korean permanent residents. They have suffered a range of discriminatory practices in employment, housing and everyday life. Short-term residents include a range of foreign workers, of whom some are skilled workers from the West in sectors such as finance, but a large number are unskilled, and in certain cases illegal, foreign migrant workers from other parts of Asia. Asian male workers have tended to take on so-called 3K jobs – *kitsui* (hard), *kitanai* (dirty), and *kiken* (dangerous) – in the construction and service industry, whereas female workers often join the service and entertainment industries. Some of these are working illegally, and cases of human rights abuses, especially exploitation of women in the sex industry, have been reported.[67]

Furthermore, three of the most important post-war Prime Ministers, Kishi, Tanaka, and Nakasone, all at one time or another declared their belief that education would be better if the values of the 1889 Imperial Rescript on Education were restored to a central place, in other words, if education served to clarify 'Japanese' notions of polity, sovereignty, and head of state rather than imbue students with a sense of their constitutional rights.[68] As the constitutional debate burgeoned in the late years of the twentieth century, conservative voices calling for a renewed stress on duties over rights were again prominent. Yamazaki Taku is one senior LDP politician who has made his position on this clear. For him, the rights described in Article 97 as 'the fruit of the age-old struggle of man to be free,' are simply matters 'accomplished within the history of modern state development,' which are too many and too much emphasized as compared to duties, which are too few and need to be given more weight.[69]

The constitutional rights to freedom of conscience, opinion, religion, and to freedom from censorship and academic freedom (Articles 19, 20, 21, 23), though central to the democratic system, are all in some measure problematic. In the context of the late twentieth-century crisis in Japanese schools, it is notable not only that homogeneous, state-centered rituals built around the flag and anthem (as noted earlier) have been steadily reinforced, but also that censorship of school texts continues. Ienaga Saburō's thirty-year-long court battle (beginning in 1965) against censorship of his school text-books in Japanese history by the Ministry of Education ended with a Supreme Court ruling in March 1997 that conceded some smaller points but held that the 'screening' of school texts did not violate constitutional guarantees of freedom of expression.[70] No regulation on the freedom of expression has ever been held unconstitutional.[71]

Article 28 guarantees to workers the right to organize, bargain, and act collectively, yet no sooner had the constitution been adopted, even before its promulgation, this right was challenged through the January 1947 order forbidding a planned general strike. At the time, the role of communists and other militants in the labor movement meant that, even more than a strike for rights or the improvement of the lives of ordinary workers, it was a political challenge to the Occupation authorities. Thereafter, both the Occupation authorities and the Japanese government sought to restrict the rights of labor, preferring instead to emphasize corporate growth. The militant union movement of the early post-war decades was unable to rely on much constitutional protection in the face of an attempt to recover from the war by placing greatest emphasis on economic growth rather than the plight of the workers. In 1973 the Supreme Court declared valid the absolute prohibition of strikes by public sector workers.[72]

Despite the provisions of Articles 31 to 38 on civil rights in relation to the criminal law, including the unequivocal Article 38 banning criminal conviction on the basis of confession, these constitutional rights have been consistently sacrificed to prosecutor pressure. Many convictions (and death sentences) in criminal cases were based on 'confessions,' and some of these verdicts only reversed during the 1980s after thirty or more years.[73] In other cases, the courts' severity towards those complaining of ill-treatment by police or detention authorities was chilling: the complaint of one prisoner (an unrepentant labour activist), citing Articles 18 and 36 of the constitution forbidding 'bondage of any kind' and 'cruel' punishments (as well as similar articles of the International Covenant on Civil Rights) against thirteen years of solitary confinement was dismissed by a judge who found such detention 'necessary and reasonable.'[74] The dismissal of this man's appeal also highlights the dilatory, not to say negative, view of the Japanese government in the matter of ratification and implementation of international treaties on human rights matters up until the 1980s. The priority given in the constitution to human rights and international responsibility is hard to square with the deeply conservative stance officially taken by Japan's government on these crucial matters.

Although not strictly speaking a matter of human rights, local government autonomy is nevertheless closely related, since it concerns the rights of local communities against the centralized power of the state. Chapter 8 of the constitution, Articles 92 to 95, spells out the principles of local self-government, but commentators agree that the nineteenth-century traditions of centralism proved tenacious and deep-rooted in the late twentieth century Japanese state.[75] Much of the popularity of Hosokawa Morihiro when he became the first post-LDP Prime Minister in 1993 derived from his pledge to revitalize the regions by a politics of decentralization, that is, to return belatedly to the principles in the constitution of the people's right to organize their affairs at the local level. Little if any progress was made in the years to the end of the century. Renegotiation of the limits of central and regional and local powers is an area which has so far figured little in constitutional debate, but this process seems central to constitutional debate throughout the democratic world, and its necessity, for the sake of the future well-being of the Japanese polity, beyond question.

In a few matters, it is true, the Supreme Court has ruled the actions of the government unconstitutional. Since 1976 it has consistently held the electoral system unconstitutional in its discrimination against urban voters, although declining to do anything to enforce that judgement, taking instead the view that in the constitutional division of powers the legislature was 'the highest organ of state power' (Article 41), and that it would cause 'unthinkable' confusion to cancel the outcome of elections.[76] This judicial conservatism, partly a product of the heavily bureaucratic structures of the judiciary during the long decades of effective one-party rule, has served to give the legislature a consistently privileged position in terms of its constitutional prerogatives.[77]

NORMATIVE IMPLICATIONS OF THE CONSTITUTION

Given the way the constitution has been contested, many of the provisions set in place fifty-three years ago have yet to be fully realized. But, although hollowed out and weakened, the constitution has still provided a normative framework informing, constraining and to some extent molding the behavior of policy-making and other political actors. This is particularly the case in respect of Article 9 and security policy.[78]

The emperor and popular sovereignty

The various official initiatives to 'flesh out' the symbolic emperor into 'head of state' or monarch seem not to have attracted much support at the popular level. The emperor system no longer serves as the core of Japanese identity, as it did in the pre-war and war-time periods. The decline in support for the emperor now means the emperor and imperial household is an irrelevance in terms of national identity on the popular level, except on the far right of the political spectrum. Attitudes towards the emperor are largely determined by age, and the levels of indifference seem to increase with each successive generation.[79]

The death of the Showa Emperor in 1989 confirmed the extent to which, for many Japanese, the emperor was not a part of their lives. While the blanket media coverage and general political pressure to preserve restraint illustrated the continuing proclivity to conform, the pragmatic response of many Japanese, as people from all walks of life chose to rent videos rather than watch the uninterrupted media coverage, showed how difficult it would be to reproduce a role for the emperor as the core of a new national identity.

State pacifism

The hollowing out of Article 9 is plain, but this does not mean that it has been without impact. Most significantly, the normative implications of this clause can be seen in the inability of policy-makers to use the military as a legitimate instrument of state policy. In the early post-war quest for identity in a bipolar, nuclearized world, progressive intellectuals and the SDPJ strove to impute positive meaning into the constitution. In the late 1940s, the 'Peace Issues Discussion Group' and the socialist party developed the idea of unarmed neutrality as their attempt to formulate in concrete terms an identity for Japan as a 'peace state': a state which deploys only non-violent resources in order to realize its interests. Article 9 was thus translated into an alternative to reliance on the US-Japan Security Treaty, albeit one that was not realized. The constitution became the normative source for political action seeking to realize a 'peace state' and to constrain policy-makers intent upon restoring legitimacy to the military as an instrument of state policy. Thus, Prime Minister Kishi's problem, when he rammed the revision through the Diet in 1960, was not just the angry crowds milling around outside, but the fact that the polls showed substantial support for either unarmed neutrality or dependence on the UN rather than the security treaty with the US.[80]

Henceforth, the pressures arising from the US-Japan security relationship to become a normal military state and those from domestic society to become a peace state have constrained the behavior of policy-makers both internationally and domestically. In sharp contrast with pre-war Japan, under Article 66 serving military officers may not become members of the Cabinet. Unlike neighboring countries such as South Korea and China, troops have not been used domestically to put down resistance, despite Prime Minister Kishi's attempt to deploy the SDF against protestors at the time of the 1960 *Ampo* demonstrations.[81] For varying periods during the Cold War the ceiling on military spending and even the third non-nuclear principle had some restraining effect, as did, and still does, the ban on weapons export. Japanese youth are also spared from conscription for armed service. During the Vietnam War, in contrast to other US allies such as South Korea and Australia, Japanese cooperation was only indirect. From their creation in 1954 until 1991, after the end of the Gulf War when the MSDF was sent on a minesweeping mission to the Gulf, the SDF were subject to a ban on overseas dispatch. During the 1990s, the SDF have been involved in other United Nations Peacekeeping Operations, but only with strict limitations being placed on their use of firearms. All of these may be seen as positive fruits of Article 9.

Human rights

The weakness of the constitution at the official or bureaucratic level in protecting human rights has gone hand in hand with a widespread acceptance on the popular level of the universal nature of rights. The constitutional enjoinder to maintain popular freedoms and rights 'by the constant endeavor of the people' (Article 12) is one that has been taken seriously by many. By the end of the 1990s, the Japanese government, under domestic and international pressure, had ratified major international conventions, including the International Covenant on Economic, Social and Cultural Rights, the International Covenant on Civil and Political Rights, the Refugee Convention, and the Convention on the Elimination of All Forms of Discrimination Against Women. It also became a member of the United Nations Commission on Human Rights and set up, within the Ministry of Foreign Affairs, a Human Rights and Refugee Division. The treatment of long-term foreign residents, especially Koreans, also improved during the 1980s and early 1990s as a result of abolition of finger-printing alien permanent residents, and other revisions to the Alien Registration Act. With a view to human rights outside Japan, moreover, the government in 1992 passed an Overseas Development Assistance Charter (ODA Charter), which specifically pays attention to the human rights situation in the country as a condition for the receipt of Japanese ODA.[82]

Furthermore, despite their weakness compared with the other major industrialized states, the activities of human rights groups, such as Amnesty International and the Asia Pacific Human Rights Information Center, point to the popular attempts being made to protect human rights outside as well as inside Japan. A range of Japanese non-governmental organizations (NGOs), such as the Japan International Volunteers (JVC), have become involved in action to enhance the life chances of people in East Asia and further afield. Although the JVC was set up in the 1980s in response to the outflow of Indochinese refugees, nearly one half of all Japanese NGOs involved in international cooperation were set up in the 1990s.[83] The Pacific-Asia Resource Center (PARC) has been active in networking through the publication of *AMPO: Japan Asia Quarterly Review* and in sponsoring visits by activists to alert Japanese domestic society to human rights and development issues in developing East Asia.[84] These NGOs play an important role in the countries of the region as well as in highlighting the issues of human rights and development in Japan.

OKINAWA

There is a further peculiarity of the Japanese Constitution: the differential treatment under it of one particular geographic region of the archipelago, Okinawa prefecture. Nowhere in Japan is the commitment to the principle of Article 9 more passionate and persistent, and yet nowhere has that commitment been more persistently frustrated, as if the government in Tokyo had made it a central policy to deny that will, defeat opposition, and enforce the long-term militarization of the islands by its US ally. Likewise, in no other part of Japan has the constitutional promise of democratic freedoms, human rights, and local autonomy, inspired such hope, and nowhere has such hope been more bitterly disappointed.[85]

Okinawa was a victim of the Second World War through the use of conventional weapons in a way only comparable with Hiroshima and Nagasaki as victims through the use of nuclear weapons. Only in Okinawa and other outlying islands was the land war fought between Japan and the allies, particularly the US. The ferocity of the fighting was unparalleled and various authors have described it in graphic terms.[86] The horror for Okinawa was multiplied by the fact that many civilians there were slaughtered, not by the enemy forces, but by the Imperial Japanese Army. In all, about one-third of the population died, either directly from the violence or from starvation. The resulting hatred of war, and commitment to the principle of Article 9, was therefore far stronger in Okinawa than elsewhere.

The US had determined two years before the war ended that long-term control of Okinawa would be necessary.[87] Okinawans firmly believe that Japan's peace Constitution would have been inconceivable without the sacrifice of Okinawa to American military control.[88] In the negotiations leading up to the 1951 San Francisco Treaty, the Emperor, Hirohito, in messages to MacArthur in September 1947 and again in February 1948 (in breach of the constitutional limitations on his role under the symbolic emperor system that had just been inaugurated), urged the US to continue its military control over Okinawa under a leasing arrangement for an indefinite period, with 'twenty-five years' or 'fifty years' suggested.[89] It was this same Emperor, Hirohito, who in February 1945 had insisted that the war, already by then a hopeless cause, be pursued in the attempt to inflict a defeat on the enemy and ensure the survival of the national polity *(kokutai)*,[90] thus making inevitable the catastrophic Battle of Okinawa that began on March 26 1945.[91] The knowledge that the horrors of war were all carried out in the name of the Emperor, that he personally had sanctioned the Battle of Okinawa and, after the war, had gone out of his way to sanction US occupation of the islands on a long-term basis, are factors which help to explain why the people of Okinawa show markedly less interest or enthusiasm over the constitutional clauses confirming the position of the emperor in the new dispensation. They also help to explain why it is in Okinawa that the pressures involved in imposing the rituals of anthem and flag have been most keenly resented.[92]

When sovereignty was restored to 'Japan' under the San Francisco Treaty in 1951, therefore, Okinawa was excluded, with only residual Japanese sovereignty recognized (possibly following up on Hirohito's suggestion). For a quarter of a century until 1972, Okinawa was completely excluded from the purview of the Constitution, the symbolic emperor system and the constitutional guarantees of human rights. Instead, it was turned into a highly militarized prefecture for the US's use. It was the 'Keystone of the Pacific': the base for the conduct of wars on the Korean peninsula and in Vietnam, and for the deployment in general readiness for global or regional, conventional and nuclear wars.

Okinawa as a 'war state' was the obverse of the 'peace state' elsewhere in Japan. As the construction of the base complex went ahead, people were ousted from their homes and villages, often by bayonet and bulldozer, and forced to derive subsistence existence in the periphery of the bases or to emigrate.[93] Through the long period under American rule, the struggle for a return to Japanese sovereignty was inspired by the belief that the peace constitution would mean a winding back of the bases, confirmation of basic human rights, and a responsible democratic local and national administration. However, after the return of administrative rights over Okinawa to the government of Japan in 1972, the bases remained. Although the prefecture makes up only 0.6 percent of Japan's total land, the thirty-nine US military facilities occupy around one-fifth of the land of Okinawa's main island, and US forces continued to enjoy the same operational freedom during the Gulf War of 1991 as during the previous wars in Korea and Vietnam. In any future 'contingency,' the Status of Forces Agreement between the US and Japanese governments ensures that the bases will maintain maximum operational autonomy, unconstrained by constitutional niceties.[94]

The peculiarity of Okinawa's status under the constitution is also attested by the extraordinary steps being taken by the national government to satisfy the desire of the US for continuance, improvement and modernization of its base facilities in the prefecture. Despite the clear outcome of the December 1997 plebiscite rejecting the proposed construction of a heliport for Nago City in northern Okinawa, the central government persisted with the plan and in 1999 rejected all alternatives and determined to build it. A December 1999 study found local opinion still heavily against this plan.[95] As the Tokyo government promised to pour in 'development' funds and committed itself to conducting the July 2000 G8 Summit in Nago City in a bid to overcome this opposition, few options seemed to be left for Okinawans to protest against the continuing militarization of their islands.

The emptiness of Article 9 in the Okinawan context during the period since reversion in 1972 is matched by the weakness of constitutional guarantees of various rights, most notably those to freedom and safety of the person and to a healthy and good life, since the bases function as virtual extra-territorial enclaves devoted to the cultivation of the 'war potential' forbidden under Article 9. They also have a marked effect on crime and other social ills in the surrounding areas. During the years since 1972, nearly 5,000 crimes, including murder, rape and robbery, have been carried out by US military personnel, civilian employees or dependents, culminating in the 1995 case of three US servicemen raping a twelve-year-old Okinawan school-girl.[96] The bases threaten Okinawa in other ways too. In 1995–6, the American military fired off 1,520 shells of armour-piercing depleted uranium in exercises on the island of Torishima, despite widespread suspicion since the Gulf War that this substance was the cause of long-term environmental toxicity and of damaging health effects on human beings.[97]

For Okinawans, two particular rights have focussed attention: local government autonomy and security of property rights. With regard to the former, an unprecedented constitutional crisis erupted in 1996, shortly after the rape crisis, which led to widespread protests involving over 85,000 people in a 1995 rally.[98] At the time, the provincial Governor for much of the 1990s, Ota Masahide, a prominent local academic and historian of Okinawa, refused to override the property rights of Okinawan landlords by renewing leasing agreements to the US against their will. Had his decision been allowed to stand, the US occupation of their bases would not only have gradually become illegal, but the very ability of Japan to perform its designated role in the alliance system would have been threatened at the most fundamental level: the provision of land for US bases. Arraigned before the Supreme Court and ordered by the Prime Minister to sign the relevant documents, Ota issued an impassioned plea, substantially based on the constitutional right to own and hold property (Article 29), to a peaceful life (Articles 13 and 25), and to provincial self-government (Chapter 8).[99] Such conflict between central and provincial governments might have been expected to draw from the Supreme Court a judgement on the limits of their respective powers. Instead, Ota's case was peremptorily dismissed in a terse two-sentence judgement, and Ota had no alternative but to yield.

Thereafter relations between his Okinawan administration and the central government in Tokyo steadily deteriorated. In February 1998, when Ota announced that he would respect the result of a plebiscite in the northern city of Nago and forbid the construction of the heliport base, they broke down altogether. Faced with steady, and unprecedented, pressure, Ota was defeated at an election in December of that same year by an opponent who placed greater emphasis on the economy and rebuilding relations with the central government.[100]

As seen in other cases where the National Diet has been used in order to deal with essentially constitutional issues, in 1997 and 1999 lawmakers went to the lengths of passing special legislation to facilitate the over-riding of local property rights in Okinawa in order to guarantee the US military security of tenure of the bases. This would appear plainly to be in breach of Article 95 of the constitution which prescribes that a law applicable to a particular region can only be passed with the consent of a majority of voters of the local public entity concerned. The new laws, curtailing and then withdrawing from provincial government authorities and placing in the hands of the Prime Minister the power to sign agreements on land leasing (in the event of refusal by the owners), had the effect of making legal what would otherwise have been illegal.[101] Landowners were deprived of their right to 'own or hold property' and of legal means of redress against forced appropriation. Ironically these provisions were passed into law as part of an omnibus bill supposedly designed to promote political decentralization and devolution of powers which was supported by all parties in the National Diet with the exception of the JCP.[102]

The Okinawan perspective on the constitution is somber. Seen from Okinawa, it looks very much as though the central government in Tokyo attaches a higher priority to the military alliance with the US than to the constitution. It looks as though state policy is to do the will of a foreign government rather than respect the clear desire of the residents of an island prefecture. Tokyo's implacable resolve to ignore or crush the local will to prefectural peace and autonomy seems explicable only in such terms. In contrast to the political and constitutional debates in Tokyo, therefore, it is not revision of the present Constitution but the struggle to implement it which absorbs all available energies in Okinawa.

For these reasons, it may be that the contradictions of constitutionalism are more sharply etched in Okinawa than anywhere else. The Japanese 'peace state' and the Okinawan 'war state' are the two, closely inter-related sides of the post-war order. If it is the case that the quality of a constitutional regime may be judged by the equality of rights which it confers to all citizens of the nation state in question, then the evidence from Okinawa – where intense political and legal efforts to get the existing Constitution implemented have been continually frustrated – suggests at best a very qualified verdict.

ANTI-CONSTITUTIONAL RADICALISM

While conservatives deplored, and radicals, by and large, embraced, the Constitution during these decades, there were those who did not fit easily into either of the main camps. One is the group known as 'Smash the Security Treaty,' which authored a document it described as 'Japan's Constitution – The Right Answers.' An abridged and translated version of this anarchistic and sarcastic document, which parodies the 1947 constitution, is reproduced here.[103]

The Constitution of Japan – the right answers

Preamble

We, the Armed Forces of the United States occupying Japan, acting on behalf of the United States and in place of the parliament chosen in Japan by menaces and bribery, determined that we shall secure for ourselves the fruits of peaceful cooperation with all nations under the control of the United States and the blessings accruing from money-making ventures throughout the Japanese archipelago, and resolved to stir up the calamities of war willingly and whenever it is in the interests of the United States, do proclaim that sovereign power does not reside in the Japanese people and do firmly establish this constitution. The governance of Japan shall be in accordance with the strict dictates of the government of the United

States, its authority stemming from the military might of the occupying army, its power exercised as proxy for the occupation forces, and its benefits enjoyed by monopoly enterprises. This is the principle established by the government of the United States upon which this constitution is founded. We reject and revoke all constitutions, laws, ordinances and rescripts in conflict herewith.

We, the Japanese people, do not desire peace for all time and are deeply conscious of the principles of connection and payoff controlling human relationship, and we have determined to maintain our own bare existence while the coffers of monopoly enterprise overflow, regardless of the justice and faith of the peace-loving peoples of the world. Should any trend emerge in international society to strive for the preservation of peace, and the banishment of tyranny and slavery, oppression and intolerance for all time from the earth, the Japanese people are determined to serve as a bulwark against it. We recognize that for the benefit of the United States of America, some among the peoples of the world are bound to lose the right to live in peace, free from fear and want.

We believe that no nation is responsible to itself alone, ignoring the United States of America, that the laws of political morality are those determined by the government of the United States, and that it is incumbent upon all nations to abandon their own sovereignty and to be subordinate to the United States.

We, the Japanese people, pledge that, in place of our national honor, we will accomplish these high interests and goals.

Chapter 1 The Emperor

Article 1
The Emperor shall be the symbol of the occupation of Japan and of the stupidity of the Japanese people, deriving his position from the orders of the Occupation Forces.

Article 2
The Imperial Throne shall be dynastic in accordance with the principle of human inequality necessary to monopoly enterprise. This principle is spelt out in the Imperial House Law passed by intimidation in the Diet.

Article 3
By his various mumbo-jumbo-like rites and rituals, the Emperor shall give the appearance of legitimacy to whatever is laid down by the body of officials known as the Cabinet. This shall be known as the conduct of matters of state. The Cabinet shall bear the responsibility for these rites and rituals. [Abridged]

Chapter 2 Choice of war

Article 9
Aspiring sincerely to an international order based on what is determined by the United States government to be just, the Japanese people shall only choose war as the sovereign right of the nation, or the threat or use of force, in accordance with the orders of the United States of America.

In order to accomplish the aim of the preceding paragraph, land, sea, and air forces, as well as other war potential, will be maintained, and they will be called Self-Defense Forces. The right of belligerency of the state shall be subordinate to the government of the United States of America.

The organization and duties of the Self-Defense Forces shall be settled by law, and since the role of the Self-Defense Forces is always to be determined in accordance with the wishes of the government of the United States of America, no further provision about it is made in this constitution.

Chapter 3 Rights and duties of the people

Article 10
All people are divided into Japanese and non-Japanese. The conditions for being Japanese are to be determined by law.

Article 11
Japanese people shall enjoy all basic human rights in so far as they do not interfere with the profit-making of monopoly enterprises or with the conduct of government. This provision does not apply to non-Japanese. [Abridged]

Article 13
All non-Japanese shall not be respected as individuals. So far as their rights to life, liberty, and the pursuit of happiness are concerned, no legal or other provision shall be made for them save as set out in the Imperial Household Law.

Article 14
All non-Japanese people shall be discriminated against in political, economic and social relations in accordance with race, creed, sex, social status or family origin or nationality.

As prescribed by the Imperial Household Law, a system of aristocracy, to be called 'imperial clan' (*kōzoku*) will be established. Its members shall enjoy the privileges accompanying awards of honor, decoration or distinction. These aristocratic privileges shall be inherited and enjoyed as a permanent right which may not be taken away. [Abridged]

Article 18
Under the rank and status system, some people will have to be confined as slaves. As distinct from punishment for crime, the drudgery of over-time work and commuting hell shall not be regarded as counter to anyone's will.

Article 19
Freedom of thought and conscience shall be recognized within those limits determined by public officials.

Article 20
Religion based on the rites and rituals performed by the Emperor is compulsory and it shall be given precedence by government.

Other religions are free in so far as they do not conflict with this.

Everybody, irrespective of their religion, must participate in the rites of the above religion, i.e. the ceremonies performed by the Emperor, the raising of the '*Hinomaru*' flag and kneeling before it, the singing in chorus of the '*Kimigayo*' anthem in praise of the Emperor. The state and its organs must take appropriate steps to ensure that the people are aware of these duties.

Article 21
All assembly and organization, and all expression of opinion or publication that has been authorized by the authorities shall be free.

All acts of censorship shall be known henceforth only as editing, and editing shall be required. The freedom of public officials to tap people's telephones shall be guaranteed.

Article 26
All people shall have the right to receive an unequal education in accordance with their financial means.

POST-COLD WAR: SEARCHING FOR NEW ARRANGEMENTS

Public opinion surveys showed a majority of people committed to the logically contradictory position of wanting to retain Article 9 while at the same time accepting the constitutionality of the SDF. Wrestling with the contradictions of public thinking on defense issues and the ongoing exigencies of the Security Treaty with the US, both the LDP and the SDPJ changed their ground in the wake of the Cold War's ending.

The SDPJ had begun its shift even before then, in the mid-1980s, when already the evidence of waning public interest in constitutional purity was clear. In 1984 the then Party Chairman, Ishibashi Masashi, proposed a formula according to which the SDF would be seen as 'unconstitutional, but legal.'[104] Thereafter, the consensus within the party around the constitutional issue further eroded. A crucial reason for the SDPJ's change of policy was the experience of the 1990–1 Gulf crisis and war. This was a watershed in the debate on Article 9 of the constitution. It confronted Japan with a peculiar conjuncture: for the first time, the government was called upon to respond to a conflict without a Cold War dimension. The Gulf War showed that the overseas dispatch of the SDF need not necessarily equate with sending them to war. Under immense pressures to join the US-led Western alliance in the Gulf, Japan responded with support that was exclusively financial. However, the huge contribution of $13 billion towards the Western war chest not only did not silence the 'free rider' criticisms of its defense policy, but simultaneously stirred calls for a human contribution (and 'blood').

After joining the coalition government in 1993, the SDPJ showed an increasing readiness to compromise on constitutional matters. By mid-1993 its then leader, Yamahana Sadao, was an advocate of 'creative constitutionalism' (*sōken*) which would call for the passage of a 'Security Law' to supplement the constitution and clarify the legitimacy of the SDF.[105] The *fait accompli* of public support for the status quo was thus conceded, despite the illogic or word-stretching, and constitutional objections were withdrawn. The problems of logic and morality were resolved by the call for supplementary legislation in the form of a 'Basic Law' on peace, security, or international cooperation. In 1994, the SDPJ held an extraordinary national convention at which it dramatically declared that it no longer held the existence of the SDF to be unconstitutional, nor did it object to the Security Treaty with the United States, or to the use of the long-contested symbols, the *Hinomaru* and *Kimigayo*, as national flag and anthem.[106] While a truncated SDPJ later opposed constitutional revision *per se*, its concession on what many members had seen as the greatest single issue of principle was irreversible. Many ordinary members, however, stood firm, persisting in their strict and literal interpretation of Article 9. To adapt the requirements of unarmed neutrality to changed circumstances, they also proposed the internationalizing of Article 9, urging its inclusion in the constitutions of all countries in the region.[107] In the nineties, however, such views lacked the political weight of major party backing that they had enjoyed during the Cold War.

One of the dominant norms embedded in domestic society is antimilitarism (more broadly anti-violence), but under the predominant norms of international society, the use of military force is accepted as a legitimate instrument of state power.[108] During the Cold War, this stand-off between domestic and international norms could be seen in the way that attempts to deploy Japanese military power were challenged by the Opposition parties as well as public opinion. Even within the governing party, Prime Minister Yoshida and others in the LDP leadership stressed an economic rather than military role in the world. The end of the international Cold War, however, was followed soon afterwards by the end of the domestic cold war political system of single party LDP rule. As the international Cold War order involved a confrontation on the four dimensions of politics, economics, security and culture (ideology), so the domestic cold war in Japan pitted the LDP against the SDPJ in these same four dimensions, and both structures of polarity collapsed within a short span of time.

For the LDP, the end of the Cold War military confrontation was a threat to the very meaning of the US-Japan security treaty system based on the existence of communism. Renewed by Kishi in 1960, the treaty thereafter was kept in place by respective LDP governments, despite a relaxation of tensions at different times during the Cold War period. But, as the alternative to the capitalist and democratic mode of organizing life collapsed, many came to question the continuing need for the treaty.

For the socialists, the end to the military confrontation created a different kind of problem. Throughout the Cold-War period, they had opposed the US-Japan Security Treaty. For them, the threat from nuclear war was greater than the threat from communism. But with the end of East–West military confrontation and the reduction in the threat of nuclear war, this fundamental premise was eroded. As a result, they were less able than in the past to use the threat of nuclear war as a political tool in support of their security policy. Second, whereas the LDP was inclined to fear abandonment – that is, that the US might withdraw from Japan and the region into isolation – the socialists viewed the US-Japan Security Treaty as a threat likely to embroil Japan in a war of the US's making; in other words, they feared entanglement. With the end of the Cold War, however, the use of the entanglement argument to oppose the security treaty also lost force. Third, the security strategy of the socialists had been premised on seeing the dispatch of the SDF overseas as meaning the use of force as an instrument of state policy, and therefore tantamount to Japan's re-emergence as a major military power and threat in East Asia. The Gulf War, however, showed that the dispatch of the SDF overseas could be in response to an international call to restore the international peace. Finally, the socialists had promoted unarmed neutrality as a key policy platform, but with the end of the Cold War the two sides between which Japan was supposed to adopt a neutral stance no longer existed. 'Unarmed neutrality' as a policy alternative to the US-Japan Security Treaty therefore ceased to mean anything.

The end of the Cold War and the 1990–1 Gulf crisis and war created increasing demands on Japan to fulfil its international obligations by making a 'human' contribution to international society, albeit 'human' here is often a euphemism for the military. The Japanese response can be seen in the case of the 1999 'Regional Contingency Law' (otherwise known as the 'Guidelines' legislation), under which support for US forces in the region was substantially reinforced. Henceforth, Japan would give 'rearguard support' in the event of 'situations in areas surrounding Japan'; an attempt to move away from a geographic understanding of the scope of Japan's obligations under the Security Treaty. In effect it committed the Japanese government to support the US in all ways short of combat in future regional and perhaps even global conflicts. This role presented obvious difficulties of reconciliation with the constitutional proscription on the use or threat of force in international conflict, as well as being difficult to square with the political and social trends towards a more assertive Japanese nationalist voice and role. Public opinion seems to have divided on this, although in the late 1990s far greater attention was being paid to economic than to strategic and military matters and this bill, despite its implications, stirred little organized opposition.[109] The constitution therefore came to function in ways that are puzzling to anyone simply reading it, or, for that matter, to its 'founding fathers.' It was not revised but yet it was revised, virtually: revision by interpretation.

Reassessing Article 9

As was seen earlier, for both conservatives and socialists, the end of the international and domestic cold wars destroyed the meaning of Article 9 in the domestic political make-up of Japan. As the Cold War no longer existed, the function of Article 9 as a rallying point for political and social forces seeking to give meaning to the identity of Japan as a peace state through the implementation of a policy of unarmed neutrality collapsed. With it collapsed the 1955 system, and Hosokawa and other 'new' political forces rose to power in the 1993 coalition government.

The 1954 ban on the dispatch of troops was based on the premise that, in order to ensure the military's role remained exclusively defensive, none should be dispatched abroad. Even Kishi Nobusuke said in April 1960 that, in his view, the constitution forbade the overseas dispatch of forces.[110] When the issue arose in the early 1990s, most (59 percent of) people agreed, opposing such dispatch on constitutional grounds. But despite minimal support, because Japan's national interest and the US alliance seemed to make it inescapable, a Peace Keeping Bill was nevertheless adopted in June 1992, with popular support running at no higher than 36 percent. Once adopted, support for it slowly rose as public opinion gradually adjusted to the *fait accompli*, and by the time Japanese troops were sent to Cambodia in September 1992, it had risen to 52 percent.[111]

In the wake of the ending of the cold and Gulf wars, moreover, a change in public opinion occurred in respect of Article 9. In 1993, for instance, for the first time just over a majority of those polled (50.4 percent) supported constitutional revision, but not necessarily of Article 9, for which public support commonly runs high.[112] From then until 1999, polls by the *Asahi* and the *Yomiuri* showed between 44 percent and 53 percent supporting revision, with the highest, a *Yomiuri* poll in 1999, showing 53 percent in favor.[113] Support for revision was even 60 percent for those in their twenties. Overall, however, the main reason was not in order to delete or revise Article 9, but to respond to new problems, such as the need to make an international contribution (46 percent). Such sentiments can be seen to link to Article 9's restriction on the dispatch of the SDF. Reflecting this, support for inserting environmental rights into the constitution (76 percent) was higher than for clarifying the state's right to self-defense (70 percent).

For the supporters of a more prominent international role for Japan, the Gulf War demonstrated conclusively that, far from the SDF being limited to the defense of Japan, their deployment could be used to fulfil Japan's international obligations, and achieve an 'honored place' in international society as called for in the Preamble to the constitution. What is more, when the Cambodian government requested the Japanese government to dispatch troops on United Nations PKO in Cambodia, the argument that Article 9 prevented Japan from again becoming a threat to its East Asian neighbors lost much of its meaning. These events turned the socialists' discourse on its head. In this way, the international norm of contribution to international society was successfully deployed against the domestic norm of antimilitarism rooted in the Constitution.

In 1998–9, moreover, various incidents occurred in and around Japan which stirred an unmistakable change in mood with regard to Article 9. In August 1998 the hitherto defense-somnolent country was awakened by the '*Taepodong*' (North Korean rocket/missile), which was launched into waters adjacent to Japan. Then, in March 1999, the MSDF engaged for the first time in its history in the unilateral exercise of force on behalf of the Japanese state – against the so-called '*fushinsen*,' the intruding 'mystery ships' which sped across Japanese waters and disappeared in the direction of North Korea. Although the action was in apparent breach of the law defining when such force might be legitimately used,[114] more than 80 percent of the population approved, finding the action to be either 'appropriate under the circumstances' or even inadequate.[115]

In the context of this burst of popular support for military action, the Chief of the Japan Defense Agency (JDA), Norota Hōsei, announced that in certain circumstances Japan enjoyed the right of 'preemptive attack.'[116] In other words, if the government so chose it could invoke the principle of self-defense to launch a pre-emptive attack on suspected North Korean missile or nuclear facilities. This statement too would once have led to uproar and resignation, but in 1999 it passed with little comment. Japan's peace constitution, by the understanding of the 1999 Obuchi Keizō government (and presumably a majority of citizens), no longer ruled out even a unilateral Japanese use of force against a neighboring state. In October 1999 the JDA's parliamentary Vice-Minister, Nishimura Shingo, carried this further by putting the case for Japan to arm itself with nuclear weapons,[117] although he was forced to resign thereafter. His statement brought to mind Kishi's earlier announcement, suggesting that in the 1990s, too, certain government officials do not consider nuclear weapons 'war potential.'

Although the peace keeping commitment from 1992, in Cambodia, Mozambique, the Golan heights, Rwanda and Honduras, was token, hedged with qualifications and conditions, and essentially symbolic – with SDF members engaged in tasks such as road construction (Cambodia), or the installation of telecommunications equipment, establishment of medical clinics and refugee camps in Zaire[118] – it still carried a considerable symbolic weight. On the one hand, it would clearly not be reversed, and marked the early stage of a new kind of Japanese engagement with the region. On the other, however, it meant that the forty-year justification for the existence of the SDF on grounds of 'inherent right of self-defense' was effectively abandoned, since no-one argued that Japan's defense was threatened in any of these places. These questions of constitutional principle were submerged in the popular desire to support what was seen as the worthy cause of the UN and to contribute to the construction of a new world order. The post-Gulf War Japanese readiness to cooperate in multilateral peacekeeping efforts was acclaimed by pundits and politicians as a sign of a new maturity and openness.[119] Pragmatism or realism was preferred to idealism or pacifism, and Japan was viewed positively by the US for adopting a 'flexible' interpretation of its constitution.

Finally, although Japan's constitution is radically different from the UN Charter in terms of the mandate to use force, with Article 2, Clause Four of the UN Charter accepting the enforced settlement of disputes, the 1990s saw a major drive to promote Japan as a permanent member of the UN Security Council (UNSC).[120] Although it has been a non-permanent member of the UNSC eight times, the existence of the 'former enemy' clause in the UN Charter means that a root and branch reform of the UN would have to take place before Japan, or Germany for that matter, can take up a permanent seat on the Council. In the 1990s the Japanese government began to advance stronger claims to a seat, pointing out that it is the second most important contributor to the UN after the US, and that it pays its contributions on time.[121] The existing permanent members have operated on the assumption that, if Japan became a permanent Security Council member, it would make every effort to behave like an 'ordinary' superpower. Whatever the actual situation, which cannot be known until UN reform takes place, Obuchi Keizō (Prime Minister 1997–2000) has stated that Japan will assume responsibilities in the UNSC so long as it does not involve 'the use of force prohibited in the Constitution.'[122]

REVISION

The inherent implausibility of a constitution drawn up and adopted in circumstances such as Japan's of 1946 remaining unchallenged for more than half a century is such that debate itself is difficult to resist. The debate is no mere narrow, or legal, matter, but goes to the heart of how Japan should see itself and its national identity and role in the coming century. Once it is opened, attention naturally focusses on what kind of revision, rather than simply on its desirability or otherwise.

No authoritative statement remains of the kind of revision the LDP contemplated during the Cold War decades, but its general tone was undoubtedly backward-looking or reactionary, characterized by resentment of the 1947 constitution and the desire to restore key elements of the Meiji state system. Typical is one influential draft published by Nakagawa Yatsuhiro in 1984.[123] It deleted reference to popular sovereignty, restored the crime of *lèse majesty* for any assault on the dignity of the Emperor, deleted the war-renouncing clauses of Article 9 and established the Emperor as Commander-in-Chief of the 'National Defense Army,' made human rights clauses conditional on requirements of public order or state security, and restored the pre-war idea of *kokutai* (national polity) by denying the right to exist to political groups which opposed the basic order and principles of state. It also established a duty for citizens to serve as required in the defense of the country (opening the way to conscription). Although the balance shifted between the various conservative revisionists, this Nakagawa draft captures their general ethos and backward-looking character.

In the 1990s, the conservative position shifted. The most widely circulating drafts and constitutional ideas all now accept the basic principles of the present constitution – symbolic emperor, popular sovereignty, no war, human rights – but argue, variously, for a clearer and more contemporary expression of those principles, for clarification of Japan's commitment to international justice and peace, or the expansion of its rights clauses to include rights to privacy or environmental amenity. Instead of looking backward in nostalgia, they look forward, offering their prescriptions for Japan's role in a world only slowly coming into existence.

The Cold War, left–right polarized division on the constitution steadily evaporated in the 1990s, but both sides of the political spectrum experienced difficulty adjusting to the changes, and behind the surface consensus of 'new' constitutional thought some old ideas still persist and are not to be written off. The neo-nationalist aspiration to restore a 'true' Japaneseness, or as some prefer a Japanese 'subjectivity' (*shutaisei*), to the center of the Japanese state and society compels

Parchment and politics 35

considerable support. With increasing stridency, nationalists and neo-nationalists insist that to restore an equilibrium requires a return to the certainties of an earlier time, in symbol, rhetoric, and educational policy. The organization which most forcefully articulates such concerns is the Nippon Conference (*Nippon Kaigi*), formed in 1997 by a merger from several pre-existing organizations. As to what exactly 'pure' Japaneseness might be, the 'Nippon Conference' is unambiguous: the emperor is its very embodiment, and he should be restored to centrality in the Japanese state. Its regular organ, *Nippon no ibuki* (Breath of Japan) declares that the post-war emperor system is the same emperor system that Japan has enjoyed from time immemorial, in which the state and Emperor are one and the same.[124] Members of Nippon Conference were vigorous campaigners for the legislation declaring the *Hinomaru* and *Kimigayo* the national flag and anthem, as was adopted in 1999, and for a new Constitution, two steps, albeit in their thinking early and provisional steps, in the restoration of a 'proud Japan.' As of 1999, they boasted of over 200 members of the National Diet among their membership.

Paralleling the Nippon Conference are two organizations with a substantial middle-class membership and a 'new liberal' agenda. The members of the 'Society for the Making of New School Textbooks in History' (*Atarashii Kyōkasho o Tsukuru Kai*) and the 'Liberal View of History Study Group' (*Jiyūshugi Shikan Kenkyūkai*) are thus far reticent about the Emperor, but their rhetoric, which like the Nippon Conference is full of reference to purifying the historical record and restoring Japanese pride and distinctiveness, suggests that it is rooted in the same privileged representations of Japanese identity.[125]

The critical question for Japanese conservatism, therefore, is whether or not the efforts to achieve a liberal-conservative consensus on an open, democratic, internationally responsible and yet still pacifist Japan would be enough to win over those who yearn still for an emperor-centered state. Furthermore, to the extent that the nationalist movement grows, the contradiction between Japanese and American conceptions of national interest is bound to diverge. Nationalist criticism continues to focus on the 'US-imposed' constitution, rather than on the US bases that constitute the fabric of continuing subordination, as well as on the 'imposition' of a system which deprived Japan of its defense autonomy rather than the imposition of the symbolic emperor system.

In theory anything might be brought forward for deliberation – including abandonment of the emperor system and declaration of a republic. Although a few individuals do declare themselves for a republic,[126] or call for the imperial institution to be radically reformed, in practice both are highly unlikely and there is little to indicate any weakening in the 'chrysanthemum taboo.' One proposal adopts the argument that the human rights under the constitution should now be extended to the Emperor. While a new Article 1 could simply state 'The sovereign authority in the Japanese nation resides with the people,' the Emperor and his family would hand over their constitutional functions (under Articles 1 to 8) to the Prime Minister and retreat to Kyoto 'to live freely as normal citizens with human rights,' as purely cultural figures, no longer 'symbol of the state and unity of the people.'[127] However, such voices are likely to be drowned by the chorus from organizations committed to restoration of a 'pure,' 'proud' Japanese identity which increasingly flourish and attract large supporting budgets from corporate and media sources. Their Japan would have a 'correct' history, the Emperor restored to a central role both in its past and its future, individual human rights subjected to limitations and conditions, and state prerogatives expanded, in particular by removal of the inhibitions currently entrenched in Article 9.[128] As of early 2000, however, it seemed unlikely that either the neo-nationalist or the republican agenda would get much of a hearing in the Constitutional Research Councils.

We here introduce four different proposals to resolve these problems, two (Yomiuri and Ozawa) favouring revision and two (Asahi and *Sekai*) opposing it but calling for legislation to clarify and supplement the constitution.

Yomiuri proposal

The *Yomiuri*, which with a circulation of around 11 million is the largest newspaper in the world, has played a leading role in campaigning nationally for revision and in radically redefining the revisionist position.[129] It was central to the campaign for revision throughout the 1990s, and there was a distinctly triumphalist note to the way it reported, in 1999, the success of its various campaigns for the passage of the anthem and flag bill and the establishment of the Constitution Research Councils in terms of a defeat for the leftwing ideology of 'post-war democracy' which for so long had been 'allowed to mislead the people.'[130] Where revisionists had traditionally favored return to the values of the pre-war constitution, the programme it enunciated from the early 1990s affirmed the principles of popular sovereignty (relegating the clauses on the Emperor to a subordinate position) and articulated a vision of Japan as a predominantly civilian power, playing a greatly expanded role in the international community while retaining the SDF and the *Ampo* treaty.[131]

On November 3 1994, the *Yomiuri* published an eight-page supplement to its regular daily edition, containing the full text of its proposed revised constitution, together with detailed arguments and the text of the constitution to be replaced.[132] The first clause of Article 9 (the abstract commitment to 'renounce war as a sovereign right of the nation and the threat or use of force as means of settling international disputes') would be retained, but the following sentence – 'land, sea, and air forces, as well as other war potential, will never be maintained' – would be deleted and replaced with an unambiguous recognition of the right to possess conventional armed forces. A new chapter would be added on international cooperation, setting out the aspiration to eliminate from the earth 'human calamities caused by military conflicts, natural disasters, environmental destruction, economic deprivation in particular areas and regional disorder,' and committing Japan to dispatch its armed forces 'for the maintenance and promotion of peace and for humanitarian support activities.'

The prefatory statement attached to the draft declared that the objective was 'not so much to maintain the principles of the existing constitution (such as pacifism) as *to reinforce them*' (emphasis added).[133] This expression by a major media group was the clearest possible testimony to the strength of popular pacifism and internationalism.[134] In other clauses, existing human rights provisions would be further elaborated, clauses on privacy and on environmental rights added, and provision made for strengthening the Diet and the role of the Prime Minister. The position of the Emperor would remain virtually unchanged but the clauses defining it would be relegated to second place after those declaring the sovereignty of the people.

The vision of Japan as a great power, with its permanent seat on the UN Security Council, is a powerful attraction for nationalists, but it is combined here with a very internationalist, peace-oriented stance, drawing deeply upon the post-war commitment to Article 9. The commitment to popular sovereignty, peace, human rights and environmental protection, on the part of the major proponent of revision, was a mark of how far the debate on constitutional revision had proceeded since Kishi and other wartime figures first launched it in the 1950s, when they entrenched in the party platform of the LDP the commitment to the 'establishment of a sovereign Constitution.'

In June 1995 the Yomiuri group proceeded to publish a further elaboration of its views, this time concentrating on measures to reinforce the powers of the Prime Minister and Cabinet to cope with emergency situations (with the Kobe Earthquake and the Tokyo subway Sarin attack of January and March 1995 in mind), involving the passage of a 'Comprehensive Security Basic Law' and the establishment of a 'Comprehensive Security Council' (under the Prime Minister) designed to be able to act quickly in response to any emergency in the areas of national defense, terrorism or natural disaster.[135] The proposal also declared the legitimacy of Japanese participation in collective security arrangements, and urged the extension of the US-Japan Security Treaty into a fully-fledged bilateral security treaty, under which Japanese forces could as much be dispatched to the defense of the United States as vice versa. These 1995 proposals were more 'dry' and defense-oriented, less idealistic, scarcely at all pacifistic in tone, quite different from the original proposals of the previous November.

Sekai proposal

The same problems addressed by the Yomiuri group were the subject of a study by a group of intellectuals associated with the Iwanami Publishing Company's monthly journal *Sekai*, long seen as the flag-bearer of the pacifist movement. This group enunciated its position in two phases in 1993 and 1994.[136] It strove to articulate a vision which would attempt the apparently impossible: to rearticulate the constitutional commitment of post-war pacifism in such a way as to preserve and develop the long tradition of constitutional pacifism but at the same time accept the constitutional basis for a defensive force (while not endorsing the existing SDF). It would be done in the context of the enunciation of a visionary, future-oriented, regional and global programme for Japan. The Group recommended that the constitution be preserved intact, but supplemented by a 'Basic

Peace Law' akin to the 'Basic Law on Education' (1947) and 'Basic Law on Agriculture' (1961), under which the constitutional legitimacy of self-defense would be proclaimed, but the existing SDF drastically reorganized. They would be divided into a 'Territorial Guard' (more like a 'citizen militia' than a standing army), which would be entrusted with the defense of Japanese soil, and a quite distinct 'International Relief Force' which would serve only under the United Nations. Article 9 would be further fleshed out by the adoption of policies appropriate to Japan as a 'peace state,' including contribution to the promotion of regional and world disarmament, and reconciliation, first with Japan's own neighbors through apology and compensation for the wounds of the war, and thereafter by building networks of peace and cooperation (involving the gradual dissolution of the existing military treaty with the US and the replacement of all such military treaties by regional collective security agreements). They also urged that Japan should elevate its international diplomatic efforts for peace by the establishment of a 'Ministry for Peace and Disarmament.'

These inter-locking proposals were presented in the context of a far-reaching critique of post-war Japanese pacifism's 'utopian' tendencies, its uncritical leaning towards the 'socialist bloc,' and its failure to address seriously the question of defense during the Cold War. This analysis aroused heated debate and highlighted the continuing tensions in the former 'socialist' camp on how to deal with the constitution in the post-Cold War era.[137]

Asahi proposal

On 'Constitution Day' (May 3) 1995, the country's second largest newspaper group, the Asahi, with a circulation of around 8 million, published its detailed plan, also endorsing the constitution as it stood but supplementing it instead with what it described as an 'International Cooperation Law.'[138] The *Asahi* proposed that Japan claim a sort of 'conscientious objector' status among nations by reason of its insistence on exclusively non-military contribution to the world community. It advanced a program for a radical overhaul of the country's defense and international relations policies to be carried out by the year 2010. Though left intact and unrevised, the Constitution would be supplemented by an 'International Cooperation Law' (paralleling the *Sekai* 'Basic Peace Law') under which Japan would adopt a particular orientation towards helping the poorest countries and addressing the global problems of militarization, population explosion and global environmental deterioration. The Cold War defense alliance relationships would be revised, the US military presence in Japan reduced and eventually eliminated, and the SDF drastically scaled down (by 50 percent in the case of the GSDF) and turned into a garrison force with the exclusive mission of defense of the Japanese islands from local aggression. A separate 'Peace Support Corps' would be established, made up of engineering, medical, rescue, communication, and civilian police units, to engage in international relief tasks, but no Japanese armed personnel should ever be sent abroad. In its essentials, this was very close to *Sekai*, and in spirit it also shares much with the Yomiuri proposals.

Ozawa proposal

Ozawa Ichirō, formerly Secretary-General of the LDP, defected from it in 1993. Thereafter he played a key role in various opposition parties, eventually rejoining the coalition government benches in 1999 as president of the Liberal Party of Japan. Though a central figure in the money and interest politics of the late 1980s and early 1990s, Ozawa showed that he was also much more than a conventional, 'parish-pump,' interest politician by the way he addressed large ideological and theoretical questions. In this respect, he stands out among contemporary politicians, and deserves much of the credit for first articulating a forward and future-oriented interpretation of the constitution, shedding the revanchist dreams of a return to Meiji. While borrowing wholesale from traditionally internationalist idealism, he did so within a vision of Japan as a 'Great Power,' thereby appealing to nationalist sentiment. Rare among Japanese politicians, he had a coherent political position, as well as a sense of theatre; the single word 'normal' in which he dressed his vision proved as evocative as the detailed fine print of his program.

For Ozawa, Japan's pursuit of narrowly economic might had turned it, in his telling phrase, into a grotesque 'one lung state.'[139] It was time to become a 'normal state' and to claim a seat on the UNSC. During the debates on UN peacekeeping, he argued that the words of the Preamble to the Constitution about Japan being 'desirous of contributing honorably to international society' should take precedence over the literal expression of Article 9.[140] Article 9, he proposed, forbade only overseas military operations without UN sanction, not the possession of forces or their deployment on UN missions and under UN command, and therefore participation in a UN standing army should present no constitutional difficulty.[141]

By tying the constitutional issue to the question of a Japanese contribution to building a better world, if not exactly a 'new world order,' Ozawa succeeded in touching a deep nerve. He argued that adherence to Article 9 amounted to a selfish and unprincipled 'pacifism in one country,' that Japan's wealth and stability was owed, to some extent, to its 'free ride' on US defense through the Cold War years, and that its economic engagement with the world obliged it to take a greater responsibility for peace and order. Initially he took the view that a 'revision by interpretation' was all that was required for Japan to be able to perform a proper role as 'world citizen.'

Through much of the evolving constitutional debate of the 1990s, Ozawa was typical of those who believed that Japan could become a 'normal' country with 'normal' armed forces, by the simple device of choosing to interpret the existing constitution as permitting it. By 1999, however, Ozawa had second thoughts, and shifted ground to join the 'constitutional revisionist' camp. On the fundamental question of constitutional interpretation it was a full 180 degree switch. Ozawa does not pretend that it resulted from a deeper scholarly understanding of legal and constitutional issues, so it must be assumed that political pragmatism was uppermost in his mind.

40 *Japan's contested constitution*

Consistent with his long-held view that Japan should strive for normalcy, Ozawa's proposals leave intact the existing Chapter 1 on the Emperor, but only for the reason that he believes those clauses already establish the role of constitutional monarch (*kokka genshu*). In Chapter 2 ('Renunciation of War') he would add a third clause to Article 9, declaring that Japan could possess 'military power' but only for defensive purposes, plus a new Article which would spell out Japan's commitment to support 'international peacekeeping activities.' So far as rights and duties are concerned, the balance would be adjusted so that people be obliged to 'refrain from abuse of their freedoms and rights' and 'respect public welfare and public order.' Ozawa would also reform the structure of the Diet, substituting for the existing Upper House a house of life-peers which he describes as modeled on the British House of Lords before the recent reforms carried out by Tony Blair's government.

CONCLUSION

The five decades of constructing this status quo have bequeathed a range of problems to the present generation. Looking back, it is plain that all of the present proposals address the same, end-of-century constitutional impasse; the result of a long series of compromises leading back to the initial shelving of the question of past war responsibility, and to the commitment to the Cold War system in a way which necessitated casuistry and obfuscation. There could be no logical way to integrate the peace system (the constitution) with the Security Treaty and the Cold War. It was done nevertheless. The first problem that all the drafts are concerned with is how to overcome the gap between the words of the Constitution and actual practice. The second is how to make the constitution relevant to the circumstances of the twenty-first century.

In imaginatively recasting the argument over the constitution, it could be said that the *Sekai* and Asahi groups performed a similar role on one side of the political spectrum as to that of the Yomiuri Group and Ozawa on the other. The four proposals reflect a world transformed beyond measure from that of the Nakagawa draft of 1984. The fragility of national mood and cultural climate of the century-spanning years is such that old agendas might still re-emerge, but for the moment these four proposals are notable as much for the values they share – idealism, pacifism, internationalism, democracy and openness – as for what divides them. Nothing could demonstrate this more clearly than the Yomiuri draft's proposal to shift the clauses relating to the Emperor to the second chapter of the constitution, following those spelling out popular sovereignty. Where they differ most, perhaps, is in the attempt to articulate an identity and role for the nation as a more-or-less conventional 'great power' (Yomiuri and Ozawa), albeit of democratic and internationalist hue, on the one hand, and the quest for something distinctive as a new sort of power, a civilian power (*Sekai* and Asahi), on the other.[142]

The difference is deeply rooted in Japan's modern history. It was the drive for great power status in the late nineteenth century that set Japan on the course for imperialism and war. It was the Meiji Constitution of 1889, together with the Imperial Rescript on Education (1891) that consolidated the infrastructure of statist, authoritarian Japan deemed necessary to power that drive to glory. There was then also an alternative vision, of a development that would give priority to human rights and needs over state rights and needs, and make a virtue of ordinariness as a small country.[143] The democratic and people-centred vision was expressed in constitutional drafts in the 1880s, drawn up in some cases by ordinary people far removed from the centers of power.[144] Again in the 1920s and 1930s, the statist, militarist drive for greatness was contested, notably in the political area by anti-war, anti-imperialist, democratic figures like Ozaki Yukiō and Ishibashi Tanzan.[145] Their efforts ended in failure, but the same, democratic, pacifist impulse for a small, ordinary, modest nation surfaced later in the immediate post-war debates on a new constitution and helped mold the provisions adopted in 1946. It is this very same issue of national identity and role that is being contested again in the contemporary debates on revision. Should Japan choose to try again to be a 'great power,' or should it opt instead to be a 'civilian power'?

The drafts all had various problems. The Yomiuri and Ozawa calls for revision of Article 9 in order to legitimize the possession of the SDF did of course imply that the existing arrangement, and the Japanese defense and alliance structures under it, were at best problematic under the constitution. If revision was *necessary* to legitimize the SDF, did that not mean that its present position was illegitimate? And if Japan declares its right to possess and exercise 'force,' ruling out only 'aggressive' war, what is there really distinctive about that? As for the *Sekai* and Asahi, their proposals for a 'Basic Peace Law' and an 'International Cooperation Law' are idealistic attempts to solve the problems short of actual revision, but are they not in fact resorting to a kind of 'revision by interpretation' to achieve their ends? And in concrete terms, the *Sekai* proposal to convert the present SDF into a 'Territorial Guard,' which would never be able to become a 'National Army,' presents obvious difficulties. Though otherwise close to the *Sekai* group, Asahi is distinct in its insistence on clinging to the literal constitutional position that Japan should be unarmed and neutral, fulfilling its responsibilities to the international community without recourse to arms as a unique pacifist or 'conscientious objector' state. Ironically, the Article 9 constitutional purist position is the one which appears most radical because it would require the largest adjustments to the present condition of Japan.

The implication of the Asahi and *Sekai* proposals is of the need to return to principles already deeply embedded in the constitution; the problem is political rather than constitutional. The one question that the Constitutional Research Councils will not be investigating is why the constitution of 1947 was so long ignored, stretched and distorted, and who should bear responsibility; yet a new constitution will be of little avail if politicians, bureaucrats, and the judiciary treat it with the same disregard as the old one. It is striking that many of those calling most vociferously for a new constitution are precisely those most responsible for subverting the old one. As Hasegawa Masayasu, Nagoya University Emeritus professor, told the House of Representatives' Constitution Research Council on March 23 2000, 'What is necessary is not discussion of this or that clause but of how the Constitution is being implemented or not implemented. Those who now make no effort to protect the constitution have no right to speak of reforming it. Even if the constitution were to be changed, such people would still not respect it.'[146] Whether Japan, even after half a century under the 1947 constitution, is actually a society ruled by law, or a 'constitutional state,' continues to be debated.[147]

The national debate on constitutional reform has long been concentrated almost exclusively on Article 9 and associated defense, security and 'international contribution' considerations. The four proposals included in this volume all make some effort to go beyond these matters and address the many issues of human rights, privacy, the environment, and devolution of powers. However, if the national debate begins to engage Japanese society more deeply, rather than the elite political, intellectual and media groups that monopolize it thus far, it is almost certain that calls for constitutional measures to extend and deepen the democratic powers of citizens would gradually come to be heard. Before the five years assigned for deliberation passes, one would expect that Japan's civil society will assert itself and attempt to regain the initiative in the debate. Whether to fight revision absolutely and cling to the existing constitution or to opt for a revision designed to radically democratize it is the dilemma faced. Might it be, for example, that constitutional endorsement will be sought of the right of citizens to direct empowerment through plebiscites, especially on local issues, and for the enforcement of clear community mandates when they emerge from them?[148] It is possible too that, with the increasing pace of globalization and the calls for greater decentralization, such engagement of Japan's civil society with the constitution will lead to a radical reconsideration of the appropriateness to the twenty-first century of the nation state itself, that pure embodiment of the values of the nineteenth and twentieth centuries. Because of the peculiar, and always peripheral, location of Okinawa within the nation state, the initiative in such rethinking may well come from there. Already the call for an 'Okinawa Basic Law' points in this direction.[149] Likewise, it may be expected that the growing democratic and universalist spirit of the new century will see a move to restore the open and universalist orientation of the early drafts of the 1947 constitution by eliminating the distinction between Japanese nationals and non-nationals and restoring the concept of *subete no shizenjin* under which equal rights would be accorded to all.

As of early 2000, however, with the debate just opened and still confined almost exclusively to politicians and intellectuals, the level of conservatism is noticeable. In essentials, the constitutional package imposed on Japan in the early days of the US occupation is not questioned. In particular the role of the Emperor is addressed only as one of whether to preserve a limited 'symbolic' emperor position or to choose 'constitutional monarchy'; republicanism is a cause little heard. The contrast between Japan and the United Kingdom, another ancient monarchy, where drastic revision of constitutional arrangements, including a possible end to the monarchy and the dissolution of the United Kingdom into its component parts, is publicly debated, is striking.[150]

The Constitutional Research Councils began their deliberations in a January 2000 national political framework that has changed drastically in the post-Cold War decade. The legislative record of 1999 was so dramatic that Ozawa Ichirō spoke of a 'bloodless revolution.'[151] What he was referring to was the passage of many bills that would have been impossible before, including the 'Regional Contingency Law' ('Guidelines'), the National Anthem and Flag Law, various laws authorizing the authorities to place wiretaps on citizens (in certain conditions) and establishing a system of numbering all citizens with a ten-digit identification code, and, of course, the decision to establish the Constitution Research Councils. In effect, the three-party conservative coalition government established by Obuchi Keizō in 1999 had the capacity to put through whatever legislation it wished. Nakasone Yasuhiro in the 1980s may have been following a more explicitly nationalist agenda in his attempt at 'comprehensive settlement of the post-war accounts' (*sengo sōkessan*), but he was blocked from realizing many of his goals by the impossibility of getting them through the Diet. From 1999, for the first time, a clear majority of Diet members – that is not only an absolute majority but in excess of the two-thirds required under Article 96 for constitutional revision – is committed to reform.[152] Even the principal opposition leader, Hatoyama Ichirō of the Democratic Party of Japan, not only supports the Constitutional Research Councils, but is explicitly 'revisionist,' insisting that the SDF should become simply the Japanese Army (*guntai*).[153]

As Tanaka Makiko (daughter of former Prime Minister Tanaka, and herself Director of the Science and Technology Agency under the Murayama government in the mid-1990s) remarked, because it had the numbers, the government, which she referred to contemptuously as a 'gulp gulp cabinet' (*pakkun pakkun naikaku*), swallowed whole whatever the bureaucrats brought forward, 'whether soap or bombs.'[154] This political vortex, in which an opposition had all but disappeared, combined with the emergence of powerful, new, mass-mobilizing, neo-nationalist organizations in society at large, alarmed others enough to arouse fear that the society was heading in the direction of 'general mobilization,' an 'Imperial Rule Assistance Association'-type regime like those of the 1930s and 1940s. Kunihiro Masao, former member of the Upper House in the national Diet, was one among many left-inclined intellectuals who spoke of the fear that what he was witnessing was 'the rush of Japanese-style fascism.'[155]

For fifty years the constitution served to root Japan in the rule of law and universalistic principles of democracy and human rights; a code that occasionally weakened but never completely lost its force. As the century ended, however, this sense of justice, peace, and human rights was drifting in the face of a rootless, situationist morality that shifted, according to calculations of interest. Increasingly Orwellian conventions of language facilitated this process. From the 1950s, the political calculations of constitutional pacifism required that tanks be known as 'special vehicles' and the national armed forces as 'Self-Defense Forces' rather than 'Army.' More recently, war itself is known as a 'contingency' – the war with

China in the 1930s is still commonly referred to as an 'incident.' Furthermore, as Yamaguchi Jirō noted in 1999, 'environs' has become a word without geographic significance, war a 'situation,' the *Kimi* whose eternal rule is prayed for in the newly adopted national anthem means 'the Emperor who is symbol of the state and unity of the people' – not the Emperor as he always used to be – and the new *Hinomaru-Kimigayo* Law would not impose any new obligations on the Japanese people, although teachers are instructed to sing the anthem at all school ceremonies and are punished if they refuse.[156]

The constitutional debate is an important window onto the way that the Japanese people think of themselves, and how they would like to be seen by the world. The steady weakening of interest in articulating a sense of being 'different' – a unique constitutional 'peace state' committed to the resolution of conflict by means other than the use of force and striving to create a New World Order based on such a distinctive value – is a testimony to the loss of idealism. Ordinariness in itself, with its associations of modesty, decency, simplicity, is no bad thing, but the 'ordinariness' of a great power, little, if at all different from other great powers; shorn of the inhibitions that were long-attached under the post-1945 settlement, and no longer a 'one lung' peace state but possessing the full complement of military enforcement powers and a seat on the UNSC, would not necessarily arouse enthusiasm on the part of its neighbors and the world.

Whether Japan's civil society will find the strength in the twenty-first century to resist the siren calls of greatness and the wisdom to discover a formula to establish the clear primacy of people's rights and interests over state rights and interests remains to be seen. Facing the emerging new world order, Japan has somehow to address the problem of the five decades of 'revision by interpretation' during which the gap between facade and reality has widened. It is up to the Japanese people to decide whether they are prepared to revise or reinterpret their Constitution and if so in what way. It is up to them, in short, to decide what they wish to offer to the new millennium. Here lies the fundamental question of Japanese democracy.

Notes

1 Among others, the German Basic Law has been revised forty-six times, and the Norwegian and Swiss constitutions 139 and 132 times respectively. (Nishi Osamu, *Nihonkoku kempō o kangaeru*, Tokyo, Bunshun Shinsho, 1999, p. 17.)
2 For authoritative studies of the process of drafting and adoption: Koseki Shoichi, 'Japanizing the Constitution,' *Japan Quarterly*, vol. 35, no. 3, July–September 1988, pp. 234–40, and Koseki Shōichi, *Shin kempō no tanjō*, Tokyo, Chūō Kōronsha, 1989, edited and translated by Ray Moore as *The Birth of Japan's Postwar Constitution*, Boulder, Colorado, Westview, 1997; and John W. Dower, *Embracing Defeat. Japan in the Wake of World War II*, New York, W. W. Norton, 1999.
3 Koseki, ibid., 1997, p. 79.
4 Dower, ibid., p. 384.
5 Yokota Kōichi, *Kempō to tennōsei*, Tokyo, Iwanami, 1990, pp. 12–38, passim. Reissued as a second edition with new preface in 1999.
6 Yasuhiro Okudaira, 'Forty Years of the Constitution and its Various Influences,' in

Percy R. Luney and Kazuyuki Takahashi (eds), *Japanese Constitutional Law*, Tokyo, University of Tokyo Press, 1993, pp. 1–38, at p. 2.
7 Koseki op. cit., 1988, p. 235.
8 Koseki, op. cit., 1997, pp. 115, 179–80.
9 John Dower's title for his Chapter Nine, *Embracing Defeat*, pp. 277 ff. See also Dower's 'Tennōsei minshushugi no tanjō,' *Sekai*, September 1999, pp. 221–32; and in English as 'The Showa Emperor and Japan's Postwar Imperial Democracy,' Japan Policy Research Institute, Working Paper no. 61, October 1999 (http://www.nmjc.org /jpri/public/wp61.html).
10 See Urata Ichirō, 'Heiwashugi no rikai no shikata,' Watanabe Osamu *et al.* (eds), *"Kempō kaisei" hihan*, Tokyo, Rōdō Junpōsha, 1994, pp. 187–241, at p. 190.
11 Dower, op. cit., September 1999, pp. 221–32.
12 Shindō Ei'ichi, *Sengo no gyakusetsu*, Tokyo, Chikuma, 1999.
13 Edwin O. Reischauer, 'Memorandum on Policy Towards Japan,' September 14 1942, document introduced and discussed in Fujitani Takashi, 'Raishawaa moto Beikoku taishi no kairai tennōsei kōsō,' *Sekai*, March 2000, pp. 137–46, and for the full text of the Memorandum: http://www.iwanami.co.jp/sekai/00.672/146.html.
14 Memorandum from the Showa Emperor, text contained in Dower, op. cit., September 1999.
15 From Congressional testimony by MacArthur, quoted in Tetsuya Kataoka, *The Price of a Constitution: The Origin of Japan's Postwar Politics*, New York, Taylor and Francis, 1991, p. 30.
16 Dower, op. cit. September 1999, p. 226.
17 Statement of June 26 1946, quoted in Tsuneoka Setsuko, 'Dai kyūjō de hatasu sengo sekinin,' *Gunshuku Mondai Shiryō*, February 1996, pp. 14–19, at p. 16.
18 Theodore H. McNelly, 'Induced Revolution: The Policy and Process of Constitutional Reform in Occupied Japan,' in Robert E. Ward and Yoshikazu Sakamoto (eds), *Democratizing Japan: The Allied Occupation*, Honolulu, the University of Hawaii Press, 1987, pp. 76–106, at p. 102.
19 Kitaoka Shin'ichi, 'The Constitutional Debate in Japan: Cutting the Gordian Knot,' *Japan Review of International Affairs*, Fall 1999, pp. 191–205.
20 Support levels running at 70 percent, according to the *Mainichi Shimbun*, May 27 1946, quoted in Tsuneoka Setsuko, 'Pacifism and Some Misconceptions about the Constitution of Japan,' in Tsuneoka Setsuko *et al.*, (eds), *The Constitution of Japan*, Tokyo, Kawade Shobo, 1993, pp. 120–53, at p. 126.
21 John M. Maki, 'The Constitution of Japan: Pacifism, Popular Sovereignty, and Fundamental Human Rights,' in Luney and Takahashi (eds), op. cit., pp. 39–56, at pp. 50–1.
22 Thus the year 2000 is known officially as 'Heisei Twelve' or the twelfth year of the Emperor who acceded to the throne in 1989.
23 Yōichi Higuchi, 'The Constitution and the Emperor System: Is Revisionism Alive?,' in Luney and Takahashi, (eds), op. cit., pp. 57–67, at p. 64; also Kōichi Yokota, 'The Separation of Religion and State,' ibid, pp. 205–20, especially at pp. 213–14.
24 Yokota, ibid., p. 205.
25 It was passed with massive parliamentary support, in the Lower House 403 (including forty-five members of the Democratic Party of Japan) in favor, 86 opposed. Opinion polls gave 68 percent in favor to 26 percent opposed (*Yomiuri Shimbun*, April 9 1999).
26 The constitutional ban on religious activity by the state was evaded by the adoption of formula to separate the religious from the political moments of imperial funeral, accession, wedding and commemorative rituals.
27 In the event, the performances by well-known musical groups, such as GLAY and SPEED, may have attracted more interest among youth than the event that was supposedly being celebrated.

46 *Japan's contested constitution*

28 Daikichi Irokawa, *The Age of Hirohito: in Search of Modern Japan*, translated by Mikiso Hane and John K. Urda, New York, Free Press, 1995, pp. 112–13; Yokota Kōichi, 'Kokumin tōgō to shōchō tennōsei,' *Sekai*, January 2000, pp. 73–86, at p. 81 (on emperor diplomacy).
29 June 29 1999 statement to the Diet by then Prime Minister Obuchi. (Kazuhiko Kajiki, 'National flag and anthem to be official,' *Nikkei Weekly*, July 19 1999.)
30 Irokawa Daikichi, 'Kokusaika ni gyakkō suru "kimigayo" hōan ga nerau kōkoku nashonarizumu,' *Ronza*, September 1999, pp. 30–9, at p. 35.
31 Yokota, 1999 (second edn of 1990 book in note 5) p. v.
32 Shimojima Tetsurō, 'Hinomaru Kimigayo ni teikō suru kyōshitachi,' *Sekai*, January 2000, pp. 134–47, at p. 139.
33 Tanaka Nobumasa, '"Kimigayo" kyōsei o kempō ni tou "kokoro saiban"' Part 1, *Shūkan Kinyōbi*, 25 February 2000, pp. 52–5; part 2, March 3 2000, pp. 30–3.
34 See Tanaka Nobumasa, 'Seikyō bunri kara tou shōchō tennōsei no jūnen,' *Sekai*, January 2000, pp. 104–12.
35 Irokawa, op. cit., 1995, p. 145; Norma Field, *In the Realm of a Dying Emperor*, New York, Vintage, 1993, pp. 177–266.
36 David Williams, *Reporting the Death of the Shōwa Emperor*, Nissan Occasional Paper Series, Oxford, Nissan Institute of Japanese Studies, 1990, p. 13.
37 Yoshikazu Sakamoto (ed.) *The Emperor System as a Japan Problem: The Case of Meiji Gakuin University*, Occasional Paper Series, International Peace Research Institute, Meigaku, 1990.
38 Field, op. cit.
39 Subsequently the album was released without deletion by an independent company ('Konshū no kono ichigen,' *Shūkan Kinyōbi*, August 27 1999).
40 Michael Schaller, *Altered States: The United States and Japan since the Occupation*, Oxford, Oxford University Press, 1997, p. 136. Also see Haruna Mikio, *Himitsu no Fuairu: CIA no Tainichi Kōsaku* (two volumes), Tokyo, Kyōdō Tsūshinsha, 2000.
41 Schaller, ibid, pp. 136, 195.
42 Nagoshi Kenrō, *Kuremurin Himitsu Bunsho wa Kataru*, Tokyo, Chūō Kōronsha, 1994.
43 See Gavan McCormack, *The Emptiness of Japanese Affluence*, New York, M. E. Sharpe, 1996, pp. 185–6.
44 Admiral Okubo Takeo, interviewed in Tokyo for Thames Television by Gavan McCormack, 16 April 1987. (See Jon Halliday and Bruce Cumings, *Korea: The Unknown War*, London, Penguin-Viking, 1988, p. 165.) Also James E. Auer, 'Article Nine: Renunciation of War,' in Luney and Takahashi (eds), op. cit., pp. 69–86, at p. 79.
45 Watanabe Osamu, 'Kempō wa dō ikite kita ka,' *Iwanami Bukkuretto* no. 85, 1987, p. 15.
46 Auer, op. cit., pp. 75–6.
47 International Institute for Strategic Studies, *The Military Balance 1999–2000*, Oxford, Oxford University Press, 2000.
48 *Mainichi Shimbun*, April 29 1987.
49 See, for example, tables in *Asahi Shimbun*, May 3 1992.
50 Nakasone, Yasuhiro, *The Making of the New Japan*, Basingstoke, Macmillan, 1999, p. 140.
51 See Gavan McCormack, 'Beyond Economism: Japan in a State of Transition,' in Gavan McCormack and Yoshio Sugimoto (eds), *Democracy in Contemporary Japan*, New York, M. E. Sharpe, 1986, pp. 56–9.
52 Odawara Atsushi, 'Kempō 9-jō wa songoku no "kanawa" buryoku fukōshi ga gensoku,' *Aera*, May 4–11 1993, pp. 66–7.
53 Gavan McCormack, '1999 nen no chikaku hendō,' *Sekai*, (Kinkyū zōkan), *Sutoppu! Ji-Ji-Kō bōsō*, November 1999, pp. 23–9, at p. 24.
54 Miyazawa Ki'ichi, *Shin gokenron sengen – 21 seiki no Nihon to sekai*, Tokyo, Asahi Shuppansha, 1995.

55 See, for example, the 'Unified View of Government,' dated November 13 1972, quoted in Urata, op. cit., p. 194.
56 Maki, in Luney and Takahashi (eds), op. cit., 39–56, at p. 41.
57 Okudaira, op. cit., 1993, pp. 23–5.
58 In regard to the SDF, 78 percent of such specialists believe so, according to a survey of October 1991. See *Asahi Shimbun*, May 3 1992. See also Yamauchi Toshihiro, *Heiwa kempō no riron*, Tokyo, Nihon Hyōronsha, 1992, and also his 'Kempōgaku no shōten,' *Asahi Shimbun*, April 15 1994.
59 Robert S. Norris, William M. Arkin, and William Burr, 'How much did Japan know?' *Bulletin of Atomic Scientists*, January–February 2000 (http://www.bullatomsci.org/issues/2000/jf00norrisarkin.html). Also Yoshitaka Sasaki, 'Secret files expose Tokyo's Double standards on Nuclear Policy, *Asahi Shimbun*, 25 August 1999, reposted by the Nautilus Institute: http://www.nautilus.org/nukepolicy/Nuclear-Umbrella/asahi_update.html.
60 John Welfield, *An Empire in Eclipse: Japan in the Postwar American Alliance System*, London, Athlone, 1988, pp. 257–8.
61 Sugihara Yasuo *et al.* (eds), *Nihonkoku kempōshi nenpyō*, Tokyo, Keisō Shobo, 1998, p. 744.
62 Glenn D. Hook, 'The erosion of anti-militaristic principles in contemporary Japan,' *Journal of Peace Research*, vol. 25, no. 4, 1988, pp. 381–94.
63 *Nihon Keizai Shimbun*, 19 December 1995. Replies to this question were as follows: bureaucrats 37 percent; politicians 22 percent; 'business' 15.5 percent; public opinion 7.2 percent.
64 Jacob Schlesinger, *Shadow Shoguns: the Rise and Fall of Japan's Postwar Political Machine*, New York, Simon and Schuster, 1997; Richard H. Mitchell, *Political Bribery in Japan*, Honolulu, University of Hawaii Press, 1996.
65 See note 8.
66 Kaizawa Kōichi, 'Ihō damu" wa nokotta,' in Urabe Noriho and Nakakita Ryūtarō (eds), *Dokyumento – Nihonkoku kempō*, Tokyo, Nihon Hyōronsha, 1998, pp. 87–94.
67 Yoko Sellek, *Migrant Labour in Japan*, Basingstoke: Macmillan, 2000.
68 Okudaira Yasuhiro, 'Some Consideration on the Constitution of Japan,' *Occasional Papers in Law and Society*, no. 3, Institute of Social Science, University of Tokyo, December 1987, pp. 32–4. See also Yamazumi Masami, 'Educational democracy versus state control,' in McCormack and Sugimoto (eds), op. cit., pp. 90–113.
69 Yamazaki Taku, *2010 nen no Nihon jitsugen*, Tokyo, Daiyamondosha, 1999, p. 38.
70 Lawrence W. Beer, 'Freedom of Expression: the Continuing Revolution,' in Luney and Takahashi (eds), op. cit., 221–54, at pp. 243–5, and, on more recent developments, Nozaki Yoshiko and Inokuchi Hiromitsu, 'Japanese Education, Nationalism, and Ienaga Saburo's Court Challenges,' *Bulletin of Concerned Asian Scholars*, vol. 30, no. 2, 1998, pp. 37–46.
71 Okudaira, in Luney and Takahashi (eds), op. cit., pp. 1–38, at p. 21.
72 Beer, op. cit., pp. 230–2.
73 Gavan McCormack, 'Crime, Confession and Control in Contemporary Japan,' in McCormack and Sugimoto (eds), op. cit., pp. 186–94; and Igarashi Futaba, 'Forced to Confess,' ibid., pp. 195–214; also D. Foote, 'From Japan's Death Row to Freedom,' *Pacific Rim Law and Policy Journal*, vol. 1, no. 1, 1992, pp. 11–101, and '"The Door that Never opens?" Capital Punishment and Post-Conviction Review of Sentences in the United States and Japan,' *Brooklyn Journal of International Law*, vol. 19, no. 2, 1993, pp. 367–521.
74 'Court rejects inmate's claim over thirteen years in solitary,' *Asahi Shimbun*, Asahi Online http\\www:asahi.co.jp (April 14 1999).
75 Yoshiaki Yoshida, 'Authority of the National and Local Governments under the Constitution,' in Luney and Takahashi (eds), op. cit., pp. 109–21, at pp. 110–12.
76 Okudaira, op. cit., 1987, pp. 18–19.

77 Okudaira op. cit., 1993, pp. 23–5.
78 Glenn D. Hook, *Militarization and Demilitarization in Contemporary Japan*, London, Routledge, 1996.
79 In a 1988 survey conducted by the Nippon Hōsō Kyōkai (NHK, the national broadcaster), for instance, only 5 percent of those born in 1972 and 9 percent of those born in 1958 expressed feelings of respect for the Emperor, whereas 70 percent of those born in 1918 and 63 percent of those born in 1923 expressed such sentiments. (*NHK Yoron Chōsa Honbu Gendai Nihonjin no Ishiki Kōzō*, Tokyo, NHK, 1991, p. 105.)
80 A January 1960 poll by the *Asahi Shimbun* showed over a third, at 35 percent, chose neutrality and just under a quarter, at 24 percent, opted for dependence on the UN as the security policy for Japan (multiple answers permitted).
81 Igarashi Takeshi, *Nichibei kankei to higashi Ajia – rekishiteki bunmyaku to mirai no kōsō*, Tokyo, Tokyo Daigaku Shuppankai, 1999, p. 166; Hara Yoshihisa, *Sengo Nihon to kokusai seiji*, Tokyo, Chūō Kōronsha, pp. 425–8.
82 Yasuaki Onuma, 'In Quest of Intercivilizational Human Rights: Universal vs. Relative Human Rights Viewed From an Asian Perspective,' in Daniel Warner (ed.), *Human Rights and Humanitarian Law: The Quest for Universality*, Kluwer Law International, London, 1995, pp. 43–78, at pp. 57–9.
83 NGO Katsudō Suishin Sentâ, *NGO Dētabukku '96*, Tokyo, NGO Katsudō Suishin Sentā.
84 Kitazawa Yoko, 'Grassroots Aid in the Work: Beyond PP21 Kanagawa International Symposium,' *AMPO*, vol. 22, no. 1, pp. 43–7.
85 For a rare consideration of Okinawa from a constitutional perspective, see Arasaki Moriteru, 'Sengo Nihon no kōzōteki sabetsu,' in Urabe and Nakakita (eds), op. cit., pp. 41–8.
86 Masahide Ota, *The Battle of Okinawa: The Typhoon of Steel and Bombs*, Tokyo, Kume Publishing, 1984; and 'Re-examining the History of the Battle of Okinawa,' Chalmers Johnson (ed.), *Okinawa – Cold War Island*, Cardiff, Ca., Japan Policy Research Institute, 1999, pp. 13–38.
87 Shindō op. cit., pp. 88–91.
88 Nakamura Masanori, 'Kempō daikyūjō to tennōsei,' *Gunshuku Mondai Shiryō*, June 1998, pp. 16–21, at p. 21.
89 The messages, penned by Terasaki Hidenari, special adviser to the Emperor, were addressed to William Seybold, head of the diplomatic section of MacArthur's GHQ (Shindō Ei'ichi, '"Tennō messçji" sairon,' *Sekai*, October 1979, pp. 104–13, Also Robert D. Eldridge, 'Shōwa tennō to Okinawa – "tennō messçji" no saikōsatsu,' *Chūō Kōron*, March 1999, pp. 152–71.
90 Shindō Ei'ichi, *Sengo no genzō*, Tokyo, Iwanami Shoten, 1999, pp. 18–19.
91 Accepting here the date given by Ota Masahide for the commencement of the fighting. (Masahide Ota, 'Re-examining the History of the Battle of Okinawa,' in Johnson (ed.), op. cit., pp. 13–38).
92 The Okinawan commitment to constitutionalism is not highly regarded in Tokyo. In an unguarded moment, the then LDP Secretary-General and future Prime Minister, Mori Yoshirō, remarked in March 2000 that he viewed the teachers' union and the two local newspapers as being under communist control. (See *Ryūkyū Shimpō* and *Okinawa Taimusu*, March 23 2000.)
93 Chalmers Johnson (ed.), op. cit., 1999.
94 Gabe Masaaki, "Sonchō" to iu na no "kyōsei", *Sekai*, January 2000, pp. 34–46, at p. 38.
95 Opinion survey conducted jointly by the *Asahi Shimbun* and the *Okinawa Taimusu*, results published in *Okinawa Taimusu*, December 19 1999 (in Nago City the outcome was 59 percent opposition to 23 percent support, and in Okinawa as a whole, 45 percent to 32 percent).
96 Tōkai Daigaku Heiwa Senryaku Kokusai Kenkyūjo (ed.), *Nichibei ampo to Okinawa mondai – bunseki to shiryō*, Tokyo, Shakai Hyōronsha, 1997.

97 Sakugawa Ei'ichi, 'Okinawa to heiwa kempō,' *Gunshuku Mondai Shiryō*, May 1997, pp. 4–9, at p. 7.
98 Okinawa Taimususha (ed.), *Okinawa kara, Beigun kichi mondai dokkyumento*, Tokyo, Asahi Shimbunsha, 1997, p. 24.
99 Ota Masahide, 'Governor Ota at the Supreme Court of Japan,' in Johnson (ed.), op. cit., pp. 205–14, at p. 213.
100 For the governor's views, see Keiichi Inamine, 'Okinawa: Reflections on the Postwar Years and a Vision for the Future, *Japan Review of International Affairs*, vol. 14, no. 1, 2000, pp. 22–37.
101 On the 1997 'Special Measures Law for Land Required by US Military bases,' see Chalmers Johnson, 'The 1995 Rape Incident and the Rekindling of Okinawan Protest against the American bases,' in Johnson (ed.) op. cit., 1999, pp. 109–29, at p. 113; Koji Taira, 'Okinawa's Choice: Independence or Subordination,' in Johnson (ed.) op. cit., 1999, pp. 171–85, at p. 175.
102 On this 1999 revision to the 'Special Measures Law,' see Arasaki Moriteru, 'Kokkai to hondo ni mushi sareta "Beigun yōchi tokushakuhō" kaitei,' *Shūkan Kinyōbi*, July 30 1999, pp. 27–9.
103 'Ampo o tsubuse! – chōchin demo no kai,' June 9 1991, in Itō Kunio (ed.), *Kempō to yoron komentāru sengo 50 nen*, Tokyo, Shakai Hyōronsha, 1996, pp. 257–8.
104 Fukushima Shingo, 'Jieitai "iken gōhō" ni hashiru Ishibashi shakaitō no shingi,' *Asahi Jānaru*, February 10 1984, pp. 14–18.
105 *Gekkan Shakaitō*, June 1993, quoted in Yoshikawa Atsushi, 'Kaikenron no dōkō to "jieiken" ron no otoshiana,' *Gekkan Fōramu*, November 1993, pp. 34–42, at p. 39.
106 Sugihara *et al.* (eds), op. cit., pp. 745–6.
107 Chuck Overby, Charles M. Overby, and Kazuma Momoi, *A Call for Peace: The Implications of Japan's War-Renouncing Constitution*, Tokyo, Kodansha International, 1998.
108 Glenn D. Hook, Julie Gilson, Christopher W. Hughes, and Hugo Dobson, *Japan's International Relations: Politics, Economics and Security*, London, Routledge, forthcoming 2001; Ueno Chizuko, 'Shiminteki bōryoku wa subete kinshi sareteiru no ni, kokka wa buryoku o kōshi shite ii nante nansensu,' *Tsūbai Seikatsu* (Tokudaigo), Spring, 2001, p. 27.
109 Support or qualified support, 37 percent; opposition or qualified opposition, 43 percent, according to the Asahi's survey ('Shin gaidorain kanren hōan – Asahi Shimbunsha Yoron Chōsa,' *Asahi Shimbun*, March 19 1999).
110 Urata, op. cit., p. 205.
111 Table of opinion poll surveys from the Asahi in Wada Susumu, 'Keizai taikoku to kokumin ishiki no henbō,' in Watanabe Osamu *et al.* (eds), op. cit., pp. 131–84, at p. 169.
112 Opinion survey conducted by *Yomiuri Shimbun* in March 1993 showed that, while defenders of the Constitution had diminished from 51.1 to 33.0 percent between 1991 and 1993, those in favor of revision had increased from 33.3 to 50.4 percent. This figure then fell (to 44.2 percent) in 1994 but rose again to the same 50.4 percent in 1995 (see Nakanō Hōkan, 'Kempō to sedai ishiki,' *This is Yomiuri*, June 1995, pp. 146–51, at p. 147).
113 *Yomiuri Shimbun*, April 9 1999.
114 Article 82 of the SDF Law spells out clear requirements for the exercise of force by the SDF, which include immediate threat to life and/or property (Maeda Tetsuo, 'Kaijō keibi kōdō "kakusareta ito",' *Sekai*, May 1999, pp. 22–6).
115 51 percent found the response 'appropriate under the circumstances,' 38 percent believed it should have been *more* severe, and only 8 percent found it excessive. (Opinion survey conducted by Kyōdō Tsūshin on April 6, quoted in Shinta Masamichi, 'Ronsō,' *Shūkan Kinyōbi*, July 9 1999.)
116 Statement of March 3 1999. Quoted in Taoka Shunji, 'Oroka na sensei kōgekiron,' *Asahi Shimbun*, March 21 1999.

117 Yamaguchi Jirō, *Kiki no Nihon Seiji*, Tokyo, Iwanami, 1999, p. 132.
118 The possibility of being involved in armed conflict was enough to rule out all but the despatch of three police officers in response to the troubles in East Timor in 1999.
119 See, for example, the 1993 deliberations of the Australian Senate Committee on Japan's defense policies: Senate Standing Committee on Foreign Affairs, Defense and Trade, *Japan's Defence and Security in the 1990s*, Canberra, Senate Printing Unit, 1993.
120 Reinhard Drifte, *Japan's Quest for a Permanent United Nations Security Council Seat: A Matter of Pride or Justice?* Basingstoke, Macmillan, 2000.
121 Hook, *et al.* op. cit., 2001 forthcoming.
122 Obuchi Keizō, 'UN General Assembly 52nd Session,' Online. http://www.undp.org/missions/japan/s_0923_7.htm (April 2 2000).
123 Nakagawa Yatsuhiro, *Shin Nihonkoku kempō sōan*, Tokyo, Yamate Shobo, 1984.
124 *Nippon no Ibuki*, May 1999, quoted in Tawara, op. cit., June 25 1999, at p. 31.
125 See Gavan McCormack, 'The Japanese Movement to "Correct" History,' in Laura Elizabeth Hein and Mark Selden (eds), *Censoring History*: P*erspectives on Nationalism and War in the Twentieth Century*, New York, M. E. Sharpe, 2000, pp. 55–73.
126 Yoshikawa Tsuneo, 'Kempō chōsakai no hossoku ni omou,' *Sutoppu! Ji-Ji-Kō bōsō*, pp. 135–6.
127 Irokawa, op. cit., 1995, pp. 145–6.
128 Fujioka Nobukatsu, central figure in the textbook revision movement, describes the peace clauses in the Constitution as 'scales' on the Japanese eyes. (Yamashina Saburō, '"Jiyūshugi shikan" wa nijūisseiki no Nihon o doko e michibiku ka,' in Matsushima Ei'ichi and Shiromaru Fumio (eds), *'Jiyūshugi shikan' no byōri*, Tokyo, Otsuki Shoten, 1997, pp. 14–48, at p. 27.)
129 Watanabe *et al.* (eds), op. cit, 1994, at pp. 22–5.
130 'Councils to help shape Japan's future,' Daily Yomiuri Online at http\\www.yomiuri.co.jp (July 30 1999), and see Ishikawa Masumi, 'Kempō rongi no katei de miete kuru kaikenha ni taisuru kimochi,' *Shūkan Kinyōbi*, August 27 1999, p. 8.
131 Inoki Masamichi *et al.* (eds), '"Kempō mondai chōsakai" no dai ichiji teigen,' (December 1992), in *Kempō mondai o kangaeru*, Tokyo, Yomiuri Shimbunsha, 1993.
132 *Yomiuri Shimbun*, November 3 1994, also reproduced in the monthly, *This is Yomiuri*, December 1994 and (as a translated English pamphlet) in *A Proposal for the Revision of the Text of the Constitution of Japan*, Tokyo, Yomiuri Shimbunsha, 1994.
133 'Kokuminteki rongi o makiokosō,' *This is Yomiuri*, December 1994, pp. 42–4, at p. 42.
134 '21 seiki e ima nani o nasubeki ka,' *Yomiuri Shimbun*, January 1 1995.
135 Yomiuri kempō mondai kenkyūkai, 'Sōgō anzen hoshō – seisaku daikō o teigen suru,' *This is Yomiuri,* June 1995, pp. 104–28.
136 'Kyōdō teigen: "Heiwa kihonhō" o tsukurō,' Koseki Shōichi *et al.*, *Sekai*, April 1993, pp. 52–67; Koseki Shōichi *et al.*, 'Ajia Taiheiyō chi'iki ampo o kōsō suru,' *Sekai*, December 1994, pp. 22–40. (See also Maeda Tetsuo, Asai Motofumi, Shindō Masayuki, *Jieitai o dō suru ka*, Tokyo, Iwanami, 1992 for the earliest formulation of some of these ideas.)
137 See the provocative essay by Wada Haruki, '55 nen taisei to heiwa no mondai,' presented to the 1993 meeting of the Japan Peace Studies Association (*Nihon Heiwa Gakkai*), November 13 1993, reproduced in revised form in 'Sengo kakushin sōkatsu to tembō,' *Rinji zōkan Sekai* ('Kiiwado sengo Nihon seiji 50 nen'), April 1994, pp. 225–30.
138 'Kokusai kyōroku to kempō,' *Asahi Shimbun,* May 3 1995. (English text in *Asahi Evening News* of the same day.)
139 Ozawa Ichirō, *Nihon kaizō kaikaku*, Tokyo, Kōdansha, 1993, p. 105 (in English as *Blueprint for a New Japan*, Tokyo, Kodansha International, 1994).
140 Watanabe Osamu, '"Kyujō" toppa e gōin na zenbun kaishaku,' *Asahi Shimbun*,

March 19 1992 (evening); also see excerpts of the Ozawa committee document in *Liberal Star*, March 15 1993.
141 Ozawa, op. cit., 1993, pp. 136–7.
142 Hans W. Maull, 'Germany and Japan: the new civilian powers,' *Foreign Affairs*, vol. 69, no. 5, 1990–91, pp. 91–106.
143 Tanaka Akira, *Shōkokushugi*, Tokyo, Iwanami Shinsho, 1999. (Also see Kunihiro Masao, 'Kempōmushi no kiwamaru tokoro,' *Gunshuku Mondai Shiryō*, May 2000, pp. 18–23.)
144 Irokawa Daikichi, *The Culture of the Meiji Period* (translated by Marius B. Jansen), Princeton, Princeton University Press, 1988. Also see Irokawa's 'Jiyū minken undō to Nihonkoku kempō,' *Gunshuku Mondai Shiryō*, May 1993, pp. 4–5.
145 Hidaka Rokurō, 'Ozaki Yukiō "Bōhyō no kawari ni" saidoku,' (part 1) *Sekai*, February 2000, pp. 184–98, part 2, March 2000, pp. 184–94.
146 Quoted in Takeda Ken, 'Kempō wa jitsugen sarete iru no ka ima kūseki medatsu chōsakai,' *Shūkan Kinyōbi*, 7 April 2000, p. 5.
147 Sugihara *et al.* (eds), pp. 769–72.
148 For the move to introduce legislation to this effect following repeated cases of government officials overruling clear expressions of local will as expressed through such plebiscites, see 'Public seeks law providing binding plebiscites,' *Japan Times*, March 14 2000.
149 Kamo Toshio, 'Okinawa – Jichi modero no sentaku,' in Miyamoto Ken'ichi and Sasaki Masayuki (eds), *Okinawa – 21 seiki e no chōsen*, Tokyo, Iwanami, 2000, pp. 249–84.
150 *Economist*, October 22 1994; Anthony Barnett, *This Time: Our Constitutional Revolution*, New York, Vintage Books, 1997.
151 Quoted in Takada Ken, 'Atarashisa o yosōtta "Sakurai Yoshiko" no fukkōshugi,' *Shūkan Kinyōbi*, 17 September 1999, pp. 32–3.
152 As of the end of 1999, the three-party ruling coalition held 71 percent of the seats in the Lower House and 56 percent of those in the Upper House. While it is true that not all of these members would necessarily support revision, it is also true that many in the opposition parties do. One estimate is that, as of January 2000, revision would be favored by 80.1 percent of members in the Lower House and 67.1 percent in the Upper House. (Yamauchi Toshihiro, '2000 nen o "kaiken gannen" ni suru na,' *Shūkan Kinyōbi*, 14 January 2000, pp. 10–13, at p. 11.)
153 Hatoyama Ichirō, 'Jieitai o guntai to mitomeyo,' *Bungei Shunjū*, October 1999, pp. 262–73.
154 Tanaka Makiko, in conversation with Sadaka Makoto, 'JiJiKō seikyoku o kiru,' *Sekai*, September 1999, pp. 41–9.
155 Kunihiro Masao, with Ishikawa Yoshimi and Chikushi Tetsuya, 'Gōman na Amerika,' *Shūkan Kinyōbi*, April 10 1998, pp. 9–15, at p. 23.
156 Yamaguchi, op. cit., pp. 74–82.

Part 2
Documents

Yomiuri Shimbun, 'A proposal for the revision of the text of the Constitution of Japan' (1994)

Preamble

Proposed text

We, the Japanese people, hold sovereign power in Japan and, ultimately, our will shall dictate all State decisions. Government is entrusted to our duly elected representatives, who exercise their power with the trust of the people.

We, the Japanese people, desire peace for all time, respect the spirit of international cooperation and pledge to use our best efforts to ensure the peace, prosperity and security of the international community.

We, the Japanese people, aspire to a free and vigorous society, where basic human rights are duly respected, and simultaneously strive for the advancement of the people's welfare.

We, the Japanese people, acknowledge the inheritance of our long history and tradition and the need to preserve our fair landscape and cultural legacy while promoting culture, arts and sciences.

This Constitution is the supreme law of Japan and is to be observed by the Japanese people.

Current text

We, the Japanese people, acting through our duly elected representatives in the National Diet, determined that we shall secure for ourselves and our posterity the fruits of peaceful cooperation with all nations and the blessings of liberty throughout this land, and resolved that never again shall we be visited with the horrors of war through the action of government, do proclaim that sovereign power resides with the people and do firmly establish this Constitution. Government is a sacred trust of the people, the authority for which is derived from the people, the powers of which are exercised by the representative of the people, and the benefits of which are enjoyed by the people. This is a universal principle of mankind upon which this Constitution is founded. We reject and revoke all constitutions, laws, ordinances and rescripts in conflict herewith.

We, the Japanese people, desire peace for all time and are deeply conscious of the high ideals controlling human relationship, and we have determined to preserve our security and existence, trusting in the justice and faith of the peace-loving peoples of the world. We desire to occupy an honored place in an international society striving for the preservation of peace, and the banishment of tyranny and slavery, oppression and intolerance for all time from the earth. We recognize that all peoples of the world have the right to live in peace, free from fear and want.

We believe that no nation is responsible to itself alone, but that laws of political morality are universal, and that obedience to such laws is incumbent upon all nations who would sustain their own sovereignty, and justify their sovereign relationship with other nations.

We, the Japanese people, pledge our national honor to accomplish these ideals and purposes with all our resources.

Chapter 1 Sovereign power of the people
(Newly chaptered)

Article 1 (The people's sovereign power)
Sovereign power in Japan resides with the Japanese people.

Article 2 (Exercise of sovereign power)
The people shall exercise their sovereign power through their duly elected representatives in the Diet, and at national referenda held to consider amendments to the Constitution.

Article 3 (The conditions for being a Japanese national)
The conditions necessary for being a Japanese national shall be determined by law.

(From Chapter 3 on rights and duties of the people)

Article 10 (The conditions for being a Japanese national)
The conditions necessary for being a Japanese national shall be determined by law.

Chapter 2 The Emperor
(Currently Chapter 1)

Article 4 (The position of the Emperor)
The Emperor shall be the symbol of the State and of the unity of the people of Japan. The Emperor's position shall be based on the sovereign will of the people.

Article 5 (Succession to the Imperial Throne)
The Imperial Throne shall be dynastic and succeeded to in accordance with the Imperial House Law passed by the Diet.

Article 6 (Limits to the Emperor's functions, delegation of his performance of state acts and Regencies)
1) The Emperor shall perform only such acts in matters of state as are provided for in this Constitution and shall have no powers related to government.
2) The Emperor may delegate the performance of his acts in matters of state as may be provided for by law.
3) When, in accordance with the Imperial House Law, a Regency is established, the Regent shall perform his acts in matters of state in the Emperor's name, and Paragraph 1 of this Article shall apply subject to necessary changes.

Article 7 (Advice and approval of the Cabinet on the Emperor's acts in matters of state)
The advice and approval of the Cabinet shall be required for all acts of the Emperor in matters of state, and the Cabinet shall be responsible therefor.

Article 1 (The Emperor's position; the people's sovereign power)
The Emperor shall be the symbol of the State and of the unity of the people, deriving his position from the will of the people with whom resides sovereign power.

Article 2 (Succession to the Imperial Throne)
The Imperial Throne shall be dynastic and succeeded to in accordance with Imperial House Law passed by the Diet.

Article 4 (Limits to the Emperor's functions; delegation of his performance of state acts)
(1) The Emperor shall perform only such acts in matters of state as are provided for in this Constitution and he shall not have powers related to government.
(2) The Emperor may delegate performance of his acts in matters of state as may be provided by law.

Article 5 (Regencies)
When, in accordance with the Imperial House Law, a Regency is established, the Regent shall perform his acts in matters of state in the Emperor's name. In this case, paragraph one of the preceding article will be applicable.

Article 3 (Advice and approval of the Cabinet on the Emperor's acts in matters of state)
The advice and approval of the Cabinet shall be required for all acts of the Emperor in matters of state, and the Cabinet shall be responsible therefor.

Article 8 (The Emperor's power to appoint officials)
1) The Emperor shall appoint Prime Minister such person as designated by the House of Representatives.
   The Emperor shall appoint Chief Justice of the Constitutional Court such person as designated by the House of Councillors.

Article 9 (The Emperor's acts in matters of state)
The Emperor, with the advice and approval of the Cabinet, shall perform the following acts in matters of state on behalf of the people:

1   As the representative of the State, receiving foreign ambassadors and ministers and attesting commissions of full power, credentials of ambassadors and ministers, instruments of ratification and other diplomatic documents as provided for by law;
2   Promulgation of amendments to the Constitution, laws, Cabinet orders and treaties;
3   Promulgation of Imperial rescripts for the convocation of the Diet;
4   Promulgation of Imperial rescripts for the dissolution of the House of Representatives;
5   Proclamation of general elections of members of the House of Representatives and ordinary elections of the House of Councillors;
6   Attestation of the appointment and dismissal of Ministers of State and other officials as provided for by law;
7   Attestation of general and special amnesties, commutations of punishment, reprieves, and restorations of rights;

Article 6 (The Emperor's power to appoint officials)
(1) The Emperor shall appoint the Prime Minister as designated by the Diet.
(2) The Emperor shall appoint the Chief Judge of the Supreme Court as designated by the Cabinet.

Article 7 (The Emperor's acts in matters of state)
The Emperor, with the advice and approval of the Cabinet, shall perform the following acts in matters of state on behalf of the people:

1   Promulgation of amendments of the constitution, laws, cabinet orders and treaties.
2   Convocation of the Diet.
3   Dissolution of the House of Representatives.
4   Proclamation of general election of members of the Diet.
5   Attestation of the appointment and dismissal of Ministers of State and other officials as provided for by law, and of full powers and credentials of Ambassadors and Ministers.
6   Attestation of general and special amnesty, commutation of punishment, reprieve, and restoration of rights.
7   Awarding of honors.
8   Attestation of instruments of ratification and other diplomatic documents as provided for by law.
9   Receiving foreign ambassadors and ministers.
10 Performance of ceremonial functions.

8   Attestation of awards of honors;
9   Performance of ceremonial functions.

Article 8 (The Imperial House's receiving and granting property)
No property can be given to, or received by, the Imperial House, nor can any gifts be made therefrom, without the authorization of the Diet.

Chapter 3 National security
(Currently Chapter 2 Renunciation of war)

Article 10 (Rejection of war and ban on weapons of mass destruction)
1) Aspiring sincerely to an international peace based on justice and order, the Japanese people shall never recognize war as a sovereign right of the nation and the threat or use of force as means of settling international disputes.
2) Seeking to eliminate from the world inhuman and indiscriminate weapons of mass destruction, Japan shall not manufacture, possess or use such weapons.

Article 11 (Organisation for self-defense, civilian control and denial of forced conscription)
1) Japan shall form an organization for self-defense to secure its peace and independence and to maintain its safety.
2) The Prime Minister shall exercise supreme command authority over the organization for self-defense.
3) The people shall not be forced to participate in organizations for self-defense.

Article 9 (Renunciation of war and ban on weapons of mass destruction)
(1) Aspiring sincerely to an international peace based on justice and order, the Japanese people forever renounce war as a sovereign right of the nation and the threat or use of force as means of settling international disputes.
(2) In order to accomplish the aim of the preceding paragraph, land, sea, and air forces, as well as other war potential, will never be maintained. The right of belligerency of the state will not be recognized.

Chapter 4 International cooperation
(New chapter)

Article 12 (The ideal)
Japan shall aspire to the elimination from earth of human calamities caused by military conflicts, natural

disasters, environmental destruction, economic deprivation in particular areas and regional disorder.

Article 13 (Participation in international activities)
In order to accomplish the aim of the preceding article, Japan shall lend active cooperation to the activities of the relevant well-established and internationally recognized organizations. In case of need, it may dispatch public officials and provide a part of its self-defense organization for the maintenance and promotion of peace and for humanitarian support activities.

Article 14 (Observance of international laws)
Japan shall faithfully observe those treaties it has concluded and those international laws well established and recognized by the international community.

(From Chapter 10 on Supreme law)

Article 98 (Observance of international laws)
This Constitution shall be the supreme law of the nation and no law, ordinance, imperial rescript or other act of government, or part thereof, contrary to the provisions hereof, shall have legal force or validity.
The treaties concluded by Japan and established laws of nations shall be faithfully observed.

Chapter 5 Rights and Duties of the People
(Currently Chapter 3)

Article 15 (Basic declaration)
The people possess all fundamental human rights. The fundamental human rights guaranteed by this Constitution are inviolable and eternal rights.

Article 11 (Basic declaration)
The people shall not be prevented from enjoying any of the fundamental human rights. These fundamental human rights guaranteed to the people by this Constitution shall be conferred upon the people of this and future generations as eternal and inviolate rights.

Article 97 (The essence of basic human rights)
The fundamental human rights by Constitution guaranteed to the people of Japan are fruits of the age-old struggle of man to be free; they have survived the many exacting tests for

Article 16 (Responsibility for maintenance of freedoms and rights)
The freedoms and rights guaranteed to the people by this Constitution shall be maintained by the constant endeavour of the people, who shall always make efforts to harmonize them with the public welfare and who shall refrain from any abuse of them.

Article 17 (Individual dignity)
All of the people shall be respected as individuals. Their right to life, liberty, and the pursuit of happiness shall, to the extent that it does not interfere with the public welfare, be the supreme consideration in legislation and in other governmental affairs.

Article 18 (Equality under the law)
1) All of the people are equal under the law and there shall be no discrimination in political, economic or social relations because of race, creed, sex, social status or family origin.
2) No peers and peerage shall be recognized.
3) No political or social privilege shall accompany the award of any honor or decoration. However, a reasonable annuity or other economic benefit may be granted when so enacted especially.
4) No such award of honor shall be valid beyond the lifetime of the individual who now holds or hereafter may receive the same.

durability and are conferred upon this and future generations in trust, to be held for all time inviolate.

Article 16 (Responsibility for maintenance of freedoms and rights)
Every person shall have the right of peaceful petition for the redress of damage, for the removal of public officials for the enactment, repeal or amendment of laws, ordinances or regulations and for other matters; nor shall any person be in any way discriminated against for sponsoring such a petition.

Article 13 (Individual dignity)
All of the people shall be respected as individuals. Their right to life, liberty, and the pursuit of happiness shall, to the extent that it does not interfere with the public welfare, be the supreme consideration in legislation and in other governmental affairs.

Article 14 (Equality under the law)
(1) All of the people are equal under the law and there shall be no discrimination in political, economic or social relations because of race, creed, sex, social status of family origin.
(2) Peers and peerage shall not be recognized.
(3) No privilege shall accompany any award of honor, decoration or any distinction, nor shall any such award be valid beyond the lifetime of the individual who now holds or hereafter may receive it.

Article 18 (Freedom from bondage and involuntary servitude)
No person shall be held in bondage of any kind. Involuntary servitude, except as punishment for crime, is prohibited.

62 *Japan's contested constitution*

Article 19 (Right of privacy)
1) Every person is guaranteed the right not to have his name, repute, honor, trustworthiness, or other aspects of his character unduly impugned.
2) Every person shall have the right to keep his private affairs, family and household safe from unreasonable interference.
3) The secrecy of communications shall be inviolable.

Article 20 (Freedom of thought and conscience)
The right to freedom of thought and conscience shall be inviolable.

Article 21 (Freedom of religion and limitation of public expenditure)
1) Every person is guaranteed freedom of religion.
2) No person shall be compelled to take part in any religious act, celebration, rite or practice.
3) The State and its organs shall refrain from religious education or any other religious activity.
4) No Religious organization shall receive privileges from the State or exercise political influence.
5) No public money or other public property shall be spent or appropriated for the use, benefit or maintenance of any religious organization or body.

Article 22 (Freedom of expression)
1) Freedom of speech, press and all other forms of expression are guaranteed.
2) No censorship shall be maintained.

Article 23 (Freedom of assembly and association)
Every person is guaranteed freedom of assembly and association.

Article 19 (Freedom of thought and conscience)
Freedom of thought and conscience shall not be violated.

Article 20 (Freedom of religion)
(1) Freedom of religion is guaranteed to all. No religious organization shall receive any privileges from the State nor exercise any political authority.
(2) No person shall be compelled to take part in any religious act, celebration, rite or practice.
(3) The State and its organs shall refrain from religious education or any other religious activity.

Article 21 (Freedom of assembly, association and expression; secrecy of communications)
(1) Freedom of assembly and association as well as speech, press and all other forms of expression are guaranteed.
(2) No censorship shall be maintained, nor shall the secrecy of any means of communication be violated.

Article 24 (Freedom to choose and change residence and to shed nationality)
1) Every person possesses the freedom to choose and change his residence to the extent that it does not interfere with the public welfare.
2) All people are guaranteed freedom to move to a foreign country or divest themselves of their nationality.

Article 25 (Academic freedom)
Academic freedom is guaranteed.

Article 26 (Individual dignity in family life and equality between the sexes)
1) Marriage shall be based only on the mutual consent of both sexes and be maintained through mutual cooperation with the equal rights of husband and wife as a basis.
2) Legislation paying due regard to the dignity of the individual and the essential equality of the sexes shall be enacted to regulate the choice of spouse, property rights, succession, choice of domicile, divorce and other matters pertaining to marriage and the family.

Article 27 (Right of subsistence and the State's social duty)
1) All people possess the right to maintain the minimum standards of wholesome and cultural living.
2) In all spheres of life, the State shall use its endeavours for the promotion and extension of social welfare and security and of public health.

Article 28 (Rights relating to the environment)
1) Every person possesses the right to

Article 22 (Freedom to choose and change residence and occupation and to divest nationality)
(1) Every person shall have freedom to choose and change his residence and to choose his occupation to the extent that it does not interfere with the public welfare.
(2) Freedom of all persons to move to a foreign country and to divest themselves of their nationality shall be inviolate.

Article 23 (Academic freedom)
Academic freedom is guaranteed.

Article 24 (Individual dignity in family life and equality between the sexes)
(1) Marriage shall be based only on the mutual consent of both sexes and it shall be maintained through mutual cooperation with the equal rights of husband and wife as a basis.
(2) With regard to choice of spouse, property rights, inheritance, choice of domicile, divorce and other matters pertaining to marriage and the family, laws shall be enacted from the standpoint of individual dignity and the essential equality of the sexes.

Article 25 (Right of subsistence and the State's social duty)
(1) All people shall have the right to maintain the minimum standards of wholesome and cultured living.
(2) In all spheres of life, the State shall use its endeavors for the promotion and extension of social welfare and security, and of public health.

enjoy a favorable environment and is obliged to preserve the same.
2) The State shall endeavour to maintain the environment in a favorable condition.

Article 29 (Right to receive education)
1) All people shall have the right to receive an equal education correspondent to their ability, as provided by law.
2) All people shall be obliged to have all children under their protection receive ordinary education as provided for by law. Such compulsory education shall be free of charge.

Article 30 (Right and obligation to work)
1) All people shall have the right and the obligation to work.
2) Standards for wages, hours, rest and other working conditions shall be fixed by law.
3) Children shall not be exploited.

Article 31 (Right of workers to organize)
The right of workers to organize, bargain and act collectively is guaranteed.

Article 32 (Freedom to choose occupation and conduct business)
Every person possesses the right freely to choose his occupation and to conduct his business to the extent that it does not interfere with the public welfare.

Article 33 (Property rights)
1) The right to own or to hold property is inviolable.
2) Property rights shall be defined by law, in accordance with the public welfare.

Article 26 (Right to receive education)
(1) All people shall have the right to receive an equal education correspondent to their ability, as provided by law.
(2) All people shall be obligated to have all boys and girls under their protection receive ordinary education as provided for by law. Such compulsory education shall be free.

Article 27 (Right and obligation to work)
(1) All people shall have the right and the obligation to work.
(2) Standards for wages, hours, rest and other working conditions shall be fixed by law.
(3) Children shall not be exploited.

Article 28 (Right of workers to organize)
The right of workers to organize, and to bargain and act collectively is guaranteed.

Article 22 (Freedom to choose occupation, duplicated for reference)
Every person shall have freedom to choose and change his residence and to choose his occupation to the extent that it does not interfere with the public welfare.

Article 29 (Property rights)
(1) The right to own or to hold property is inviolable.
(2) Property rights shall be defined by law, in conformity with the public welfare.

3) Private property may be taken for public use upon just compensation being made therefor.

Article 34 (Liability to taxation)
The people shall be liable to taxation as provided by law.

Article 35 (Guarantee of due legal procedure)
No person shall be deprived of life or liberty, nor shall any other criminal penalty be imposed, except according to procedure established by law.

Article 36 (Right of access to the courts)
All persons possess the right of access to the courts.

Article 37 (Conditions for arrest)
No person shall be apprehended except upon warrant issued by a judge which specifies the offense with which the person is charged, unless he is apprehended while committing a crime.

Article 38 (Conditions for arrest or detention and guarantee against unjust arrest or detention)
No person shall be arrested or detained without being at once informed of the charges against him, or without the immediate privilege of counsel; nor shall he be detained without adequate cause. Upon demand of any person such cause must be immediately shown in open court in his presence and the presence of his counsel.

Article 39 (Searches and seizures)
1) The right of all persons to be secure in their homes, papers and effects against entries, searches and seizures shall not be impaired with-

(3) Private property may be taken for public use upon just compensation therefor.

Article 30 (Liability to taxation)
The people shall be liable to taxation as provided by law.

Article 31 (Guarantee of due legal procedure)
No person shall be deprived of life or liberty, nor shall any other criminal penalty be imposed, except according to procedure established by law.

Article 32 (Right of access to the courts)
No person shall be denied the right of access to the courts.

Article 33 (Conditions for arrest)
No person shall be apprehended except upon warrant issued by a competent judicial officer which specifies the offense with which the person is charged, unless he is apprehended, the offense being committed

Article 34 (Guarantee against unjust arrest or detention)
No person shall be arrested or detained without being at once informed of the charges against him or without the immediate privilege of counsel; nor shall he be detained without adequate cause; and upon demand of any person such cause must be immediately shown in open court in his presence and the presence of his counsel.

Article 35 (Searches and seizures)
(1) The right of all person to be secure in their homes, papers and effects against entries, searches and seizures shall not be impaired except upon

out warrant issued for adequate cause or except as provided by Article 37.
2) Each search or seizure shall be made upon separate warrant which shall describe the place to be searched or the things to be seized.

Article 40 (Ban on torture and cruel punishments)
The infliction of torture by any public officer and cruel punishments are absolutely forbidden.

Article 41 (Rights of an accused)
1) In all criminal cases the accused shall enjoy the right to a speedy trial by an impartial tribunal.
2) The accused shall be permitted full opportunity to examine all witnesses, and shall have the right of compulsory process for obtaining witnesses on his behalf at public expense.
3) At all times the accused shall have the assistance of competent counsel who shall, if the accused is unable to secure the same by his own efforts, be assigned to his use by the State.

Article 42 (Invalidity of forced testimony and confession)
1) No person shall be compelled to testify against himself.
2) Confession made under compulsion, torture or threat, or after unduly prolonged arrest or detention, shall not be admitted in evidence.
3) No person shall be convicted or punished in cases where the only proof against him is his own confession.

Article 43 (Prohibition against retroactive punishment and double jeopardy)
No person shall be held criminally liable for an act which was lawful at

warrant issued for adequate cause and particularly describing the place to be searched and things to be seized, or except as provided by Article 33.
(2) Each search or seizure shall be made upon separate warrant issued by a competent judicial officer.

Article 36 (Ban on torture and cruel punishments)
The infliction of torture by any public officer and cruel punishments are absolutely forbidden.

Article 37 (Rights of an accused)
(1) In all criminal cases the accused shall enjoy the right to a speedy and public trial by an impartial tribunal.
(2) He shall be permitted full opportunity to examine all witnesses, and he shall have the right of compulsory process for obtaining witnesses on his behalf at public expense.
(3) At all times the accused shall have the assistance of competent counsel who shall, if the accused is unable to secure the same by his own efforts, be assigned to his use by the State.

Article 38 (Invalidity of forced testimony and confession)
(1) No person shall be compelled to testify against himself.
(2) Confession made under compulsion, torture or threat, or after prolonged arrest or detention, shall not be admitted in evidence.
(3) No person shall be convicted or punished in cases where the only proof against him is his own confession.

Article 39 (Prohibition against retroactive punishment and double jeopardy)
No person shall be held criminally liable for an act which was lawful at

the time it was committed, or of which he has been acquitted, nor shall he be placed in double jeopardy.

Article 44 (Right to receive criminal redress)
Any person, acquitted after arrest or detention, may sue the State for redress as provided by law.

Article 45 (Right to choose and dismiss public officials, characterization of public officials, guarantee of universal suffrage and ballot secrecy)
1) The people have the inalienable right to choose and dismiss their Diet members, municipal heads and assembly members and other public officials.
2) All public officials are servants of the whole community and not of any group thereof.
3) Universal adult suffrage is guaranteed with regard to the election of public officials.
4) The secrecy of the ballot shall not be violated in any election. No voter shall be answerable, publicly or privately, for the choice he has made.

Article 46 (Right of petition)
Every person shall have the right of peaceful petition for the redress of damage, for the removal of public officials, for the enactment, repeal or amendment of laws, ordinances or regulations and for other matters, nor shall any person be in any way discriminated against for sponsoring such a petition.

Article 47 (Redress for damage from the State or a public entity)
Every person who has suffered damage through the illegal act of any public

the time it was committed, or of which he has been acquitted, nor shall he be placed in double jeopardy.

Article 40 (Right to receive criminal redress)
Any person, in case he is acquitted after he has been arrested or detained, may sue the State for redress as provided by law.

Article 15 (Right to choose and dismiss public officials, characterization of public officials, guarantee of universal suffrage and ballot secrecy)
(1) The people have the inalienable right to choose their public officials and to dismiss them.
(2) All public officials are servants of the whole community and not of any group thereof.
(3) Universal adult suffrage is guaranteed with regard to the election of public officials.
(4) In all elections, secrecy of the ballot shall not be violated. A voter shall not be answerable, publicly or privately, for the choice he has made.

Article 16 (Right of petition)
Every person shall have the right of peaceful petition for the redress of damage, for the removal of public officials, for the enactment, repeal or amendment of laws, ordinances or regulations and for other matters; nor shall any person be in any way discriminated against for sponsoring such a petition.

Article 17 (Redress for damage from the State or a public entity)
Every person may sue for redress as provided by law from the State or a

official may sue for redress as provided by law from the State or a public entity.

public entity, in case he has suffered damage through illegal act of any public official.

Chapter 6 The Diet
(Currently Chapter 4)

Article 48 (Legislative power of the Diet)
Power to legislate shall pertain exclusively to the Diet.

Article 41 (Status and legislative power of the Diet)
The Diet shall be the highest organ of state power, and shall be the sole law-making organ of the State.

Article 49 (Bicameral system)
The Diet shall consist of two Houses, namely the House of Representatives and the House of Councillors.

Article 42 (Bicameral system)
The Diet shall consist of two Houses namely the House of Representatives and the House of Councillors.

Article 50 (Composition of the Diet)
1) Both Houses shall consist of elected members
2) The members of the Houses shall represent all the people.
3) The number of the members of each House shall be determined by law.

Article 43 (Composition of the Diet)
(1) Both Houses shall consist of elected members, representative of all the people.
(2) The number of the members of each House shall be fixed by law.

Article 51 (Qualifications of members of both Houses and their electors)
The qualifications of members of both Houses and their electors shall be determined by law. However, there shall be no discrimination on grounds of race, creed, sex, social status, family origin, education, property or income.

Article 44 (Qualifications of members of both Houses and their electors)
The qualifications of members of both Houses and their electors shall be fixed by law. However, there shall be no discrimination because of race, creed, sex, social status, family origin, education, property or income.

Article 52 (Term of office of members of the House of Representatives)
The term of office of members of the House of Representatives shall be four years. However, if the House of Representatives is dissolved, the term shall be terminated before the full term has expired.

Article 45 (Term of office of members of the House of Representatives)
The term of office of members of the House of Representatives shall be four years. However, the term shall be terminated before the full term is up in case the House of Representatives is dissolved.

Article 53 (Term of office of members of the House of Councillors) The term of office of members of the House of Councillors shall be six years, and elections for half the members shall take place every three years.	*Article 46 (Term of office of members of the House of Councillors)* *The term of office of members of the House of Councillors shall be six years, and elections for half the members shall take place every three years.*
Article 54 (Matters pertaining to elections) Electoral districts, method of voting and other matters pertaining to the method of election of members of both Houses shall be determined by law.	*Article 47 (Matters pertaining to elections)* *Electoral districts, method of voting and other matters pertaining to the method of election of members of both Houses shall be fixed by law.*
Article 55 (Ban on being members of both Houses of the Diet) No person shall be permitted to be a member of both Houses simultaneously.	*Article 48 (Ban on being members of both Houses of the Diet)* *No person shall be permitted to be a member of both Houses simultaneously.*
Article 56 (Annual salary for Diet members) Members of both Houses shall receive appropriate annual payment from the national treasury in accordance with law.	*Article 49 (Annual salary for Diet members)* *Members of both Houses shall receive appropriate annual payment from the national treasury in accordance with law.*
Article 57 (Diet members' exemption from apprehension) Except as provided by law, members of both Houses shall be exempt from apprehension while the Diet is in session, and any members apprehended before the opening of a session shall be freed during the term thereof upon demand of the House of which he is a member.	*Article 50 (Diet members' exemption from apprehension)* *Except in cases provided by law, members of both Houses shall be exempt from apprehension while the Diet is in session, and any members apprehended before the opening of the session shall be freed during the term of the session upon demand of the House.*
Article 58 (Non-liability outside the House of its members for their speeches, debates or votes inside the House) Members of both Houses shall not be held liable outside the House for speeches, debates or votes made, participated in, or cast inside the House.	*Article 51 (Non-liability outside the House of its members for their speeches, debates or votes inside the House)* *Members of both Houses shall not be held liable outside the House for speeches, debates or votes cast inside the House.*

Article 59 (Ordinary session of the Diet)
An ordinary session of the Diet shall be convoked once per year.

Article 60 (Extraordinary sessions of the Diet)
The Cabinet may determine to convoke extraordinary sessions of the Diet, and shall do so when a quarter or more of the total members of either House so demands.

Article 61 (Dissolution and special sessions of the House of Representatives and emergency sessions of the House of Councillors)
1) When the House of Representatives is dissolved, there shall be a general election of members of the House of Representatives within forty (40) days from the date of dissolution, and the Diet shall be convoked within thirty (30) days from the date of the election.
2) When the House of Representatives is dissolved, the House of Councillors shall simultaneously be closed. However, the Cabinet may in time of national emergency convoke the House of Councillors in emergency session.
3) Measures taken at such session as is mentioned in the proviso to the preceding paragraph shall be provisional and shall lapse unless agreed to by the House of Representatives within a period of ten (10) days after the opening of the next session of the Diet.

Article 62 (Adjudication of disputes about the qualification of members)
Each House shall judge disputes related to the qualifications of its members. However, in order to deny a seat to any member, it shall be necessary to

Article 52 (Ordinary session of the Diet)
An ordinary session of the Diet shall be convoked once per year.

Article 53 (Extraordinary sessions of the Diet)
The Cabinet may determine to convoke extraordinary sessions of the Diet. When a quarter or more of the total members of either House makes the demand, the Cabinet must determine on such convocation.

Article 54 (Dissolution and special sessions of the House of Representatives and emergency sessions of the House of Councillors)
(1) When the House of Representatives is dissolved, there must be a general election of members of the House of Representatives within forty (40) days from the date of dissolution, and the Diet must be convoked within thirty (30) days from the date of the election.
(2) When the House of Representatives is dissolved, the House of Councillors is closed at the same time. However, the Cabinet may in time of national emergency convoke the House of Councillors in emergency session.
(3) Measures taken at such session as mentioned in the proviso of the preceding paragraph shall be provisional and shall become null and void unless agreed to by the House of Representatives within a period of ten (10) days after the opening of the next session of the Diet.

Article 55 (Adjudication of disputes about the qualification of members)
Each House shall judge disputes related to qualifications of its members. However, in order to deny a seat to any member, it is necessary to pass

pass a resolution by a majority of two-thirds or more of the members present.

Article 63 (Quorum and voting)
1) The quorum required for the transaction of any business in either House shall be one-third or more of all current registered members.
2) All matters shall be decided, in each House, by a majority of those present, except as elsewhere provided in the Constitution, and, where there is no clear majority, the presiding officer shall decide the issue.

Article 64 (Deliberations to be public; record of proceedings; record of votes)
1) Deliberations in each House shall be public. However, a secret meeting may be held where a majority of two-thirds or more of those members present passes a resolution therefor.
2) Each House shall keep a record of proceedings. This record shall be published and given general circulation, excepting such parts of the proceedings of secret session as may be deemed to require secrecy.
3) Upon demand of one-fifth or more of the members present, the votes of the members on any matter shall be recorded in the minutes.

Article 65 (Selection of officials; rules for the Houses; punishments)
1) Each House shall select its own president and other officials.
2) Each House shall establish the rules pertaining to its meetings, proceedings and internal discipline, and may punish members for disorderly conduct. However, in order to expel a member, a majority of two-thirds or more of those members present must pass a resolution to that effect.

a resolution by a majority of two-thirds or more of the members present.

Article 56 (Quorum and voting)
(1) Business cannot be transacted in either House unless one-third or more of total membership is present.
(2) All matters shall be decided, in each House, by a majority of those present, except as elsewhere provided in the Constitution, and in case of a tie, the presiding officer shall decide the issue.

Article 57 (Deliberations to be public; record of proceedings; record of votes)
(1) Deliberation in each House shall be public. However, a secret meeting may be held where a majority of two-thirds or more of those members present passes a resolution therefor.
(2) Each House shall keep a record of proceedings. This record shall be published and given general circulation, excepting such parts of proceedings of secret session as may be deemed to require secrecy.
(3) Upon demand of one-fifth or more of the members present, votes of the members on any matter shall be recorded in the minutes.

Article 58 (Selection of officials; rules for the Houses; punishments)
(1) Each House shall select its own president and other officials.
(2) Each House shall establish its rules pertaining to meetings, proceedings and internal discipline, and may punish members for disorderly conduct. However in order to expel a member, a majority of two-thirds or more of those members present must pass a resolution thereon.

Article 66 (Voting on bills, and precedence of the House of Representatives)
1) A bill becomes law when passed by both House except as otherwise provided by the Constitution.
2) A bill which is passed by the House of Representatives, and upon which the House of Councillors makes a decision different from that of the House of Representatives, shall become law when passed a second time by the House of Representatives by a majority of three-fifths or more of the members present.
3) The provision of the preceding paragraph shall not preclude the House of Representatives from calling for a meeting of a joint committee of both Houses, as provided for by law.
4) Failure by the House of Councillors to take final action within sixty (60) days after receipt of a bill passed by the House of Representatives, time in recess excepted, may be determined by the House of Representatives to constitute a rejection of said bill by the House of Councillors.

Article 67 (Precedence of the House of Representatives in deliberations and decisions on the budget bill)
1) The annual budget bill must first be submitted to the House of Representatives.
2) Upon consideration thereof, when the House of Councillors makes a decision different from that of the House of Representatives, and when no agreement can be reached even through a joint committee of both Houses, as provided by law, or in the case of failure by the House of Councillors to take final action within thirty (30) days, periods in recess excluded, after the receipt of the budget bill passed by the House of

Article 59 (Voting on bills, and precedence of the House of Representatives)
(1) A bill becomes a law on passage by Houses, except as otherwise provided by the Constitution.
(2) A bill which is passed by the House of Representatives, and upon which the House of Councillors makes a decision different from that of the House of Representatives, becomes a law when passed a second time by the House of Representatives by a majority of two-thirds or more of the members present.
(3) The provision of the preceding paragraph does not preclude the House of Representatives from calling for the meeting of a joint committee of both Houses, provided by law.
(4) Failure by the House of Councillors to take final action within sixty (60) days after receipt of a bill passed by the House of Representatives, time in recess excepted, may be determined by the House of Representatives to constitute a rejection of said bill by the House of Councillors.

Article 60 (Precedence of the House of Representatives in deliberations and decisions on the budget)
(1) The budget must first be submitted to the House of Representatives.
(2) Upon consideration of the budget, when the House of Councillors makes a decision different from that of the House of Representatives, and when no agreement can be reached even through a joint committee of both Houses, provided for by law, or in the case of failure by the House of Councillors to take final action within thirty (30) days, the period of recess excluded, after the receipt of the budget passed by the House of Representatives, the decision

Representatives, the decision of the House of Representatives shall be the decision excepted, may be determined by the House of Representatives to constitute a rejection of the said bill by the House of Councillors.

Article 68 (Precedence of the House of Councillors in treaty approval)
1) Treaties must first be submitted to the House of Councillors.
2) Upon consideration of treaties, when the House of Representatives makes a decision different from that of the House of Councillors, and when no agreement can be reached even through a joint committee of both Houses, as provided by law, or in the case of failure by the House of Representatives to take final action within thirty (30) days, periods in recess excluded, after the receipt of the treaties passed by the House of Councillors, the decision of the House of Councillors shall be the decision of the Diet.

Article 69 (Precedence of the House of Councillors in personnel matters)
1) Appointments to important public posts provided for by law shall require the approval of the Diet.
2) The approval specified in paragraph 1 hereof shall be subject to the provisions of the preceding article.

Article 70 (The Diet's power to investigate governmental matters)
Each House may conduct its own investigations in relation to government, and may demand the presence and testimony of witnesses, and the production of records.

Article 71 (Ministers' right to, and duty of, presence in the Diet)

of the House of Representatives shall be the decision of the Diet.

Article 61 (Precedence of the House of Representatives in treaty approval)
The second paragraph of the preceding article applies also to the Diet approval required for the conclusion of treaties.

Article 62 (The Diet's power to investigate governmental matters)
Each House may conduct investigations in relation to government, and may demand the presence and testimony of witnesses, and the production of records.

Article 63 (Ministers' right to, and duty of, presence in the Diet)

74 *Japan's contested constitution*

The Prime Minister and other Ministers of State may, at any time, appear in either House for the purpose of speaking on bills, regardless of whether they are members of the House or not. Further, they shall appear when their presence is required in order to give answers or explanations.

Article 72 (Judge impeachment court and judge indictment committee)
1) The House of Councillors shall set up a judge impeachment court from among its members for the purpose of trying those judges against whom removal proceedings have been instituted by the following paragraph.
2) The House of Representatives shall set up a judge indictment committee from among its members for the purpose of indicting those judges described in the preceding paragraph.
3) Matters relating to judge indictment and judge impeachment shall be provided for by law.

The Prime Minister and other Ministers of State may, at any time, appear in either House for the purpose of speaking on bills, regardless of whether they are members of the House or not. They must appear when their presence is required in order to give answers or explanations.

Article 64 (Judge impeachment court)
(1) The Diet shall set up an impeachment court from among the members of both Houses for the purpose of trying those judges against whom removal proceedings have been instituted.
(2) Matters relating to impeachment shall be provided by law.

Chapter 7 The Cabinet
(Currently Chapter 5)

Article 73 (Executive power)
Executive power shall be vested in the Cabinet.

Article 74 (Composition of the Cabinet and its collective responsibility to the Diet)
1) The Cabinet shall consist of the Prime Minister and other Ministers of State, as provided for by law.
2) The Prime Minister shall represent the Cabinet and exercise control and supervision over Ministers of State.
3) The Prime Minister and other Ministers of State must be civilians.
4) The Cabinet, in the exercise of

Article 65 (Executive power)
Executive power shall be vested in the Cabinet.

Article 66 (Composition of the Cabinet and its collective responsibility to the Diet)
(1) The Cabinet shall consist of the Prime Minister, who shall be its head, and other Ministers of State, as provided for by law.
(2) The Prime Minister and other Ministers of State must be civilians.
(3) The Cabinet, in the exercise of executive power, shall be collectively responsible to the Diet.

executive power, shall be collectively responsible to the Diet.

Article 75 (Designation of the Prime Minister and the House of Representatives' precedence)
The Prime Minister shall be designated from among the members of the House of Representatives by a resolution thereof. This designation shall precede all other business.

Article 67 (Designation of the Minister and the House of Representatives' precedence)
(1) The Prime Minister shall be designated from among the members of the Diet by a resolution of the Diet. This designation shall precede all other business.
(2) If the House of Representatives and the House of Councillors disagree and if no agreement can be reached even through a joint committee of both Houses, provided for by law, or the House of Councillors fails to make designation within ten (10) days exclusive of the period of recess, after the House of Representatives has made designation, the decision of the House of Representatives shall be the decision of the Diet.

Article 76 (Appointment and dismissal of Ministers of State)
1) The Prime Minister shall appoint the Ministers of State. However, a majority of their number must be chosen from among the members of the Diet.
2) The Prime Minister shall have sole discretion in the removal of Ministers of State.

Article 68 (Appointment and dismissal of Ministers of State)
(1) The Prime Minister shall appoint the Ministers of State. However, a majority of their number must be chosen from among the members of the Diet.
(2) The Prime Minister may remove the Ministers of State as he chooses.

Article 77 (The Cabinet's power to dissolve the House of Representatives and the consequence of a non-confidence decision against the Cabinet)
1) The Cabinet may dissolve the House of Representatives.
2) If the House of Representatives passes a nonconfidence resolution, or rejects a confidence resolution, the Cabinet shall resign en masse, unless the House of Representatives is dissolved within ten (10) days.

Article 69 (The consequences of a nonconfidence decision against the Cabinet)
If the House of Representatives passes a nonconfidence resolution, or rejects a confidence resolution, the Cabinet shall resign en masse, unless the House of Representatives is dissolved within ten (10) days.

Article 78 (Vacancy in the post of Prime Minister, convocation of a new Diet, and resignation of the Cabinet en masse)
When there is a vacancy in the post of Prime Minister, or upon the first convocation of the Diet after a general election of members of the House of Representatives, the Cabinet shall resign en masse.

Article 79 (The Cabinet after its resignation en masse)
In the cases mentioned in the two preceding articles, the Cabinet shall continue its functions as defined in this Constitution until a new Prime Minister shall be appointed, provided always that it shall not exercise its power to dissolve the House of Representatives until such appointment has been made.

Article 80 (The Prime Minister's duties)
The Prime Minister, representing the Cabinet, submits bills, including the annual budget bill, and other measures to the Diet and reports on general national affairs and foreign relations to the Diet.

Article 81 (The Prime Minister's power of command and control)
The Prime Minister shall exercise general control and supervision over the various departments of the executive branch.

Article 82 (The Prime Minister pro tempore)
1) When the Prime Minister is incapacitated or where there arises a vacancy in his post a Minister of State designated as prime minster pro tempore shall discharge the Premier's duties.

Article 70 (Vacancy in the post of Prime Minister, convocation of a new Diet, and resignation of the Cabinet en masse)
When there is a vacancy in the post of Prime Minister, or upon the first convocation of the Diet after a general election of members of the House of Representatives, the Cabinet shall resign en masse.

Article 71 (The Cabinet after its resignation en masse)
In the cases mentioned in the two preceding articles, the Cabinet shall continue its functions until the time when a new Prime Minister is appointed.

Article 72 (The Prime Minister's duties)
The Prime Minister, representing the Cabinet, submits bills, reports on general national affairs and foreign relations to the Diet and exercises control and supervision over various administrative branches.

2) In order to anticipate the contingencies described in the preceding paragraph, the Prime Minister shall designate in advance a Minister of State as his pro tempore.

Article 83 (The Cabinet's duties)
The Cabinet, in addition to other general administrative functions, shall;

1 Administer the law faithfully and exercise due control over, and management of, administrative affairs of the state;
2 Manage foreign affairs;
3 Conclude treaties, subject to prior, or, in appropriate circumstances, subsequent, approval of the Diet;
4 Administer the civil service, in accordance with the standards established by law;
5 Convoke the Diet;
6 Draft the annual budget bill and present it to the Diet;
7 Enact Cabinet orders in order to implement the provisions of this Constitution and of the law. Such orders may not include penal provisions unless authorized by law;
8 Decide on general and special amnesties, commutations of punishment, reprieves, and restorations of rights;
9 Decide on the conferment of honors.

Article 84 (Privileges of the Ministers of State)
The Ministers of State, during their tenure of office, shall not be subject to

Article 73 (The Cabinet's duties)
The Cabinet, in addition to other general administrative functions, shall perform the following functions:

1 Administer the law faithfully; conduct affairs of state.
2 Manage foreign affairs.
3 Conclude treaties.
4 However, it shall obtain prior or, depending on circumstances, subsequent approval of the Diet.
5 Administer the civil service, in accordance with standards established by law.
6 Prepare the budget, and present it to the Diet.
7 Enact cabinet orders in order to execute the provisions of this Constitution and of the law. However, it cannot include penal provisions in such cabinet orders unless authorized by such law.
8 Decide on general amnesty, special amnesty, commutation of punishment, reprieve, and restoration of rights.

Article 74 (Signature of laws and Cabinet orders)
All laws and cabinet orders shall be signed by the competent Minister of State and countersigned by the Prime Minister.

Article 75 (Privileges of the Ministers of State)
The Ministers of State, during their tenure of office, shall not be subject to

legal action without the consent of the Prime Minister. However, the right to take that action shall remain intact after his dismissal.

legal action without the consent of the Prime Minister. However, the right to take that action is not impaired hereby.

Chapter 8 The Judiciary
(Currently Chapter 6)

Article 85 (Judicial power, courts and ban on extraordinary tribunals)
1) Judicial power shall be vested exclusively in a Constitutional Court, a Supreme Court and in such inferior courts as are established by law.
2) No extraordinary tribunal shall be established, nor shall any organ or agency of the Executive be given ultimate judicial power.

Article 76 (Judicial power, courts and ban on extraordinary tribunals)
(1) The whole judicial power is vested in a Supreme Court and in such inferior courts as are established by law.
(2) No extraordinary tribunal shall be established, nor shall any organ or agency the Executive be given final judicial power.

Article 86 (Constitutional Court's power to determine the constitutionality of legislation)
The Constitutional Court shall be the sole arbiter of the constitutionality of any treaty, law, order, rule or other official act.

Article 81 (Supreme Court's power to determine the constitutionality of legislation)
The Supreme Court is the court of last resort with power to determine the constitutionality of any law, order, regulation or official act.

Article 87 (Jurisdiction of the Constitutional Court)
The Constitutional Court shall perform the following functions;
1 Judge the constitutionality or lack thereof under the law of matters related to any treaty, law, order, rule or other official act upon demand by the Cabinet or a one-third or more majority of the members of the House of Representatives or of the House of Councillors;
2 Judge the constitutionality under the law of matters related to specific trials upon request by the Supreme Court or an inferior court;
3 Determine, as provided for by law, appeals founded on points of

constitutional law raised by appellants against Supreme Court decisions in specific trials.

Article 88 (Validity of the judicial decisions by the Constitutional Court)
Where the Constitutional Court pronounces unconstitutional any treaty, law, order, rule or other official act, such decision, except as provided for by law, shall thenceforth be binding upon all the organs of the State.

Article 89 (Term of office, retirement age and compensation of Constitutional Court Justices)
1) The Constitutional Court shall consist of a Chief Justice and eight other Associate Justices. The Justices excepting the Chief Justice shall be designated by the House of Councillors and appointed by the Cabinet.
2) The term of office of Constitutional Court Justices shall be eight years, with no provision for re-appointment.
3) Constitutional Court Justices shall be retired upon the attainment of the age fixed by law.
4) Constitutional Court Justices shall receive adequate compensation, at regular stated intervals; such compensation shall not be decreased during their terms of office.

Article 90 (The Supreme Court as a court of last non-Constitutional resort)
The Supreme Court shall be the court of last resort in matters outwith the jurisdiction of the Constitutional Court.

Article 91 (Term of office, retirement and compensation of Supreme Court Judges)
1) The Supreme Court shall consist of a Chief Judge and such number of

Article 79 (Composition of Supreme Court; its Judges' reviews by the people; Judges' retirement age and compensation)
(1) The Supreme Court shall consist of a

Associate Judges as may be determined by law, all such Judges excepting the Chief Judge shall be appointed by the Cabinet.
2) The term of office of Supreme Court Judges shall be five (5) years with the privilege of reappointment.
3) Judges of the Supreme Court shall be retired upon the attainment of the age fixed by law.
4) All such Judges shall receive, at regular stated intervals, adequate compensation which shall not be decreased during their terms of office.

Article 92 (Term of office, retirement and compensation of inferior court judges)
1) The judges of the inferior courts shall be appointed by the Cabinet from a list of persons nominated by the Supreme Court. All such judges shall hold office for a term of ten (10) years with the privilege of reappointment, provided that they shall be retired upon the attainment of the age fixed by law.
2) Judges of the inferior courts shall receive, at regular stated intervals, adequate compensation which shall not be decreased during their terms of office.

Chief Judge and such number of judges as may be determined by law; all such judges excepting the Chief Judge shall be appointed by the Cabinet.
(2) The appointment of the judges of the Supreme Court shall be reviewed by the people at the first general election of members of the House of Representatives following their appointment, and shall be reviewed again at the first general election of members of the House of Representatives after a lapse of ten (10) years, and in the same manner thereafter.
(3) In cases mentioned in the foregoing paragraph, when the majority of the voters favors the dismissal of a judge, he shall be dismissed.
(4) Matters pertaining to review shall be prescribed by law.
(5) The judges of the Supreme Court shall be retired upon the attainment of the age as fixed by law.
(6) All such judges shall receive, at regular stated intervals, adequate compensation which shall not be decreased during their terms of office.

Article 80 (Terms of office, retirement age and compensation of inferior court judges)
(1) The judges of the inferior courts shall be appointed by the Cabinet from a list of persons nominated by the Supreme Court. All such judges shall hold office for a term of ten (10) years with privilege of reappointment, provided that they shall be retired upon the attainment of the age as fixed by law.
(2) The judges of the inferior courts shall receive, at regular stated intervals, adequate compensation which shall not be decreased during their terms of office.

Article 93 (The Constitutional Court's and Supreme Court's rule-making power)
1) The Constitutional Court and the Supreme Court are empowered to make rules governing practice and procedure, matters relating to attorneys, the internal discipline of the courts and the administration of judicial affairs.
2) Public procurators shall be subject to the rule-making power described in the preceding paragraph.
3) The Supreme Court may delegate the power to make rules for inferior courts to such courts.

Article 94 (Judges' independence and security of tenure)
1) All Justices and judges shall be independent in the exercise of their conscience and shall be bound only by this Constitution and the laws of the land.
2) No Justices or judges shall be removed except by due impeachment process unless judicially decided mentally and physically incompetent to perform official duties. No disciplinary action against judges shall be administered by any executive organ or agency.

Article 95 (Open trial)
1) Trials shall be conducted, and judgments declared, publicly.
2) Where a court unanimously determines publicity to be dangerous to public order, good morals or the interests of the private lives of those persons concerned, a trial may be conducted privately, but trials of political offenses, offenses involving the press or cases wherein the rights of the people as guaranteed in Chapter 5 of this Constitution are in question shall always be conducted publicly.

Article 77 (The Supreme Court's rule-making power)
(1) The Supreme Court is vested with rule-making power under which it determines the rules of procedure and of practice, and of matters relating to attorneys, the internal discipline of the courts and the administration of judicial affairs.
(2) Public procurators shall be subject to the rule-making power of the Supreme Court.
(3) The Supreme Court may delegate the power to make rules for inferior courts to such courts.

Article 76 (Judges' independence)
(1) All judges shall be independent in the exercise of their conscience and shall be bound only by this Constitution and the laws.

Article 78 (Judges' security of tenure)
Judges shall not be removed except by public impeachment unless judicially declared mentally or physically incompetent to perform official duties. No disciplinary action against judges shall be administered by any executive organ or agency.

Article 82 (Open trial)
(1) Trials shall be conducted and judgment declared publicly.
(2) Where a court unanimously determines publicity to be dangerous to public order or morals, a trial may be conducted privately, but trials of political offenses, offenses involving the press or cases wherein the rights of people as guaranteed in Chapter 3 of this Constitution are in question shall always be conducted publicly.

Chapter 9 Finance
(Currently Chapter 7)

Article 96 (Basic principles of financial management)
The power to administer national finances shall be exercised by the Cabinet as the Diet shall determine. The State shall endeavor to maintain and manage its finances in a sound and proper manner.

Article 97 (Taxation)
No new taxes shall be imposed or existing ones modified except by law or under such conditions as law may prescribe.

Article 98 (State expenditure and financial obligations)
No money shall be expended, nor shall the State obligate itself, except as authorized by the Diet.

Article 99 (Budget bills)
1) The Cabinet shall prepare and submit to the Diet for its consideration and decision a budget bill for each fiscal year.
2) When a continuing expenditure is needed in special circumstances, it shall require the Diet's approval as a continuing expense, but the period during which it is permitted to continue shall be limited.

Article 100 (Reserve fund)
1) In order to provide for unforeseen deficiencies in the budget, a reserve fund may be authorized by the Diet to be expended upon the responsibility of the Cabinet.
2) The Cabinet must get subsequent approval of the Diet for all payments from the reserve fund.

Article 83 (Basic principles of financial management)
The power to administer national finances shall be exercised as the Diet shall determine.

Article 84 (Taxation)
No new taxes shall be imposed or existing ones modified except by law or under such conditions as law may prescribe.

Article 85 (State expenditure and financial obligation)
No money shall be expended, nor shall the State obligate itself, except as authorised by the Diet.

Article 86 (Budget)
The Cabinet shall prepare and submit to the Diet for its consideration and decision a budget for each fiscal year.

Article 87 (Reserve fund)
(1) In order to provide for unforeseen deficiencies in the budget, a reserve fund may be authorized by the Diet to be expended upon the responsibility of the Cabinet.
(2) The Cabinet must get subsequent approval of the Diet for all payments from the reserve fund.

Article 101 (Imperial Household property and expenditures)
All property of the Imperial Household shall belong to the State. All expenses of the Imperial Household shall be appropriated by the Diet in the budget.

Article 102 (Final accounts audit and a Board of Audit)
1) Final accounts of the expenditures and revenues of the State shall be audited annually by a Board of Audit and submitted by the Cabinet to the Diet, together with the statement of audit, during the fiscal year immediately following the period covered.
2) The organization and competency of the Board of Audit shall be determined by law.

Article 103 (Report of national finances)
At regular intervals and at least annually the Cabinet shall report to the Diet and the people on the state of national finances.

Chapter 10 Local self-government
(Currently Chapter 8)

Article 104 (Basic principle of local autonomy)
Regulations concerning organization and operations of local public entities shall be fixed by law paying due regard

Article 88 (Imperial Household property and expenditures)
All property of the Imperial Household shall belong to the State. All expenses of the Imperial Household shall be appropriated by the Diet in the budget.

Article 89 (Limits to public property expenditure and its use)
No public money or other property shall be expended or appropriated for the use, benefit or maintenance of any religious institution or association, or for any charitable, educational or benevolent enterprises not under the control of public authority.

Article 90 (Financial account audit and a Board of Audit)
(1) Final accounts of the expenditures and revenues of the State shall be audited annually by a Board of Audit and submitted by the Cabinet to the Diet, together with the statement of audit, during the fiscal year immediately following the period covered.
(2) The organization and competency of the Board of Audit shall be determined by law.

Article 91 (Report of national finances)
At regular intervals and at least annually the Cabinet shall report to the Diet and the people on the state of national finances.

Article 92 (Basic principle of local autonomy)
Regulations concerning organization and operations of local public entities shall be fixed by law in

to the principle of self-government by local residents and local public entities.

Article 105 (Election of chief executive officers, assemblies, and officials of local public entities through direct popular vote)
1) The local public entities shall establish assemblies in accordance with law.
2) The chief executive officers of all local public entities and the members of their assemblies shall be elected by direct popular vote within their several communities.

Article 106 (Functions and regulation-making power of local public entities)
Local public entities shall have the right to manage their property, affairs and administration and to enact their own regulations within the spirit of the law.

Article 107 (Plebiscite on special law)
A special law, applicable only to certain local public entities, cannot be enacted by the Diet without the consent of the majority of the voters of the local public entity concerned, obtained in accordance with law.

Chapter 11 Amendments
(Currently Chapter 9)

Article 108 (Amendment procedure; promulgation of amendments)
1) Amendments to this Constitution shall require to be approved by the concurrence of the majority of valid votes cast by the members of each House present and voting, and shall be submitted to the people for ratification. Such amendments shall be considered at a meeting of the Diet at

accordance with the principle of local autonomy.

Article 93 (Election of chief executive officers, assemblies, and officials of local public entities through direct popular vote)
(1) The local public entities, shall establish assemblies as their deliberative organs, in accordance with law.
(2) The chief executive officers of all local public entities, the members of their assemblies, and such other local officials as may be determined by law shall be elected by direct popular vote within their several communities.

Article 94 (Functions and regulation-making power of local public entities)
Local public entities shall have the right to manage their property, affairs and administration and to enact their own regulations within law.

Article 95 (Plebiscite on special law)
A special law, applicable only to one local public entity, cannot be enacted by the Diet without the consent of the majority of the voters of the local public entity concerned, obtained in accordance with law.

Article 96 (Amendment procedure and its promulgation)
(1) Amendments to this Constitution shall be initiated by the Diet, through a concurring vote of two-thirds or more of all the members of each House and shall thereupon be submitted to the people for ratification, which shall require the affirmative vote of a majority of all votes cast

which two-thirds or more of all current registered members are in attendance.
2) Notwithstanding the terms of paragraph 1 of this Article, if, at a meeting of the Diet at which two-thirds or more of all current registered members are in attendance, a majority of two-thirds or more of the members of each House present and voting vote in favor of the amendment under consideration, such amendment shall be passed.
3) Such ratification as is mentioned in paragraph 1 of this Article shall require a concurring majority of the valid votes cast either at a national referendum held specially for the purpose, or at a special voting held concurrently with such election as the Diet may specify.
4) Amendments to this Constitution may be proposed by members either of the Diet or of the Cabinet.
5) An amendment ratified under paragraph 1, or passed under paragraph 2, of this Article shall immediately be promulgated by the Emperor in the name of the people.

We have deleted the current Constitution's Chapter 11 on Supplementary Provisions (Articles 100–3), since it contained only transitional provisions which were to apply until the current Constitution came into force. Any new supplementary provisions will be similar, if not identical, and purely procedural in phraseology. Hence, we feel no need to duplicate Supplementary Provisions in this book.

---

thereon, at a special referendum or at such election as the Diet shall specify.
(2) Amendments when so ratified shall immediately be promulgated by the Emperor in the name of the people, as an integral part of this Constitution.

Supreme law
(Currently Chapter 10)

(All the articles below duplicated for reference)

Article 97 (The essence of basic human rights)
The fundamental human rights by this Constitution guaranteed to the people of Japan are fruits of the age-old struggle of man to be free; they have survived the many exacting tests for durability and are conferred upon this and future generations in trust, to be held for all time inviolate.

Article 98 (Supreme law)
(1) This Constitution shall be the supreme law of the nation and no law, ordinance, imperial rescript or other act of government or part thereof, contrary to the provisions hereof, shall have legal force or validity.
(2) The treaties concluded by Japan and established laws of nations shall be faithfully observed.

Article 99 (Obligation to respect and uphold the Constitution)
The Emperor or the Regent as well as Ministers of State, members of the Diet, judges, and all other public officials have the obligation to respect and uphold this Constitution.

Commentary

Since the enactment of the current constitution, the focal point of constitutional debate for some fifty years has been 'the Article 9 (renunciation of war) problem,' more specifically its 'constitutionality' or 'unconstitutionality' of the Self-Defense Forces. In fact, it can be said that the major element characterizing the framework of Japan's post-war politics has been interpretations of Article 9, or the confrontation between those who are for, and those against, its revision. As a result of the great changes in world history manifested by the collapse of the East-West Cold War structure, the Socialist Party (Social Democratic Party of Japan) made a fundamental change in its policy on the Self-Defense Forces and switched from labelling it 'unconstitutional' to labelling it 'constitutional,' thus politically settling the so-called Article 9 issue.

Yet, the truth is that Article 9 of the current constitution remains in its phraseology too confusing to be properly interpreted. Therefore, in our consideration of constitutional review, we must, first, frame the wording of the proposed Article to place the existence of our Self-Defense Forces and its significance in a precise constitutional context and, second in order to maintain the spirit of 'everlasting peace' well-expressed in Article 9 of the current constitution, we must also curb firmly any effort to turn Japan into a major military power. This is an important step, which will operate to avoid the creation of unnecessary anxieties around the world, particularly among neighboring Asian nations.

We propose to name this chapter 'National Security' with a view to capturing the meaning of the nation's security as being something far broader than that of 'renunciation of war.'

Main points of our revision

1   Rejection of aggressive wars.
2   Ban on possession of weapons of indiscriminate mass destruction.
3   Clarification of possession regarding an organization for self-defense.
4   Clarification of civilian control.
5   Ban on conscription.

Rejection of aggressive wars

The current constitution's Article 9, paragraph 1 follows basically the wording of the Treaty for the Renunciation of War of 1928 signed in Paris, and similar wording has been adopted by the constitutions of Italy, the Philippines and other countries. All those nations accept the spirit of the Paris Anti-War Treaty of 1928 as renouncing the use of force 'as means of settling international disputes,' i.e. aggressive wars. From the fundamental point of view that the spirit of this treaty should be the central factor in the ideal of everlasting peace, we propose to keep it as it is, in paragraph 1 of our proposed Article 10.

In the original Article 9, the idea of renunciation was expressed by the word *hōki*, which means to give up something to which one is entitled. We felt that, because there is no justification for the use of aggressive war, or of force which is not recognized by International Law, an alteration had to be made to the wording, and we have suggested the use of *mitomenai* which has been rendered into English as 'not recognize.'

Elimination of weapons of indiscriminate mass destruction

Paragraph 2 of our proposed Article 10 stipulates our determination not to possess weapons of indiscriminate mass destruction. Our purpose is to express our basic concept and premise that weapons of indiscriminate mass destruction ought to be eliminated from the earth, thus reinforcing Japan's firm determination to renounce aggressive wars and maintain peace.

Needless to say, the expression 'weapons of indiscriminate mass destruction' will include not only nuclear but also biological and chemical weapons.

Around the world in recent years, science and technology have developed and propagated to a degree unforeseen at the time of the enactment of the current constitution: consequently, we are entering an age when chemical weapons can easily be produced by the application of the manufacturing technology of daily consumer goods. Even the major problems related to nuclear weapons are not necessarily only those related to qualitative and quantitative control talks among major nuclear nations. In fact, the probability of nuclear proliferation among smaller powers is now a task to be dealt with by the international community as a serious threat to world peace.

In view of the circumstances outlined above, it will, we believe, lead to an enhancement of Japan's moral prestige if it incorporates in the revised constitution an article explicitly calling on the world to eliminate the means of indiscriminate mass destruction, and denying itself possession thereof, despite its economic and technological advancement.

Noteworthy are similar articles which may be found in the Columbian Constitution banning the manufacture, introduction, possession and use of nuclear weapons and the Constitution of the Philippines declaring 'the adoption and implementation of a non-nuclear policy.'

Organization for self-defense

The central debate on how to interpret 'the so-called Article 9 problem' is whether Article 9, paragraph 2 of the current constitution should be read as

(i) banning only the possession of war-fighting capability as a 'means of settling international disputes,' and not as prohibiting the possession of a military force for self-defense or
(ii) denying the possession of any military force, including one designed for self-defense.

This difference of interpretation has led to a division of opinion between those who regard the Self-Defense Forces as constitutional and those who do not.

The Japanese government takes the position that it does not ban the possession of military force for self-defense and is proceeding with a military preparedness program. Conversely, those factions represented by the Socialist Party (Social Democratic Party of Japan) under the political regime of 1955, have upheld a 'Self-Defense-Forces-are-unconstitutional' thesis in opposition to the Liberal-Democratic Party. This political landscape has continued to date with no truly meaningful or fruitful debate on Japan's security.

It is our view that Japan as an independent nation is naturally entitled to possess the necessary minimum force for self-defense and that the current constitution does not prohibit its possession as such, and we have expressed this view on various occasions. On this point 'The First Intermediate Proposal' of 'The Yomiuri Constitution Study Council' (chaired by Dr Inoki Masamichi), published in December 1992, detailed the deliberation process of the current Constitution during which Chairman Ashida Hitoshi of the House of Representatives' Special Committee on the Bill for Revision of the Japanese Constitution added the expression 'In order to accomplish the aim of the preceding paragraph.' Mr. Ashida himself testified that this 'Ashida Paragraph' was designed as 'a device to allow the possession of a military force for self-defense.'

In recent years, public opinion, as expressed through various polls, show that some 80 percent of the populace regards the Self-Defense Forces as constitutional. Further, after the inauguration of the LDP-Socialist-Sakigake's three-party coalition regime in late June 1994, the Socialist Party (Social Democratic Party of Japan) changed its position to 'the SDF are constitutional' thesis, thus making the SDF's constitutionality no longer a national political issue. Nonetheless, in our view, it is undesirable that any article of the constitution pertaining to basic issues of national survival should remain expressed in a way both confusing and open to various interpretations.

Therefore, our proposed Article 11, paragraph 1 states: 'Japan shall form an organization for self-defense.'

We considered adding the expression 'minimum necessary' to 'an organization for self-defense.' However, we took the view the notion of 'self-defense' has the implication of 'minimum necessity,' and made up our minds not to word the Article in a tautological fashion.

Civilian control

In order to make clear that control over 'the organization for self-defense' is held by civilian politicians, paragraph 2 of our proposed Article 11 defines the Prime Minister's supreme command authority.

The current constitution, in its Article 66, paragraph 2, states that the Cabinet Ministers of State must be 'civilians,' while Article 7 of the Self-Defense Forces Law stipulates that the Prime Minister, representing the Cabinet, possesses the supreme command authority over the SDF, and Article 8 prescribes that a civilian

Minister of State should assume the post of Director-General of the Defense Agency – all of these are designed to assure civilian control.

Therefore, at present, there is legally no problem whatsoever as to civilian control. Nonetheless, we think it better to confirm more explicitly the principle of civilian control in an article of the constitution, since the presence of 'an organization for self-defense' is clearly stated as well.

Ban on introduction of conscription

Accompanying the article on 'an organization for self-defense,' our proposed Article 11, paragraph 3 stipulates a ban on the introduction of conscription as a measure against the possibility of Japan's turning into a major military power.

The current constitution nowhere directly bans conscription. However, a majority view of constitutional scholars and the government's interpretation to date is that both the current constitution's Article 13 (individual dignity) and the Article 18 provision prohibiting involuntary servitude do disallow the introduction of conscription.

To that extent, it can be argued that there is no need to create an article banning conscription. Nonetheless, since this proposal specifically permits the maintenance of 'an organization for self-defense,' and since we feel it essential to eliminate any possible argument in favor of the introduction of conscription, and taking into account the terms of Article 18 of the current constitution (no involuntary servitude), we propose that 'a ban on conscription' be clearly stated.

Interestingly enough, at present the constitutions of major nations either prescribe the people's liability to conscription or include articles excusing conscientious objectors, and none apparently upholds a ban on conscription.

Right of belligerency

Article 9 of the current constitution makes reference to 'the right of belligerency of the state,' and there has been much discussion about the meaning of the phrase. Three theories have emerged:

1   The first theory, prevalent among scholars, is a broad concept, which says that it embraces all the rights admissible under international law, including, for example, the detention and inspection of enemy ships, the administration of occupied territories, and everything done to overcome an enemy's will to resist.
2   The second theory presents a more literal interpretation, and restricts the meaning to the nation's right to wage war. Scholarly opinion differs: some say that the phrase is mere tautology, while others argue that it lends further meaning to the first paragraph of Article 9 (the nation's renunciation of war).
3   The third theory incorporates elements of theories 1 and 2. It says that the true meaning of the right of belligerency is to be understood as every right related to war which a country has, but including also the rights of belligerents which international law inevitably recognizes.

90 *Japan's contested constitution*

If Article 9 of the current constitution is interpreted as an absolute prohibition on the maintenance of any kind of armed force, it matters little which theory one favors. However, if it is interpreted as permitting acts of self-defense, then the first theory is to be preferred, and it follows from that, that if the right of belligerency (so defined) of a nation is not recognized, then that nation will, in the event of an attack upon it, find itself in a position where it can neither claim the rights of a belligerent recognized by international law, nor demand that its opponent observe the rules laid down for the conduct of war.

This proposal for a revised constitution affirms the need for a self-defense capability on the one hand, while specifically rejecting the use of aggressive force on the other, and therefore we have deemed it unnecessary to refer to a non-recognition of the right of belligerency.

International cooperation

Concept

One of the three-point principles of the current constitution is 'everlasting peace.' This principle goes beyond the so-called 'one-country pacifism,' i.e. a country being satisfied with its own internal peace and tranquility alone, and is based on the spirit of international cooperation and harmony as expressed in the Preamble to, and, paragraph 1 of Article 9 of, the current constitution.

For Japan, so very dependent on the free trade system possible only under conditions of world-wide peace, its contribution to world peace is motivated not only by moral obligation but also by the maintenance of the basis of its survival.

Moreover, circumstances today are so different from those obtaining at the time of the enactment of the current constitution. Japan today is an economic superpower occupying 15 percent of the world's GNP. The international community is placing increasing pressure on Japan, now such an influential presence, to play a commensurate role in various fields in its contribution to the maintenance of world peace.

We are, therefore, proposing a new chapter on international cooperation.

Main points of our revision

1 Declaration of our ideal of international cooperation.
2 Cooperation with the activities of international organizations.

Ideal of international cooperation

The Preamble to the current constitution states:

> We desire to occupy an honored place in an international society striving for the preservation of peace, and the banishment of tyranny and slavery,

oppression and intolerance for all time from the earth. We recognize that all peoples of the world have the right to live in peace, free from fear and want.

Our proposed chapter on international cooperation stipulates this ideal at its outset.

The expression 'human calamities caused by economic deprivation and regional disorder' is included, since in recent years the relief of mass refugees in many parts of the world has become a serious task confronting the international community.

How best to participate in international activities

The proposed Article 13 in manifesting its determination to implement the ideal of international cooperation empowers Japan actively to participate in, and cooperate with, 'the activities of the well-established international organizations.' The substance of our cooperation naturally includes not only the dispatch of SDF personnel for UN PKO (peacekeeping operations) but also the economic cooperation and humanitarian support by both governmental and non-governmental organizations. The reason for inserting the expression 'in case of need, it may dispatch public officials' is that we presume that when such contingencies occur, we may have to dispatch civilian officials to the scenes thereof.

At present, there is only one well-established international organization to which we can provide a part of our organization for self-defense – the United Nations. However, in view of the proliferation of its functions, the resultant possibility of organizational reforms and a change of name should not be neglected. In addition, regional organizations may emerge in Asia, as in Europe, and the possibility that Japan may be asked to participate in, and cooperate with, their activities also, cannot be excluded. Hence, we have not used the expression 'the United Nations.'

Observance of international laws

We propose to place at the end of our chapter on international cooperation an article on 'observance of international law' and to transfer thereto the second paragraph of Article 98 of Chapter 10 (Supreme Law) of the current constitution.

When the constitution and international law contradict each other, there are two possibilities open: one is to grant precedence to international law and the other is to give priority to the constitution. However, it is universally accepted that constitutions are constrained by treaties codifying well-established international law or those defining territorial boundaries.

Given the international scene today, it is all the more important that we accept this principle so that the world may maintain order and each nation may achieve its own security. In Japan's case, this means the observance of the UN Charter, the San Francisco Peace Treaty and the main articles of the US-Japan Security Treaty. This is why we have placed the current constitution's provisions on Supreme Law in Article 14 of our proposed constitution, under the heading Chapter 4 (International Cooperation).

Sekai, 'Peace and regional security in the Asia-Pacific'
A Japanese proposal (1993–4)

Koseki Shōichi, Maeda Tetsuo, Suzuki Yūji, Takahashi Susumu, Takayanagi Sakio, Tsuboi Yoshiharu, Wada Haruki, Yamaguchi Jirō, and Yamaguchi Sadamu[1]

PART ONE

A Proposal for a basic peace law:
Towards a resolution of the problem of Japan's Self-Defense Forces in keeping with the spirit of the constitution[2]

> Aspiring sincerely to an international peace based on justice and order, the Japanese people forever renounce war as a sovereign right of the nation and the threat or use of force as means of settling international disputes.
>
> In order to accomplish the aim of the preceding paragraph, land, sea, and air forces, as well as other war potential, will never be maintained. The right of belligerency of the state will not be recognized.
>
> (Article 9, Constitution of Japan)

The Cold War era, which for nearly half a century gripped the world within its tensions, has ended. It is also the end of that 'age of world wars' which from the beginning of this century led the great powers to pour out vast sums in military expenditure, and to form alliances opposing one another on a global scale.

The end of the Cold War on a global scale demands an end in Japan to the various arguments and confrontations which have long continued within its domestic politics. It goes without saying that the biggest argument in the post-war period has been that regarding the issues of Article 9 of the Japanese Constitution, the Japanese Self-Defense Forces (SDF), and the US-Japan Security Treaty. Because of Article 9, which, under the flag of 'pacifism,' makes clear its stance of 'renunciation of war' and 'non-possession of war potential,' the Japanese Self-Defense Forces lack the dimensions of a conventional military force in terms of command, operations, and deployment, and the right to wage war, although they possess huge war-making potential. Similarly, the US-Japan Security Treaty has had to function as an irregular system, not in the form of a conventional military alliance.

Herein lies the reason for the continuing dissatisfaction of those, mainly in conservative and government circles, who demand a 'normal state.' While the spirit of the constitution has been distorted by the SDF and the security treaty, so, conversely, the SDF and the security treaty may also be said to have been distorted by the existence of the constitution (at least from the point of view of the conventional modern state). Furthermore, since the security debate died down in the 1970s, this structure was simply set aside without any pretence of a solution, and on the surface appeared to be forgotten.

However, the contradictions and the gap between the Constitution, the SDF and the treaty cannot simply be set aside in this way. The problem henceforth is whether to try to correct the distortions while adhering to the spirit of the constitution, or alternatively to correct them by holding fast to the security treaty and the SDF.

The latter position is that of constitutional revision, which is now vociferously advocated. The common strain of thinking in this argument is that which advocates 'normal statehood' with a 'normal army' for Japan, along with international 'great power' status in the international community represented by a permanent seat on the UN Security Council, and to that end international contribution and the overseas dispatch of armed forces.

Basically, we advocate the former position. Apart from the fact that the main consensus among the Japanese people is the aspiration for peace and justice, the renunciation of war and the ability to wage war, and respect for international cooperation, all set out in the constitution, we consider it a position that most adequately reflects the spirit of the present age in which wars on a world scale are a thing of the past.

Classical warfare, in the sense of state armies being pitted against each other, or wars fought by the forces of several states forming military alliances as was once the case, has become unimaginable, at least among the advanced industrial countries. The best chance for the spirit of the Japanese Constitution to match that of the current age has arrived. It must be stated however, that our position is not that of the established constitutional defense party, *gokenron*, which calls for the immediate abolition of the Self-Defense Forces as unconstitutional. As will be explained further on, we are advocating not complete disarmament, but a new type of Self-Defensive Defense, wielding the minimum necessary defensive force, which, subject to meeting various conditions, could be maintained constitutionally. This position could be described as *sōkenron*, or 'creative constitutionalism.'

While still adhering to the spirit of the constitution, how are we to resolve the contradiction between the Self-Defense Forces and the constitution that has divided public opinion for so long, and achieve a national consensus on this matter? We wish to propose the creation of a semi-constitutional law that in legal terms would be derivative from Article 9, and which would adhere to its spirit, which we have named the Basic Peace Law.

This Basic Peace Law as we propose it is not merely the exposition of an ideal, but a practical foundation to consolidate Article 9 of the constitution, specifying procedures and processes to embody its ideals. Furthermore, it reverses the gradual erosion of the ideals of the constitution consistently practiced by successive post-war conservative governments, and would amount to a vow of 'non-use of force,' 'renunciation of war' and 'disarmament' to both the Japanese people and the people of the entire world, most particularly the peoples of Asia. The Japan Defense Agency (JDA) and Self-Defense Forces based on the present Defense Law would be re-structured and incorporated under this law. From the moment of inception of this law, the Self-Defense Forces, which, because of unconstitutional elements contained within them, could be described as in an unconstitutional state, would be re-structured into a new organization, provisionally named the National Guard (*Kokudo keibitai*). This could be regarded as a transitional entity pointing towards the Minimum Defensive Force that would be constitutional and lacking in any attacking capacity. So far as Japan's international contribution of a non-military kind is concerned, that would be entrusted to a separate organization. Furthermore, the Japanese people would be able to launch court actions based on this law, hence shifting the current debate over interpretation from the constitution to this Basic Peace Law.

Firstly, we will present the following points which we feel should be incorporated into the Basic Peace Law. It goes without saying that the following is not a formal draft law, and as such it is not presented in strictly legal form. Then secondly, we will explain its background.

Outline of a Basic Peace Law (Draft)

A. Objectives

This law affirms the basic principles and ideals regarding security embodied in the Japanese Constitution, and is here promulgated in order to detail concrete methods and procedures by which to maintain the security of the Japanese people and contribute positively towards world peace, striving for the implementation of the universal ideals embodied in the constitution, in particular the spirit of those sections of the constitution which state that the Japanese people have

> resolved that never again shall we be visited with the horrors of war through the action of government
>
> (Preamble)

> [that] We, the Japanese people . . . have determined to preserve our security and existence, trusting in the justice and faith of the peace-loving peoples of the world
>
> (Preamble)

> [that] Aspiring sincerely to an international peace based on justice and order, the Japanese people forever renounce war as a sovereign right of the nation and the threat or use of force as a means of settling international disputes . . . land, sea, and air forces, as well as other war potential, will never be maintained. The right of belligerency of the state will not be recognized.
>
> (Article 9)

B. Relationship with the constitution

THE RIGHT TO LIVE IN PEACE

The Japanese people are guaranteed 'the right to live in peace' under the Constitution of Japan. The government bears the responsibility of security in order to protect the people's lives from various threats.

THE RIGHT TO SELF-DEFENSE

Although Article 9 of the constitution by paragraph one rejects aggressive war and prohibits the use of force as a means of settling international disputes, the right to individual self-defense is recognized by Article 51 of the United Nations Charter. Sufficient force may be maintained to defend the people's lives from any invasion of sovereignty. However, because paragraph 2 of Article 9 prohibits all war potential and renounces the right to Defensive Force, the mode of its organization and equipment, and the methods by which it may exert force, must be limited and restricted.

PROHIBITION OF CONSCRIPTION

Since the Constitution of Japan forever renounces war as a sovereign right of the nation, no emergency powers for such purpose may be adopted, the government does not have the right to declare war or sue for peace, the establishment of courts martial is prohibited, and the duty of state defense shall not be imposed upon the people. Based on the spirit of the constitution, the government shall not impose conscription or any other analogous duties upon the people.

OBLIGATION OF DISARMAMENT

Since the constitution prohibits our nation from the use of force as a means of settling international disputes, the duty to strive ceaselessly for disarmament, both in Japan and in the world, is imposed on Japan.

C. Security not reliant on military force

RELATIONS WITH NEIGHBORING COUNTRIES

The basis of the security to which the Constitution of Japan aspires is 'trust in the justice and faith of the peace-loving peoples of the world.' Previously, Japan committed the error of employing force to make colonies of its neighboring countries, threatening and invading them with force, and inflicted numerous sufferings and losses upon them. The first thing that Japan must do to regain the trust of these nations and to secure the peace and security of Japan by trusting in the 'justice and faith of the peace-loving peoples of the world' is to pledge never to repeat those errors, and to apologize and compensate for them. The Japanese people must not be allowed to forget this reality.

COMMON SECURITY

Regional collective security   The peace and security of the Asia-Pacific region is an indispensable factor in the security of Japan. By avoiding the construction of hypothetical enemies, deepening of mutual economic, political, and cultural exchange, and gradual and continuous effort toward building and encouraging mutual trust in this region, Japan should exert itself to get mutual declarations and treaties of non-aggression and non-war. Every effort must be made to construct a regional collective security apparatus, as was prescribed in a future-oriented way in the United Nations Charter. Furthermore, every effort shall be made to inform the other peoples of Asia of the ideals embodied in Article 9 of the constitution, and of the Japanese people's sincere commitment to these ideals.

Common security based on the United Nations Charter   The United Nations Charter and the Constitution of Japan are both rooted in the common spirit of the same period in terms of their renunciation of the use of force as a means for settling international disputes and their aspiration toward international security based on rejection of war. Furthermore, the peace of Japan cannot be realized without a stable international peace and order. From this perspective, along with positive participation in the various United Nations activities, every effort shall be made toward what can be termed common security on a global scale in the form of a UN-centered collective security apparatus. Also, every effort shall be made toward the democratic reform of the United Nations, and a position of responsibility should be adopted to pursue such reform.

However, so far as the 'use of military forces' against threats to peace or against aggressors as prescribed by Article 7 of the UN Charter is concerned, in consideration of the fact that the 'war potential' and war methods employed by United Nations member-states is completely different from that envisaged in the period during which the Charter was established, we make this concrete proposal for cooperation with other states towards the establishment of a 'United Nations Army' suited to the contemporary world.

Comprehensive security   Security means the protection of the lives of the people from all sorts of threat. To accomplish it, we must strive by diplomatic effort, stabilizing and improving domestic politics, stressing the non-military aspects of scientific and technological, economic and industrial progress, to transform the international environment in desirable directions and to promote a security which will ease antagonisms in order to effect favorable change on the international environment. Furthermore, we recognize that the increasing wealth gap between North and South is the major source of conflict, and shall make every effort to rectify it.

Prohibition of military alliances   In accordance with its constitution, Japan should not belong to any military alliances. Taking note of the new post-Cold War circumstances, we look to the demilitarization of the post-Cold War US-Japan Security Treaty and its development and merger into a regional collective security system (see 2A).

The three non-nuclear principles   Japan shall never possess, store, or develop either nuclear weapons or the means to transport them. Furthermore, Japan shall not export armaments to any country, nor repair or modify the weapons possessed by another country.

D. Minimum defensive force

TASK

Its task is to respect the spirit of the constitution and defend the people from any act in violation of territorial sovereignty.

COMMAND

The Prime Minister shall command and supervise it.

MINISTRY FOR PEACE AND DISARMAMENT

As for the possession and management of a strictly-controlled minimum defensive force, a provisionally named Ministry of Peace and Disarmament (or alternatively, Ministry of Peace and Security) shall be established. A civilian shall be appointed to head this Ministry (Article 66: 2, Constitution of Japan).

BASIC PRINCIPLES

The Minimum Defensive Force cannot engage in defense activities beyond the boundaries of Japanese sovereign air, sea, or land space. The position of resort to the use of force only after prior use by an opponent shall be maintained.

Furthermore, the decision to deploy the Minimum Defensive Force shall be subject in principle to the prior resolution and approval of the National Diet.

COMPOSITION AND EQUIPMENT

Levels of personnel, budget, composition and equipment appropriate within the limits appropriate to conducting the tasks outlined by the Basic Peace Law require the decision and approval of the Diet. Furthermore, in regard to scale, every effort shall be made to adhere to the principle of consultation with neighboring countries and mutual approval.

CIVILIAN PRIORITY

The Ministry for Peace and Disarmament shall be managed according to the principle of civilian priority.

PUBLIC DISCLOSURE OF INFORMATION

The Minimum Defensive Force shall have a duty to publish for the Diet all information pertaining to matters of equipment, operations and information collection.

RIGHTS OF MEMBERS

The democratic rights (including the right to public association) of personnel who volunteer to participate in the Minimum Defensive Force shall be respected in the same manner as the normal rights of all public servants.

OBLIGATION OF FULLFILLMENT AND PENALTIES

This law imposes upon the government concrete obligations – including in respect of disarmament – of fulfillment, and appropriate penalties for breach. Accordingly, in the event that either the general public or the members of the Minimum Defensive Force have reason to believe that these principles have been violated, they may resort to the courts.

E. Transitional measures

Following the establishment of the Basic Peace Law, the current Self-Defense Forces shall be reorganized into a National Guard (*Kokudo keibitai*: a provisional title) with different duties. Furthermore, an International Relief Force (*Kokusai kyūnantai*: a provisional title) shall be hived off as a separate organization, comprising volunteers, for non-military activities associated with UN Peacekeeping Operations and other duties relating to international contribution. Continuing employment will be guaranteed to all personnel.

A disarmament program, designed to bring about the Minimum Defensive Force, shall be spelled out, according to which reductions of equipment and personnel shall be effected in harmony with the disarmament processes of neighboring countries. (At the time of establishment of the Basic Peace Law, the Diet shall proclaim the constitutionality of the National Guard.)

F. Non-military methods for a positive contribution towards world peace

The Japanese government and the Japanese people must contribute towards world peace through non-military methods in accordance with the spirit of the constitution. We must deepen mutual understanding and trust through diplomacy, striving for a global nuclear ban and for reductions in conventional armaments and the banning of weapons exports, and also for the implementation of an Official Development Assistance (ODA) policy that will contribute toward the narrowing of the North–South gap in a way without harming the environment or the peoples of any other country, and through the positive advancement and promotion of Non-Government Organizations (NGOs) and the positive promotion of things like textbook exchanges.

HOW TO INTERPRET THE PRESENT AGE

The end of the Cold War may be considered as the conclusion of an age of worldwide war that spanned the entire twentieth century. Great powers formed global military blocks and confronted each other; regional conflict always threatened to expand into global hostilities between the military blocks, and on two occasions – the First and Second World Wars – did actually evolve into world war. Such an age has now finished.

State socialism, which was born out of the hostilities of the world wars and became one of the major actors of this age, met its end in Russia and Eastern Europe. Furthermore, with the dissolution of the Soviet Empire, the military superpower, the Soviet Union, and the other military superpower, the United States, have also in a sense come to an end. It could be described as the end of the American empire. Upon the end of the Cold War, former US president Bush spoke of the victory of the United States but this can scarcely be considered to be true.

During the nuclear arms race, the main resources of the former Soviet Union were poured into the production of weapons. At the same time, the economy of the United States also became a grossly weapons-centered system. Now that the two countries have ceased to be enemies, large numbers of overseas-deployed troops, huge nuclear capacity, chemical weapons, the Central Intelligence Agency and KGB and other specialist organs, are all becoming redundant. What is called for now is to move away from a world of military confrontation rooted in hate and fear. The basic orientation of the history that begins now is that of disarmament and demilitarization.

What begins with the passing of the age of world wars is the age of economics. The economic center of this age is Japan, which has built up a highly-efficient, growth economy through non-military development, and Germany, which in the same manner through non-military development became the economic leader of Europe.

Japan suffered defeat in the Second World War, and was democratized under the occupation of the US, its military forces disbanded. With its peace constitution, Japan was promptly able of its own accord to remove itself from the age of world wars. The anti-war and anti-military feelings of being fed-up with war and sick of armies were sentiments only to be expected from a people that had been the first in history to suffer the horror of nuclear weapons. The Japanese people had sung the praises of its army and supported overseas expansion for half a century after the Sino-Japanese War (1894–5). The transformation into a country without conscription was remarkable.

However, we must also acknowledge that the unprecedented spiritual demilitarization of the Japanese people might actually have been based upon a lack of genuine feeling of responsibility about the war. This can be well understood if Japan and Germany are compared.

At the end of street-fighting in the German capital, the parliament was occupied, and Germany finally surrendered. As a result of the defeat, the country, and even the capital Berlin, was divided. West Germany later revised its new constitution and established a conscription army, but this army was part of the North Atlantic Treaty Organization (NATO) and in the main only operated under NATO command, not sending troops outside of NATO territory. Germany has created relations of such trust with France, a country with which it fought two world wars, as to be able to constitute a joint force with it. This state of affairs however, is linked firmly to the fact that in West Germany the war responsibility of the Hitler regime and Nazism was pursued thoroughly, and de-Nazification was carried out autonomously by the German people themselves. The statute of limitations was lifted with respect to the pursuit of Nazi war criminals, and compensation to the victims of Nazism undertaken through the responsibility of the German people and industry. The German people punished Nazi crimes and thereby reflected upon their own responsibility. Furthermore, it may well be that through continuing to question their own responsibility for the war, they have managed to put the responsibility of the military into proportion, without going so far as to negate it outright.

In Japan, as part of the Cold War strategy of the US, all responsibility for the war was ascribed to Tōjō and the military, and the war responsibility of the Showa Emperor [Hirohito] was not pursued. In addition, because it was easier for most Japanese not to question their own responsibility but to blame the military, the idea of compensating the victims of Japan's aggressive war never occurred to them. The military was completely negated, but at the same time their own responsibility was forgotten.

Emotionally, the Japanese people turned their backs on wars and armies, even though the age of worldwide conflict continued. The US and the Soviet Union became centers of this age, forming world-wide military blocks and confronting each other with nuclear weapons. Japan was denied the exercise of collective self-defense rights under its constitution, but basically belonged to the US camp, allowed the establishment of US bases within its territory, and in this way chose to entrust its security to a quasi-military alliance with the US. Also, within this security arrangement it constructed on a limited scale a quasi-army known as the Self-Defense Forces. Although such a move was inherently in conflict with the constitution, it explained it to the people in terms of the right to individual self-defense. This was the beginning of constitutional revision by interpretation. In addition, the policy of concentration upon economic growth through non-military development was taken by the Yoshida government.

Later, the Liberal-Democratic Party (LDP) called for constitutional revision in order to resolve the contradiction between the constitution and the military, but the people did not give the constitutional reform proposal the necessary two-thirds of parliamentary seats. In due course, popular support for Article 9 of the constitution became fixed, and support within the LDP for express constitutional revision weakened. Nevertheless, the constitution was systematically belittled by the governing party. Under this weak state in which conscription did not exist, 'companyism' advanced with great strides, and economic high growth was achieved through development of mass production of consumer goods based on non-military, civilian technologies. The fact that the political opposition, and almost a third of the general public, insisted that the existence of the Self-Defense Forces was unconstitutional under Article 9, both made the Yoshida doctrine possible in the first place and sustained it, but also served as a constraint and a brake on its expansion, and served to hold military cooperation with the US to a minimum.

So, what does the end of the age of world conflict portend?

First of all, because the military blocks have been dissolved, or lost their meaning, the concept of collective self-defense by military alliances has also become meaningless. The US-Japan alliance has likewise lost its meaning as something confronting the 'Soviet threat.' It is 'common security' on a global scale that must now be aimed for.[3] It is only natural that the concept of collective security conceived at the formation of the United Nations should now be reconsidered.

The fact that the age of world wars has now passed does not mean that there is no more war but that regional wars are more possible since there is no fear of them escalating into world war. Superpower Soviet-American controls no longer operate, and with the force of ideology diminishing, ethnic emotions and long-held resentments that had been held down by this power explode and regional warfare becomes rampant. The neglected questions of the influence of colonial control, and the scars of aggressive wars, again generate antagonisms. In addition, in the age of the world economy, as the wealth gap between North and South widens it carries the potential for even greater conflicts. Disputes over resources and territory are already occurring.

Even considering such antagonisms and wars, the activities of a UN which stood on the principle of common security become important. Without being one-sidedly swayed by the interest of the larger powers, the UN should continue its activities, taking a stance of fairness and respecting the equal status of all its constituent states. However, the deeply-rooted antagonisms or wars which stem from them will not be resolved by military means. There cannot be true resolution other than by exercising political, economic and cultural effort designed to stir the people of the region concerned to a new awakening and to make their own effort.

Also important are factors which make it impossible for the US and the (former) Soviet Union to push ahead with arms reduction, despite its urgency. The disposal of these (military) white elephants is enormously expensive, and people get laid off as a result, swelling the ranks of the unemployed. The process of transformation of the munitions industry to civilian industry is fraught with difficulties, whether in the former Soviet Union or in the US. Disarmament must proceed slowly but surely, through the deepening of mutual trust between both countries, and it needs to be expanded into a framework of regional cooperation. It is necessary for countries other than the USSR and the US to cooperate positively in the disarmament process.

What does this current situation mean for Japan?

Although the end of the age of world wars means that Japan must endeavor to fulfil its responsibility as a leading power, Japan is not ready for this. It has neither a political position nor a philosophy which is sensitive to this new era and so has issued almost no message to the world. Under these circumstances, it is fatal for there to be no consensus regarding the Constitution, and precisely because this is the case we must now tackle the main point of constitutional contention, the problem of the Self-Defense Forces.

The problems of apology, reflection and compensation for war and colonial rule ought to have been settled after the end of the Second World War, but were set aside and left unresolved. Above all else, we must first begin the effort to establish at a national level an understanding of Japan's colonialism and aggressive war, and show repentance over them. The history of aggression must be taught to the next generation, and compensation made to those who suffered.

The Self-Defense Forces and the security treaty are problems left over from the Cold War. They must be resolved in a new spirit appropriate to our third 'post-war' constituted by the end of the age of world wars. We will not be able to enter this new period unless we do this.

TOWARD THE IMPLEMENTATION OF ARTICLE 9

Although the 'left' in post-war Japan adopted the preservation of Article 9 as its *raison d'être*, their explorations of what concretely was meant by preservation of Article 9 did not go very deep.

Domestically, as a result of having renounced armaments and the use of force, little concrete consideration was given to the question of how to advance Japan's security. Unarmed neutrality may have been one of the possibilities considered, but it was assumed to be unrealistic amid the realities of the Cold War, and subsequent opinion surveys and elections show that the majority of the people did not choose this option. The people firmly rejected constitutional revision, but they accepted the contradictory reality involved in recognition of the existence of the SDF.

Internationally, concrete consideration was not given to how Japan might contribute to the resolution of world conflict. Whatever fears there may have been about being embroiled in another war, little practical consideration was given to how to manifest to the world its peace constitution spirit of 'aspiring sincerely to an international peace based on justice and order.'

For this reason, the word 'constitutional defense' came to be ridiculed as meaning 'one country pacifism.' The main responsibility, however, should attach to governments which, faced with this situation, high-handedly possessed and expanded 'war potential' whose possession was clearly forbidden by the constitution, without amending the constitution, merely saying 'we can possess it because it is not war potential.' Not once was the contradiction between constitution and armed forces made clear to the people, and not once were they given the opportunity to choose to resolve it. The people simply gave up thinking deeply about the issue and lapsed into thinking they might as well just enjoy the 'peace' they had.

Now that the age of world wars is over, what is required of us, both nationally and internationally, in order to preserve the spirit of the constitution, is the wisdom to implement Article 9. We must put an end to the sterile arguments about what is 'constitutional' or 'non-constitutional,' and shift the focus of the debate towards finding a 'creative constitutionalist' path to breathe life into the spirit of the constitution.

As mentioned earlier, the peace constitution was historically prophetic in character. When considering how to implement it this is a point which should first be recognized. That force is of no use in the settlement of conflict has been demonstrated anew both by the way the Cold War ended and by the course of post-Cold War regional disputes. Unlimited military expansion exhausts economies and comes to threaten security itself. If we look at the examples of the Gulf War and the civil war in Yugoslavia, we should be able to understand that the fundamental causes of conflict cannot be eliminated by force. Although it is still possible to imagine situations where force might be necessary, the spirit of the peace constitution, which rejects force as a means of settling disputes, is not only not 'outdated' but is very much in keeping with the times.

Furthermore, another perspective to keep in mind when considering the implementation of the constitution is that the gap between legal norms and reality should not be ignored any longer. That the court has used the argument of *'tōchi kōi'* to avoid making any judgement on the constitutionality of the Self-Defense Forces means that there are limits to the extent to which any resolution of the problem may be sought through the legal system.[4] Since the courts defer their judgement to the government, there is no alternative to entrusting the political wisdom of the people to find a solution. The constitution is the basic norm which determines the way politics should be conducted and the condition of the state, and as such it must be clear and understandable to the people. What is needed is to strive towards formulation of clear norms, not an explanation of reality by means of interpretations.

Let us here set out the main categories of interpretation of the constitution.

It goes without saying that there are two positions with respect to Article 9, that the SDF is constitutional and that it is unconstitutional, but within both of these there are differences of nuance about interpretations of the right to self defense and of war potential.

The established view of those who affirm the existence of the SDF is that since 'Article 9 paragraph One of the constitution does not go so far as to deny the existence of the right to self-defense, accordingly a minimum necessary force (*hitsuyō saishōgendo no jitsuryoku*) may be maintained based on paragraph Two.' This is the constitution interpretation favoured by the conservative mainstream, and it became the official viewpoint of successive Liberal-Democratic Party governments (argument A).[5] Although belonging to the same affirmative view, there is another interpretation of this genre which claims that 'Understanding that Article 9 prohibits wars of aggression, but not defensive wars, a defensive force may be maintained under paragraph Two.' This was the interpretation of Prime Minister Ashida, and until recently was also favored by a majority of scholars. Of late the Ozawa Study Group's understanding of the constitution is of the same type, arguing that Self-Defense Forces may participate in exercising force for security in accord with the decision of the United Nations (argument B). Interpretation B takes the view that, as a normal state, Japan's possession of an army is natural, and restricts the meaning of the constitution to a certain restraint on the exercise of that force.

Even among those who believe that the existence of the SDF is unconstitutional, there are differences of interpretation. The conventional understanding interprets Article 9 as meaning 'Article 9 paragraph One renounces all forms of war, and the maintenance of war potential of any kind is forbidden under paragraph Two' (argument C). A further interpretation (D) claims that 'Article 9 does not deny the right to self-defense, but because the possession of war potential is prohibited in paragraph Two, in effect even defensive war is prohibited.' According to D, in the case of aggression, defense would be pursued through non-military police forces and civilian sabotage. This argument was adopted in the first judgement in the Naganuma case.

Our own stance, which rates highly the constitution's pacifism, and tries to pursue its implementation, is this D position. This is because we feel that position C does not permit room for the realization of any other security option than immediate unarmed neutrality, leaving no room for discussion of methods of security to realize the ideal.

Furthermore, the core of implementation of Article 9 is the pursuit of security through methods other than traditional military force. What is necessary towards this end is a transformation in the established ideas of war and army, based on the large historical turning-point of the end of the age of world wars. In this age, even if another country were to be invaded and subdued by force, there is no state able to bear the cost of such war and the costs of controlling the conquered territory. Accordingly, at least among advanced countries, classical warfare in which soldiers of rival state armies engage in fighting based on the right of state belligerency, has become inconceivable.

Military blocs have broken down, and the threat to be faced has changed from enemy states or blocks of states seeking conquest to the level of international terrorism and armed refugees. If so, then what this means is that the sort of self-defensive organization would be much smaller than that required in the traditional scenario of confrontation with another country's regular army, and the scope to construct a new type of defensive organization not prohibited by Article 9 may be discerned.

What was problematic about the interpretation of Article 9 by previous governments was its possession of inherent attack capability as its equipment was steadily upgraded despite the words 'Self-Defense.' In so far as the SDF was for defense against the regular forces of some other country, there was nothing to hold its expansion in check. This aroused suspicion among both the Japanese people and the peoples of neighboring Asia. In keeping with the change in the nature of the threat, the possibility has emerged for constructing henceforth a self-defense organization without attacking capability.

We wish to call this new type of defensive organization 'Minimum Defensive Force' (saishōgen bōgyoryoku). Since much discussion will be needed on the actual scale, equipment, and personnel of such a force, and because there will be changes in accord with international circumstances, we have avoided spelling it out too clearly within the substance of the law. So far as the basic principles are concerned, we have restricted ourselves to what is outlined above. The sort of spider-web defensive organization proposed by Maeda Tetsuo could serve as a draft proposal.[6] It would be a defensive organization without offensive equipment or orientation, but equipped to deal with disasters and conflicts beyond the scope of a conventional police force or fire brigade.

The gap between the present Self-Defense Forces and our proposed Minimum Defensive Force is large. The SDF, under pressure from the US, expanded greatly during the Cold War and especially during the 1980s, to the point where they could not possibly be described as 'constitutional.' In order to switch the SDF to a constitutional Minimum Defensive Force, transitional measures, in accordance with a demilitarization program to be debated in the Diet, will be necessary.

What is necessary in sum is to establish a formula for subjecting the new-style military to the control of civil society. Most pressing is to put an end to mobilisation for keeping the public peace (with certain political movements in mind) as prescribed under Articles 3 and 78 of the Self-Defense Force Law. Furthermore, for civilian control of the military, openness of information is vital. In addition, the enshrinement of the dead at Yasukuni Shrine, which is evocative of the former Imperial Japanese Army, and illegal gathering of intelligence on the civil society should probably also be stopped.

Furthermore, the scale of the Minimum Defensive Force will also change depending on the extent to which the UN's collective security system and East Asian regional security systems are provided. If a regional security organization encompassing the US, Russia, China, North and South Korea (or a united Korea) is formed, it could be that a coastguard plus small numbers of ground troops would be enough for the defense of Japan's territory.

The Constitution of Japan orders the Japanese people to make 'ceaseless effort' toward the accomplishment of security and the resolution of disputes by more peaceful means and by increasing avoidance of force. Continuing discussion on concrete constitutional means will be needed to cope with this permanent movement.

Restriction of the Self-Defense Forces

Until now, the Japanese government has held that it was internationally understood that the SDF were maintained as an 'inherent right' of a sovereign state prescribed under the UN Charter. It has continued to develop its position on the constitutionality of the SDF. However, although this idea of individual self-defense has been accepted in Japan as an absolutely self-evident national right, we should realize that there is no clear definition of it, and it is not only vague but potentially dangerous as a basis for legitimacy.

This is because, as pointed out by Prime Minister Yoshida at the Constitutional Reform Committee (June 26 1946) 'Many of the wars of recent years have been waged in the name of self-defense.' Furthermore, because the geographical limits of self-defense are not defined, one cannot rule out the possible emergence of irresponsible politicians claiming that Japan's self-defense right extends from 1,000 nautical miles to the Malacca Straits or even the Gulf area.

Certainly, Article 51 of the UN Charter states that 'In the interim before the UN Security Council takes necessary steps for the preservation of peace and security, nothing in the present Charter shall impair the inherent right of individual or collective self-defense if an armed attack occurs against a member of the United Nations.' (Even the 1928 Treaty of Non-Aggression includes the qualification that 'Since all sovereign states possess a self-defense right, and since it is assumed in all treaties, therefore all states, regardless of what is stipulated in any treaty, possess the freedom to defend their own territory from attack or aggression.')

However, the reason why we propose a reinterpretation of the notion that the 'self-defense right' is an 'inherent right' of a sovereign state, lies in the collective security system envisaged by the United Nations. In that self-defense is recognized as a temporary measure pending the adoption of measures based upon the collective security system, the judgement of whether or not something is a self-defense right is entrusted to each sovereign state. The problem inherent in this is that of abuse of the self-defense right.

If pacifist Japan can be said to have the right to self-defense, the problem of how to interpret excessive use of this right must be seen as inescapable, and the scale, deployment, and any restrictions on the military force of the proposed Minimum Defensive Force becomes relevant to it.

The use of force and even resort to war in case of conflict between states used to be recognized, but in the course of the present century the view that war is illegal has progressed, and within this trend the United Nations has outlawed both the 'use of force' and the 'threat of force' permitting force only for sanctions or self-defense.

Within the UN collective security system, broad restrictions have been imposed upon the 'use of force,' especially war. The collective sanctions by the UN against illegal 'use of force' or 'threat of force' have been recognized as legal responses, and the exercise of a self-defense right recognized as a temporary measure pending the coming into operation of such sanctions. However, even if the right to self-defense is exercised as a temporary measure, the possibility remains that the self-defense power may be abused if it is seen as an 'inherent right' of sovereign states.

To construct a system which would prevent such abuse, the 'self-defense right' might be seen as a right stemming from the UN's collective security system rather than as an 'inherent right' of a sovereign state. The possession by a sovereign state of a 'self-defense right' does not vary in accordance with whether the right is inherent or given, but, if the self-defense right were to be reconstituted as a right bestowed under the collective security system it should be easier to prevent its abuse.

The 'Basic Peace Law' which we have proposed here can be described as the first step toward a political declaration on the limitation of the self-defense right, and in order to realize it, it might be worth considering the international exchange of documents pertaining to the Basic Peace Law, either through the United Nations or on a regional level.

At the heart of the current UN collective security system is the recognition of the 'use of military force' against breaches of the peace and aggressive acts. However, the essence of an army is 'victory over the enemy,' 'annihilation' and 'destruction.' In principle, what collective security requires should be not the use of the military, but police activity based upon the law to restrain the breaches of the law. There should be no such thing as an 'enemy.'

In addition, in the event of such international (UN) policing activities, it should be possible to establish a new-type Japanese unit, not an army and completely separate from the Minimum Defensive Force, which could be internationally, or UN, trained and led.

In fact, if Japan is to entrust its security to such an international policing system, one would expect that it would want to participate positively in it. This is because as the international police system grew in strength, the Minimum Defensive Force protecting Japanese territory could gradually be reduced. (So far as any United Nations army is concerned, our position is that great prudence should be exercised regarding any participation by Japan, and that participation in any other multinational force is out of the question).

Of course, we realise that conditions in either the UN or East Asia are not conducive to the immediate formation of a collective security system involving a strengthened police along these lines. However, if we are to be committed to the pacifism demanded by the constitution in this new post-world war age, we must strive to move the reality in the direction of the ideal.

Japan is indeed a 'special state' which has voluntarily relinquished part of its military sovereignty. There are voices, not only from the Liberal-Democratic Party but also from within the political opposition, which would have this 'special state' become a 'normal state.' Even in some circles in Germany the call to become again an 'ordinary state' is gaining strength. But what is wrong with being a 'special state'? Might not the abandonment of part of our sovereignty indicate rather a certain foresight? This is after all the age in which the modern state itself, its borders, its centralized government, its education system and its national economy, are being seriously questioned.

We believe that it is precisely through inheriting and further developing the idea of a 'collective security system' that was born out of the horrors of repeated war, and by exploring both in juridical theory and in practice the idea of UN-based collective security and regional security, that our 'special state' may be made into a 'normal state' while retaining its 'specialness.'

What we have developed here is not an argument for the constitutionality of the Self-Defense Forces. Even less is it an argument for leaving things be, by accepting the current situation as it is. It is instead a prescription for putting an end to the Cold War era within our country by our own efforts. For the resolution of conflict, both political wisdom and sincere effort on both sides is necessary. We must attempt to disentangle ourselves from the inertia of the 'Cold War mentality' and 'confrontational thinking' that were nurtured within the Cold War structure.

The political parties that are the political expression of the will of the people, in particular the Social Democratic Party of Japan and the Liberal-Democratic Party, are called upon to exert the utmost efforts towards achieving a mutual understanding and a consensus on this problem.

Furthermore, without the participation and supervision of the people, whatever laws are drawn up will be meaningless. This is so much more the case in dealing with the problem of the military, the most difficult of all problems facing a democracy. A lively debate is called for from the people on this issue.

PART TWO

A Proposal for Asia-Pacific regional security[7]

Introduction

The main points of the proposal we made in April 1993 were as follows:

1   The Soviet-American Cold War, with its threat of the extinction of the world, is over, and the age of world wars has also ended.
2   Thanks to the end of the Cold War, the Warsaw pact armies have ceased to exist and the meaning of NATO has changed greatly. The context surrounding the US-Japan Security Treaty has also greatly changed. On the other hand, regional wars and ethnic conflicts are intensifying. Under these circumstances, attention has come to focus on the notion of a collective security system, which was the original meaning of the United Nations.
3   In Japan the contradictions over the constitution and the Self-Defense Forces, which were born of the Cold War and have divided public opinion, must be resolved.
4   To achieve this, a national debate and effort, transcending Cold War inertia, is necessary to construct a national consensus over how to contribute positively and by non-military means to world peace, to construct a 'Basic Law of Peace' in accordance with Article 9 of the constitution, and to cut

back the scale and the structure of the existing Self-Defense Forces so that their military force becomes 'Minimum Defensive Force' of a level allowed by the constitution.
5 For this purpose it is also necessary to accomplish a true reconciliation with the countries of Asia that Japan once invaded.
6 The idea of 'Minimum Defensive Force' is based on the right of national self-defense, but the self-defense right is not an 'inherent right' but a right bestowed in accordance with the collective security system and as such obviously subject to constraint.

After the publication of this proposal, we received many responses from various quarters. So far as political quarters are concerned, the opinions of ten members of the Diet who responded to the solicitation of the editors of *Sekai* may be consulted in the June 1993 issue of the journal. Mr Hosokawa Morihiro, who was to become Prime Minister two months later, responded that he 'could well understand' the proposal. Asked whether he was in agreement or not he replied that 'you could say that I am in agreement,' and called for the creation of a UN Police Unit. Tanaka Shūsei, then a member of the Liberal-Democratic Party, who later established the 'Harbinger' (*Sakigake*) party and became a special adviser to Prime Minister Hosokawa, said, 'I have no particular disagreement with the proposal. I respect the aspiration, but must say that I do not see its necessity at the present juncture.' He proposed planning towards an international security system under UN auspices. From the Social Democratic Party of Japan, Uehara Kōsuke, who was to become a member of Cabinet two months later, declared his 'complete agreement with the gist of what has been proposed and the political line it embodied,' saying that he intended to have his party work on the drawing up of drafts. Endō Otohiko of the Kōmeitō said it was most important to devise a clear guide in the form of a 'Basic Law on Peace' and a 'Basic Law on Security,' but that, while he 'recognized the proposal as a clarification of the problem,' he himself stood for the constitutionality of the Self-Defense Forces and the continuation of the US-Japan Security Treaty.

As against these views, the Japan Communist Party's Ueda Kōichirō said the proposal was 'a kind of constitutional revision by legislation.' He called for a repudiation of the security treaty and for 'a non-nuclear, non-aligned path.' Apart from the Japan Communist Party, it seems to us that the proposal was widely recognized, irrespective of party, as worthy of deliberation.

Next, the views of politicians and activists living in the vicinity of the bases were solicited, and carried in the August issue. These views were many and various, ranging from 'complete agreement' to 'determined to block it completely' and 'had to groan while reading it.' What was most resisted was the idea that 'Minimum Defensive Force' was constitutional. How was it different from the Liberal-Democratic Party's understanding of Article 9, and did it not amount to an abandonment of the view of the constitution as 'giving up the right of self-defense' and 'completely renouncing war'? However, positive responses to the proposal may be seen as coming from the demands of reality, in that its existence would have to be clearly recognized if the size of the SDF was to be reduced.

The response from constitutional scholars was also mixed. In '"The Basic Law on Peace" from a Constitutional law perspective' (*Sekai*, July 1993 and March and May 1994), Fukase Chūichi, professor of Japanese Constitutional Law at Hokusei Gakuen University, while surveying the constitutional cases of the post-war period, took the view that the constitutionality of the Self-Defense Forces remained unsettled, drew attention to the importance of the role of the courts in blocking any threats to the basic human right of the people to live in peace arising from national defense and military purposes of the Self-Defense Forces, and concluded that the proposal for a 'Basic Law on Peace' had important and positive meaning as 'a model for implementing the peace constitution.' However, he added that he could not help feeling opposed to the constitutionalising of 'Minimum Defensive Force,' stressed the need for reconsideration of the right of self-defense based on it, and called for further scholarly research on the question. On the other hand, Okudaira Yasuhiro, professor at International Christian University, offered the criticism that, while he appreciated that this was 'an attempt to systematize and give life to the spirit of Article 9,' it was hard to see how 'Minimum Necessary Force' was different from the government's 'necessary minimum for self-defense,' and 'could not help thinking that it amounted to no more than a play on words' (*Sekai*, June 1993).

Our proposal met with a fierce response and criticism from one sector of the 'constitutionalists.' Watanabe Osamu, professor at Hitotsubashi University, criticised us in his book *Seiji kaikaku to kempō kaisei*[8] saying that the kernel of the proposal was 'the constitutionality of the Self-Defense Forces' and that the objective of the proposal was 'to have the Social Democratic Party of Japan adopt a position of clear support for the constitutionality of the Self-Defense Forces.'

Many of the critical opinions oppose the thrust of the proposal to seek positively for a new direction to mark an end to world war. It seems that they feel the problem of this moment is 'how to resist' the trend for a strengthening of unipolar US control accompanying the end of the Cold War, and the increasingly strong tendencies for Japan to be tugged along the path of war and militarization.

However, the fact is that great global changes have occurred and are continuing. No-one can escape these changes. The resistance which certainly was meaningful in the context of the structure of events as they existed till now becomes meaningless under the new circumstances. If we are to recognize as positive the situation brought about by that resistance till now, are we not called upon to propose an alternative, to give life to it, and to take part in the construction of a new world?

So, what is it that can be recognized as positive in the situation brought about by our resistance? Is it not, so far as the security dimension is concerned, the Japanese people's psychological transcendence of militarism, the existence of a society in which the military is not given priority, and the character of the Self-Defense Forces as a special military force greatly constrained by the Constitution? The prohibition on collective defense, the three non-nuclear principles, the ban on export of weapons, and the ban on the overseas dispatch of Japanese troops, should probably also be included. What is now required of us, we believe, is to preserve and reform these assets and expand them by linking them to new directions.

In the one and a half years since we proposed the 'Basic Law on Peace' we have not seen any need to revise the proposal itself in its fundamentals. However, while in our proposal we called for a debate of the utmost intensity, the Social Democratic Party of Japan for its part thereafter entered government and, without any new debate at all, switched its position to 'constitutionality of the Self-Defense Forces' and 'support for the Security Treaty.' The peacekeeping organization [units] of the Self-Defense Forces which were then deployed in Cambodia were withdrawn, and now the Self-Defense Forces are active in Zaire. On the other hand, implementation of the heavily armed 'Peace Enforcement Units' under the Ghaly plan seems, after the stalemate in Somalia, to have receded into the distant future. The United Nations' peacekeeping operations are undergoing severe trials.

Faced with such changes in the situation, we would like here to supplement, or make more concrete, our original proposal and to indicate what are the problems we now face.

The meaning of 'Minimum Defensive Force'

The criticisms of our proposal have been manifold, but the greatest criticism has attached to our idea of 'Minimum Defensive Force' (*saishōgen bōgyoryoku*). That is to say, it is a matter of how recognition of the constitutionality of 'Minimum Defensive Force' differed from the established government position that 'necessary minimum force for self-defense' (*jiei no tame no hitsuyō saishōgen no jitsuryoku*) was constitutional.

We classify the main interpretations so far of Article 9 under the following four headings.

A   Since Article 9, paragraph 1 does not go so far as to rule out self-defense powers, the necessary minimum force for self-defense may be possessed under paragraph 2 (the government position).

B   Since paragraph 1 of Article 9 forbids aggressive war but not defensive war, defensive forces may be possessed (the view of Ashida).

C   Paragraph 1 of Article 9 rejects all war, and paragraph 2 rules out possession of all war potential (*senryoku*) (the established view of the Constitutional Lawyers' Society).

D   Paragraph 1 of Article 9 does not rule out defensive war but, since paragraph 2 forbids the possession of force, the upshot is that even defensive war is forbidden (the judgement in the Naganuma case).

112 *Japan's contested constitution*

In our proposal we said that we adopted the 'D' position, and we were criticized on the ground that, if we recognized 'Minimum Defensive Force' as constitutional, we were so close as to be almost identical with the 'A' position. It is our position that 'Minimum Defensive Force' does not mean the air, land, and sea forces which are ruled out under paragraph 2 of Article 9, or any similar war-potential. However, it is not denied that Minimum Defensive Force means armed force (*busōryoku*) that could be directed against any invader. Our position is that an army, or 'special armed force' analogous to an army but not 'war potential,' may be possessed under the constitution.

What becomes important here is the question of what is an army. In our view, an army is an armed unit for combat,

i   mostly against foreign enemies, possessed by a state for the protection of the state, whose main purpose is to destroy and annihilate the enemy
ii   which recruits troops by a voluntary system or by conscription
iii in which orders from command are absolute
iv in which insubordination is punished by court-martial or military tribunal
v   which possesses voluminous secrets that are protected by special laws
vi which during combat operations is more-or-less freed of the constraints of the law.

In the definition of an army, Professor Fukase Chūichi draws attention not just to the quality and scale of the armed force (*busōryoku*) but to its use in battle of force freed from the restraint of the law. Yamauchi Toshihiro, Professor of Japanese Constitutional Law at Hitotsubashi University, also believes that one basic distinguishing characteristic of an army, along with its purpose and its essence, is its distinctive principle of organization and activity.[9]

However, iv, v and vi above do not apply even to the existing Self-Defense Forces. That is why, in our proposal, we used the expression 'distorted by the existence of the Constitution.'

Apart from the Self-Defense Forces, there also exist in Japan the armed organizations of the coastguard and the police force. Despite the fact that the coastguard has 12,000 men and is equipped with automatic cannon and Vulcan cannon, which are classified as 'conventional weapons' (having thirty-eight patrol boats equipped with 40 mm automatic cannon, four with 35 mm and forty-nine with 20 mm) commonly no question is raised about whether these are constitutional or not.

Along with difference in purpose and organizational principle, while the coastguard and the police are subject to regulation of the laws even in subjugation operations, an army in battle exercises force, freed from the restraint of the law. This seems to us to be a fundamental distinction. (Under the *Keisatsukan shokumu shikkōhō* or Police Duties Implementation Law, the use of weapons by the coastguard is limited to the extent reasonably necessary to subdue resistance.)

Traditionally, Japan has clearly distinguished between an army, which is used externally, and police which are used for maintenance of the peace. We are used to this concept, but in many foreign countries this distinction has ceased to hold good, at least since the First World War. In other words, in between army and police, there are armed units of various scale and possessing various functions.

For example, there are coast guards, border police, national guards, and constabulary. In the case of the United States, the coastal police, which is equivalent to the Japanese coastguard, is under the command of the Ministry of Transport in ordinary times but in wartime shall be subject to the order of the Ministry of the Navy (14 USC.A., para. 3). Likewise, the Militia, ordinarily under the command of the governor, in wartime come under the command of the president. Under Article 80, clause 1 of the Self-Defense Law, even Japan's coastguard would in wartime come under the command of the Director-General of the JDA.

In other words, these armed organizations may in certain circumstances be incorporated into the army, which means the real difference between such armed organizations and an army is not a matter of size or scale of equipment.

The American constabulary was basically a peace preservation force set up in the colonies, and were not the Police Reserve Forces which the United States set up in Japan during the Korean War exactly such a constabulary, both in function and in name? In 1953, the year that the Police Reserve Forces became the National Safety Forces (*Hōantai*), Kimura, the Yoshida Cabinet's Minister for State, explained in a Diet interpellation that since this was not 'a force capable of the efficient or appropriate prosecution of modern warfare,' it was therefore not a *senryoku* or war potential such as was forbidden by the Constitution (House of Representatives Budget Committee, February 1). In concrete terms this meant that there was at the time no air-force, but when soon afterwards the three Self-Defense Forces of land, sea, and air, were set up under the Defense Laws and Japan came to possess the 'capacity for implementing modern war,' the government changed its explanation. From 1954, the 'minimum force necessary for self-defense' was held not to amount to 'war potential' or *senryoku*.

The transition from police reserves to Self-Defense Forces, and the history of the expansion of the SDF till it came to have its present 233,000 members provided with the utmost modern arms in the world, is a process of becoming an armed organization which is virtually an army.

From these considerations we are led to the idea of 'Minimum Defensive Force.' We believe the present SDF is in an unconstitutional state. To turn it into a 'Minimum Defensive Force' which would not be unconstitutional, it will be necessary to go against the current of recent history by turning an armed organization which is virtually an army into an armed organization which is virtually a police force or coastguard.

A disarmament involving a considerable reduction in equipment and personnel will naturally be necessary, but that alone will not be enough. What is indispensable is (i) restriction of the role and purpose, and (ii) restriction of the defensive force and geographic scope, and (iii) reform of the organizational principles. In our thinking, so far as role is concerned this means the protection of the lives and property of the people; so far as geographical scope is concerned it means confinement to national territory and the territorial seas and skies; and so far as organizational principle is concerned, the principles of democracy and openness apply. However, in fact what the Self-Defense Forces protect is not the lives and property of the people but the security of the state, and, as is clear from the notion of 'sea-lanes to 1,000 nautical miles,' its military presence has been expanded well beyond the geographical confines of either territorial seas (twelve nautical miles) or exclusive economic zones (200 nautical miles).

Under the government's 'minimum necessary for self-defense' the possibility of expansion is inherent in the idea of resistance to any supposed threat, and in fact such expansion has occurred. In the notion of 'blockade of the three straits' and the '1,000 nautical miles defense' mentioned above, the 1980s expansion of armaments by the Self-Defense Forces proceeded by leaps and bounds. By contrast, no hypothetical enemy is even assumed by the idea of 'Minimum Defensive Force.' Another way of putting it is to say that this means force enough to symbolically represent the people's sense of defense and resistance.

The essential quality of an army is to crush the enemy and thoroughly implement the ideology of the state. The essential quality of 'Minimum Defensive Force' is utterly defensive and includes no intent to crush any enemy.

Such 'Minimum Defensive Force' is subject to international law, that is to say it is predicated upon consultation with neighboring countries, on the idea that a defense right cannot just be exercised in one's own country, and on organizational democratization and the non-possession of secrets from the people.

Is this notion of ours absurdly idealistic? At any rate, the effort to solve these problems has already begun in the world.

On the meaning of 'army' in the contemporary world

A reconsideration of the meaning of an army is under way in the countries of Western Europe that constituted the front line in the Cold War, and at least in some quarters it involves not just a matter of restructuring the state but also a profound theoretical reconsideration of the nature of an army in a democracy.

There are some countries in Western Europe which practice conscription, but the feeling is strong that for a democracy the system of citizen-soldier, based on the militia tradition, is preferable. However, the idea of citizen-soldiers which is rooted in democracy is predicated on the view that national defense can be implemented in a single country, yet from the time of the Cold War, defense became, in practice, collective. Thereafter this has remained the mainstream defense posture among the advanced countries. Whether in NATO or the Western European Union (WEU) or the Common Security Conference for Europe (CSCE), doubts have been raised over whether military service could be compelled for the defense of the collective unit.

On the other hand, the idea of promulgating an European Community (EC) conscription system and encouraging loyalty to the defense of the EC has emerged. An alternative prescription is to leave intact the conscription system of particular countries, but to attach part of the personnel to a newly established force such as an environmental protection force (Green Helmets). In a related debate, the notion that a 'democratically-rooted citizen-soldiery' should not serve for the defense of national territory and was inappropriate for an intervention force in regional conflicts has surfaced. In all cases, the debate stresses the gap between the equation of democracy and defense of national territory on the one hand and actual defense tasks on the other.

On the other hand, focusing on actual armies, the argument has developed that since armies have become highly specialized and require highly specialised technical training, they have become unsuited to the conscription system. It is a debate which slices through the gap between the idea of citizen-soldiers and the reality of armies. However, the question that has come to be asked is what to do about the democratic control of an army made up of professionals when that which gives the best guarantee of the democratic control of the army is the citizen-soldier who stands in the tradition of the militia.

In either case, the legitimacy of the army in a democracy is at issue. The background to this is the large transformation of the Western European sovereign national state. In other words, the tradition of one country militarism is severely shaken. In the European Union (EU), which is at the stage of developing a common foreign policy and defense policies, consideration is being given to assigning, sharing, or pooling part of that military sovereignty.

Ideas about 'structural incapacity to attack' and 'defensive defense' (*bōgyoteki bōei*) are seriously debated. What the EU and the CSCE are trying to do may seem to be part of a project for the distant future, yet it seems as though in the post-Cold War present Japan too shares the common problems of constructing a shared military sovereignty and a non-offensive defensive force. This suggests that a truly world-wide transformation is under way in the established framework of the sovereign state.

For both East and West camps in the Cold War, security was thought to lie either in influencing the behaviour of the other side, or in blocking or repulsing an attack from it. To achieve that, the core of security was military security, and central to that was the building of military force and strategy and tactics.

However, in the post-Cold War age the likelihood of armed struggle arising out of East–West confrontation has become very slight, and so-called regional conflict grounded in racial, cultural, religious or economic causes has become the problem. To deal with these, military-centered thinking has already become ineffective, as should have become clear from recent experience in Cambodia, Somalia, Bosnia, Palestine or Haiti.

In case of a war of annihilation such as the recent Gulf War against Iraq, the military force accumulated during the Cold War period might have been effective, but in places such as Somalia, however much the attempt is made to impose peace by intervening in civil wars with military force alone, it does not work. Politics – the capacity for diplomacy, negotiation, dialogue – has come to play an extremely large role in security.

Of course it would be an illusion to think that peace could be established by political power alone, or that the meaning of military force had completely evaporated.

Regional conflicts stem from many different causes and cannot all be accounted for by a single concept. Responses to conflict have to be considered on a case-by-case basis. All sorts of interventions by countries or organizations not directly involved in regional conflict, including the United Nations, may be contemplated, from cases in which politics is paramount and military force minimal to those in which politics is minimal and military force paramount, but in any case no solution is to be achieved by input from one side only.

However, the recent tendency to deal with regional conflicts by simply sending in armed forces has strengthened. Even for activities such as maintenance of public peace and order, medical and sanitation tasks, or the provision of infrastructure which can scarcely be considered military, the army has been sent in. And to cope with this, armies have also begun to reorganize and revamp themselves into a dual-purpose (military and non-military) model. Reorganizing and revamping in this way would further increase the tendency for armies to be sent in. There is a danger that this tendency may lead to an excessive expectation of the capacity of armies to solve regional conflict and lead instead to military escalation of regional conflicts.

We believe it is necessary to put an end to the sort of thinking which responds to regional conflict by wanting to resort to military intervention legitimized by the United Nations. What is more important than anything is to find pre-emptive measures to avoid conflict and ways to achieve coexistence. In addition, should conflict occur, through an analysis of the distinctive causes, character and underpinnings of each conflict, we should draw up a menu of measures deemed necessary and out of that consider what sort of body would be appropriate to each.

Accordingly, we are extremely critical of the recent dispatch of Japanese Self-Defense Forces peacekeepers (including 'humanitarian aid' such as to Zaire). It is not just because of the constitutional ban on the overseas dispatch of military forces but because of doubt about the efficacy of such interventions by military force.

The Self-Defense Forces have no political force (especially no capacity to mediate), and no such capacity can be expected of them. Nor do they have any capacity for either medium or long term regional economic development. What is needed for Japan is to prepare bodies appropriate for various activities in accord with different scenarios. International emergency relief forces made up from NGOs, local government aid, ODA, governmental diplomacy, would be included among such measures. Probably the Self-Defense Forces, for the time being and subject to five conditions, might have to be included as one possibility, but for everything to be left to the SDF, as at present, can only be described as unfortunate, whether for the SDF itself or for the people of the regions they are sent to.

In our view, overseas dispatch of the 'Minimum Necessary Force' entrusted with the defense of the lives and property of the people should be ruled out. Our proposal is for the present SDF to be split up and reduced in size, and for an 'unarmed, separate organization' to be established, suitable for overseas dispatch. Our proposal has been criticized as unrealistic, but is not its realism being progressively demonstrated by the realities?

Going beyond the US-Japan Security Treaty

What was scarcely mentioned in our original proposal was the US-Japan Security Treaty (system). The US-Japan Security Treaty system was established during the Korean War (1950–3) which was the 'hot war' that occurred in the middle of the Cold War, and it was predicated on cold war or actual war. The Self-Defense Forces were also produced and sustained by this US-Japan Security Treaty system. It began as a force for the maintenance of public order after US forces were dispatched to Korea, became a support group for the American forces to the point where they became capable of fighting jointly with them, and fundamentally this character of being a supplementary unit to the US forces has not changed. It is impossible to talk about the Self-Defense Forces without talking about the US-Japan Security Treaty.

The US-Japan Security Treaty was maintained during the Cold War as the fixed compass-needle of Cold War Japanese diplomacy. Together with the San Francisco Treaty which was adopted at the same time, this should probably be seen as constituting a '1952 system.' This '1952 system' constituted the kernel of Japan's post-war foreign policy and its Cold War Asia policy. It was like the opposite side of the same coin to the '1955 system' in domestic politics. Now that the Cold War is over and we are confronting the collapse and reorganization of the '1955 system,' it would be strange if the '1952 system' were not also to change.

The US-Japan Security Treaty has to be reappraised and redefined in the new security context. Under the '1952 system,' Japan clearly chose to join the Western camp of which the United States was core, and militarily, by the gratis provision of bases within Japan, accepted the role of the United States' advance base against the Soviet Union and against Asia. From bases in Japan, the United States fought the Korean War, kept watch on China, and bombed Vietnam. Till its 1960 revision, the US-Japan Security Treaty included a 'civil disturbance clause' under which US forces could intervene in domestic disturbances in Japan, and the sense of a protective treaty relationship was strong. At the time it was enough that Japan remained a member of the West and that it (the US) be able freely to use the bases.

Under the Japanese Constitution, Japan was denied the right to exercise the right of collective self-defense. Accordingly, while the Self-Defense Forces, which were the 'minimum necessary force for self-defense,' protected the territories under Japan's jurisdiction (individual self-defense right), the exercise of this individual self-defense right was structured so as to incorporate the US bases which were capable of sending (and did actually send) armed forces into Asia. In other words, a spear was contained within the shield.

The structure may be explained in terms of two partially overlapping circles. The small circle is the treaty zone of joint US-Japan response to any armed attack on territories under the administration of the government of Japan, according to the provisions of 'joint defense' in Article 5 of the US-Japan Security Treaty. The large circle is the separate treaty zone in which the US forces contribute, unaided, to 'the maintenance of international peace and security in the Far East' as prescribed in Article 6 on 'provision of bases.'

According to the government's interpretation, these two zones are clearly differentiated. The small circle is the sphere of 'collective self-defense right' in which Japanese involvement is forbidden. However, both in principle and in practice, this distinction is unstable and filled with contradictions which have grown larger with time.

The large circle, or the sphere within which US forces could operate from Japanese bases, was at first 'inclusive of the area to the north of the Philippines, Japan and its vicinity, Korea and Taiwan' (Unified Government Explanation of February 1960). Vietnam, which was outside this sphere, became part of it from the late 1960s, and in the 1980s, in the fierce contest with the Soviet Union to establish 'nuclear control of the seas' in the North-West Pacific, Japan became the indispensable 'unsinkable aircraft carrier.' Later, in the 1990s, the bases of Okinawa, Sasebo and Yokosuka played an important role in the Gulf War in the Middle East, 10,000 kilometres away. By then, the large circle covered half the world.

Accompanying this expansion, the small circle also grew. The '1,000 nautical miles sealane defense' which was designed to resist the activities of the Soviet Navy in the Pacific in the 1980s, expanded this circle to 'North of the Philippines and West of Guam.' The activities of anti-submarine patrol vessels and convoy ships were brought within the scope of 'individual self-defense.'

The 1960 treaty revision and the 'US-Japan Defense Cooperation Guidelines' (or simply 'Guidelines') adopted by the government in 1978 mark distinct epochs in the US-Japan Security Treaty. According to the Guidelines, the security treaty, which till then had been basically no more than an agreement for the provision of bases, changed into a system under which Japan and the US could jointly engage in military activities. Under it, joint responsive activities became possible even in peacetime, including not only an emergency in Japan but an emergency in the Far East beyond the scope of Article 5. Joint operations were studied and joint manoeuvres carried out repeatedly. The coordination of command and rear support in terms of supply and transport was agreed and arrangements for Japan and the US actually to conduct war jointly were put in place. It was for this reason that a senior JDA official spoke of life having been breathed into the Buddha (the security treaty) by the Guidelines.

Since the Cold War front line was at this time in the Japan region and in Europe, it could almost be said that the Japanese individual self-defense sphere and the US strategic operational activities zone became blurred, virtually overlapping or merged.

Accompanying this qualitative transformation, considerable changes were also evident in the Self-Defense Forces' equipment and operations. What it amounted to was that 100 Japanese P-3C anti-submarine planes, a staggering number in world terms, were tracking Soviet submarines, Japanese convoy ships were engaging in joint manoeuvres with US aircraft carriers which were in a state of readiness to attack the Soviet Union, and US bases were protected by 170 Japanese F-15s. The Self-Defense Forces acted as supplementary components of US forces and by that very fact had become an extremely distorted organization.

The Self-Defense Forces took part in the biennial RIMPAC (Rim of the Pacific) naval exercises for the purpose of 'upgrading their strategic ability,' but little-by-little this 'strategic ability' grew till in the 1990s it was obviously in excess of the level of the government's explanation, and had become something very close in practice to the exercise of a collective defense power, with ANZUS (Australia, New Zealand, and the United States), NATO (US and Canada), the US-Japan security treaty (Japan), and the US-ROK Joint Defense Treaty (South Korea) having become parts of a single system.

Furthermore, from 1978, under the name of 'thanks payment,' Japan began to cover the costs of stationing US forces in Japan. In 1994 this item amounted to 250 billion yen. Neither Germany nor Korea makes any appropriation under such a vague formula as 'thanks payment.' This burden is clearly contrary to the terms of the 'US-Japan Status Agreement.' In defense expenditure too, the two circles have become blurred.

Also not to be overlooked are moves to establish a legal system for coping with a state of emergency.[10] Even though the joint US and Japanese forces were to achieve combat readiness they could not actually fight a war without the control and mobilization of the Japanese people. At the end of the 1970s an 'Emergency Bill' was proposed by the government, at the same time as the adoption of the Guidelines, and research was begun in the JDA. The argument that an emergency legislation system is necessary thereafter surfaced whenever anything happened, and even in the 1990s it appeared again on the occasion of the suspicions over the North Korean nuclear program. A system of emergency law rule is a system of wartime law in which it is implicit that the Self-Defense Forces become an army (as the criteria of army listed earlier under iv to vi are satisfied), the military is given priority, people are mobilized under conscription and corvee, the mass media are controlled by laws such as a Secrets Protection Law, and rights including the right to strike are suspended.

Fortunately, after reaching a peak in the early 1980s, the Soviet-American confrontation gradually eased, and in 1989 the end of the Cold War was announced without military conflict or war having broken out in the vicinity of Japan. A dangerous fusion of the 'two circles' was accomplished, but a situation that would have shaken the roots of the Constitution – such as an emergency law system or a secrets protection law – was avoided.

The end of the Cold War could be the occasion heralding a transformation in this US-Japan Security Treaty system structure, and we should try to move things in that direction. With the collapse of the Soviet Union and the loss of a 'common enemy' from the security treaty, the *raison d'être* and need for the US bases in Japan as advance base to restrain the Soviet Union has greatly diminished.

The security system based on a combination of individual self-defense power and collective self-defense power which had become the keystone of the international relations of the Cold War and the East–West confrontation (as, for example, in the WTO or Warsaw Treaty Organization, NATO, US-Japan Security Treaty, US-ROK Mutual Defense Treaty), in other words the 'threat–response' model of security system, has lost its efficacy and change has become unavoidable. Dissolution of the Warsaw Pact, the transformation of NATO into an all-European organization, the anticipation of a strengthening of the functioning of the United Nations, constitute evidence of this. Moves in the direction of 'common security' which are under way in Europe – including the multilateral Common Security Conference for Europe (CSCE), the European Conventional Force Reduction Treaty (CFE), and the Open Skies Treaty – are gropings towards imagining and then implementing a new security system.

Even in the Asia-Pacific region, which includes Japan and its environs, the structure as known till now has greatly eroded. The Soviet-American *rapprochement*, the simultaneous entry of North and South Korea into the United Nations and their reaching of agreements on reconciliation, non-aggression and cooperation, the normalization of relations between the Soviet Union and South Korea and China and South Korea, the beginnings of negotiations between North Korea and Japan and North Korea and the United States, the end to the Cambodian civil war, and the opening of the ASEAN Regional Forum (ARF), constitute evidence of this. The process of groping for a way to move from a 'threat–response model' towards a 'common security' model has begun. Japan too must participate and cooperate in planning for and actually constructing it. It is not enough just to 'cling to the US-Japan Security Treaty.'

In our proposal last time, we did not go beyond saying of the US-Japan Security Treaty that we 'looked to its demilitarization and its development and dissolution into a regional security system.' In this essay we now propose to consider in more concrete fashion what we mean by demilitarization and a regional security system.

We do not favor immediate abrogation of the US-Japan Security Treaty, for the reason, first of all, that the preamble and Article 2 of the treaty include a clause on 'promotion of economic cooperation.' There is no economic cooperation clause in the security and mutual defense treaties contracted by the US with other Asian-Pacific countries, such as ANZUS, US-Republic of Korea Mutual Defense Treaty, US-Philippines Treaty, and the US-Republic of China [Taiwan] Treaty. Article 2 of the security treaty is a new sprout which should be cultivated in place of military cooperation. When one considers that the two countries, located on opposite sides of the Pacific, are both major centres of the world economy and indispensable members of the emerging Asia-Pacific region, the transformation of the US-Japan Security Treaty into a different framework with strengthened and diversified economic cooperation becomes highly desirable.

The second reason is because, after the Cold War, it is China and Japan that are perceived as threatening by the countries of Asia, and the US-Japan Security Treaty is seen as a restraint on Japanese militarization (or any revival of Japanese militarism) and even as functioning to stabilize the Asia-Pacific region. It would be nothing but a nightmare for the people of Asia if Japan were to expand militarily again and come to exercise a renewed hegemony over Asia in the wake of a US withdrawal. It may be seen as a reflection of the fact that Japan has not renounced militarization and has neglected efforts to build a new peaceful order that even now, fifty years on, it is still not able to gain the trust of the people of

Asia. Another reason for this is Japan's post-war path in which the 'Greater East Asian War' has been seen exclusively as a war against the United States, and attention focussed only on Japan's own losses. Japan's role as aggressor in Asian wars has been overlooked. The reinforcement of military preparations by post-war conservative governments counter to the principle of Article 9, and the widening of the gap between the official position and the reality, have intensified doubts and suspicions about Japan.

It is precisely because we believe it is a matter crucial to the recovery of the trust of the peoples of Asia that we make our proposal for a 'Basic Peace Law,' urge a process of progressive reduction of the Self-Defense Forces, and try to show in concrete terms a non-aggressive defense policy and new-style security policy.

Towards demilitarization

The process of demilitarization begins from the shrinking and separating of the merged 'two circles.' In a situation that has escalated to 'combat-ready posture' it may be described as 'abandoning combat-readiness.' It is not a revision or abrogation of the security treaty so much as a return to 'the situation that ought to be,' and it can, and must, be begun forthwith.

Among the issues that could be discussed even now with the Americans are the strict interpretation of the 'Far East clause' (to shrink the large circle to its proper size), the recognition that 'advance consultations' may be proposed from the Japanese side, and the abolition of the 'thanks payments.'

It is also desirable to shake free of the 'Guidelines,' to reduce and then stop joint operational research and exercises and to make clear separate lines of command. The Soviet Far Eastern Fleet, which was always described as threatening the sealanes, has already collapsed and the threat of the Chinese navy is over-emphasized. 'Sealane Defense Operational Research' based on the Guidelines should be opened to scrutiny and then returned to a clean slate, joint operations in 'maritime anti-air defense' stopped, and participation in joint exercises including RIMPAC suspended (while calling for the suspension of the exercises themselves). The 'small circle' too should be reduced to Japan's sovereign land, sea, and air territory.

This process of shaking free of the 'Guidelines' will also contribute to an accompanying disarmament of the Self-Defense Forces. And if deployment and exercises outside the territories remote from Japan are ended, a scalpel can also be taken to large-scale, expensive, and huge support systems and maintenance costs for the frigates equipped with AEGIS defense systems and the P-3Cs. With Russia obviously engaged in demilitarization, and the US too quite dramatically engaged in the same process, it would not do for Japan alone to be satisfied with minimal budget cuts.

Apart from such 'demobilization,' the basic contours of the US-Japan Security Treaty system itself will have to be reconsidered.

A fundamental reconsideration of the Security Treaty and Status Agreement and related domestic laws (hereafter referred to as the US-Japan Security Treaty system) is necessary. This system is predicated on cold war and war, and the disarmament of the Self-Defense Forces is impossible without taking a good second look at it. This is because Article 3 of the security treaty calls for 'continuous and effective self-help and mutual aid [to] . . . maintain and develop . . . their capacities to resist armed attack.'

Article 6 of the security treaty determines the provision of bases, but the United States may also ask for the provision of bases anywhere on Japanese territory without restriction as to disposition or equipment if it is to contribute to the security of Japan or to 'maintenance of international peace and security in the Far East.' Although the restriction of 'prior consultations' was established by the Exchange of Notes in 1960, no such consultations have been held for more than thirty years, and the clause might just as well not exist. The particulars of 'provision of bases' are determined by the Status Agreement under this clause.

One characteristic of the security treaty is that it is not just a state-to-state agreement, like a friendship treaty, but it comprises a system made up of security treaty, Status Agreement, and related domestic laws. For example the Criminal Special Law accompanying the Status Agreement makes the divulgence of US military secrets a crime punishable by up to ten years penal servitude. This is an extremely heavy penalty, compared to less than one year under the Self-Defense and public service laws.

Accompanying the Status Agreement, a Land Use Special Measures Law applies to US military bases, and makes possible the compulsory expropriation of land for US military bases only. However, land for Self-Defense Forces use cannot be expropriated in the main islands of Japan since the (ordinary) Land Expropriation Law, reversing the law that used to operate under the Meiji Constitution, rules out expropriation for military purposes.

Quite apart from this, there is a series of laws and regulations which confirm the preferential position of US forces, such as the Special Civil Law, according to which the Japanese government pays for any damage inflicted on Japanese people by US forces, and the Tariff Special Law, under which not only US military personnel and employees but also their families are exempted from tariffs on imported goods. All of these domestic laws date from 1952, when the old Security Treaty system was in operation, and have not been revised for more than forty years. Furthermore, most of these domestic laws are simply a continuation of US occupation orders.

This Cold War Security Treaty system deserves to be thoroughly overhauled and in due course completely abolished.

Especially worthy of note is the 'Korea-United Nations Status Agreement' which is in a similar category to the Security Treaty system. In the Korean War, which broke out during the occupation of Japan, all US bases in Japan became 'United Nations Forces' bases. This was the result of America being allowed by the United Nations Security Council the use of the term 'United Nations Forces' and of the United Nations flag. This residual vestige from the occupation period still continues today and is still effective under the 'Agreement Regarding the Status of UN Forces in Japan' (which came into effect in June 1954). By Article

5 of this Agreement, US bases in Japan could be provided for the usage of 'UN forces' in the event of a crisis in Korea. At present the rear command of the UN Forces in Korea is established at Camp Zama US base in Kanagawa prefecture, and Japan would automatically become involved in the event of a crisis in Korea.

The situation on the Korean peninsula has greatly changed, as is evident from the understanding reached between the US and North Korea. It is no longer necessary to uphold this agreement, and indeed it should not be upheld. Now that conditions are ripe for its abrogation, it is up to Japan to take the initiative.

So far as manoeuvres by US forces are concerned, these have continued because they were taken to be important, despite the great inconvenience and danger they cause to Japanese people, but they must now be reduced in scale and in due course stopped. For example, the low level flight practice in the mountains by aircraft carrier planes, the night landing practice flights at Atsugi, the F16 training flights from Misawa, and the firing of artillery across main roads in Okinawa should be stopped forthwith.

In Okinawa in particular, it is necessary to commence at the earliest possible moment a reconsideration of the various systems giving priority to US forces. US air traffic control, which has continued despite revision, should be completely turned over to Japanese civilian aviation control, and all air and maritime zones which give priority to US military exercises should be abolished. The unfairness of the concentration of 75 percent of US military exclusive (or regular use) facilities in Okinawa which has only one percent of Japan's land area and population, should not be tolerated any longer. Those who suffered most from the Cold War should be first to benefit from the 'peace dividend' deriving from the conclusion of the Cold War.

So far as the bases are concerned, it is necessary that the right of inspection and investigation be acquired and exercised by the Japanese government, not only because of Japan's non-nuclear policy but also in order to verify whether the 'two circles' of the security treaty system referred to earlier are being kept distinct.

In addition, the return of the bases becomes a central issue.

Now that the Cold War is over, the retrenchment of US bases both on the US mainland and overseas is under way. A complete check of bases provided to the US forces under the security treaty should be carried out and a process of return undertaken in accord with Article 2 of the Status Agreement, beginning with unnecessary and idle bases. First of all, should not those which are already strategically unnecessary, such as the communications base at Yokota on the outskirts of Tokyo, Misawa, which confronted the Soviet Union, and Iwakuni, which is the air base for the marines, be targeted for reduction and return?

For the demilitarization of the US-Japan security treaty not only will time be necessary, but the building of a consensus on the strengthening of the broad cooperative relationship with America will be an indispensable factor. Efforts to ensure that it will not be seen as anti-American, and to seek a new US-Japan regional cooperative *modus vivendi* while at the same time not causing unease to the countries of Asia, will be absolutely essential.

124   *Japan's contested constitution*

Towards a regional security system

While thus helping the US-Japan Security Treaty system to grow beyond its military dimension, it is desirable that it be incorporated within a new regional security system. This should be a 'multilateral regional collective security,' in which the Asia-Pacific countries participate on the basis of equality, irrespective of capacity or means of involvement, rather than 'US-centered multilateral security' as spelled out in the 'Report on Japanese Defense Problems.' This new system should stand firmly on precisely this shared security, and must also meet the condition of being 'without enemy.'

Already various schemes based on such thinking have been proposed, such as Australian Foreign Minister Evans's proposal for the establishment of a CSCA (Conference on Security and Cooperation in Asia) modeled on CSCE, or Canadian Foreign Minister Clark's proposal for a North Pacific regional security framework. Of course, there are also plans which strive to promote multilateral cooperation still centered on the regional powers, such as (former) Korean president Ro Tae Woo's proposal for the creation of a Northeast Asian Peace Conference which would include the US, Russia, China and Japan, plus North and South Korea. Various comprehensive regional cooperation framework proposals have also been made, such as US President Clinton's idea of a 'New Pacific Community.'

In practice, however, it was the loose consultative group on political cooperation and security called the ASEAN Regional Forum, which was convened at the initiative of ASEAN and met for the first time this year [1994], which started things moving. The fact is that in this region, which is characterized not only by Cold War confrontation and different experiences of colonialism but by differences in history, politics, society, economics and culture, the process of cultivating a common security sense has to begin with confidence-building measures. In this sense, the ARF, which would probably best be described as a small power initiative, may be seen as hinting at the nature of a common regional security system for Asia.

Of course there is no contradiction between the ARF and the various other security conceptions. It is probably true to say that the search for a new Asia-Pacific regional collective security has just begun. Still quite captive to the framework of the US-Japan Security Treaty system, Japan lacks either the will or the ability to propose a new idea, despite the considerable Japanese role in constructing in this region what seems to have become almost an inbuilt economic interdependence and an infrastructure allowing continuing peace and equal participation.

However, what is required of Japan is not, as we have said above, to lend a shoulder to the burdens of the United States, but on the contrary to respect the initiatives of regional states such as the ARF and to come up with plans for multilateral regional collective security. This means that effort will be required to conceive of a model for the transformation of the current Cold War US-Japan, US-South Korea, US-Philippines, and ANZUS security treaty system into a security system 'without enemy.' At the same time, effort will be required towards resolution of present-day problems which even now are severe, such as the problem of peace on the Korean peninsula, China-Taiwan relations, and territorial issues between Japan and Russia, in a form which will make possible a truly continuing peaceful and equal participation.

Even though no mean time and effort will be required, without effort along these lines and a strengthening of mutual trust there cannot be any prospect of resolving them. In this sense it could be said that what is required is the ability to think along fresh, new lines.

Demilitarizing the US-Japan Security Treaty and reincorporating it within a multilateral security system will inevitably have consequences for Japan's own defense policy. The Basic Peace Law which obliges disarmament and lays down rules for democratic control and organizational democracy will be a legal expression of Japan's new posture to Asia. The division and reduction of the SDF and their transformation into a 'minimum defensive force' will be the practical expression of that new posture. It is a finely honed position, in which Japan will not threaten its neighborhood, nor be threatened by it. If Japan does not trust its neighboring countries, Japan itself will not be trusted and no multilateral security system will be able to take shape.

Here we want to demonstrate a concrete plan for multilateral security. If Europe is a continent and East–West confrontation was concentrated in land forces, Asia is linked by oceans and its confrontation is concentrated in naval forces. If multilateral security is land-based CSCE in Europe, will not Asia's multilateral security be in the form of a maritime CSCA? However, this will have to take a step beyond CSCE and show a strong orientation towards demilitarization.

To the extent that the 'sealane defense policy' of the Nakasone government of the 1980s had any persuasive force it was because Japan's economy depended on the network of maritime communications. Now that particularly large threats have disappeared, is it not time to consider the idea that maritime regions of the Pacific and South China Seas be patrolled through cooperation between the coastal countries, in other words, the idea of 'East and Southeast Asian maritime defense cooperation'? The Maritime Safety Board from Japan and the Maritime Police from ASEAN could contribute to sea rescue, prevention of ocean pollution, control of smuggling and drugs. If a joint presence enough to defeat pirates but not enough to defeat a navy could be implemented from the Malacca Straits to the South China Sea, the P-3C and large frigates would become unnecessary. Not only that, but this could actually become one step towards the realization of a truly new ideal of common security, through the cultivation of mutual trust and political negotiation in relation to the racial confrontation and territorial problems of the kind that have caused most of the post-Cold War disputes and that cannot be settled by military force.

Future-oriented planning

Till now we have dealt with the plan to demilitarize, disarm, and transform the military alliance mould of the 'US-Japan Security Treaty' system into a multilateral security system, and to expand upon the peculiarities of the Japanese military forces so that they are transformed into a 'Minimum Defensive Force' which does not breach the constitution and is worthy of the respect of other Asian countries, and we have referred to the peculiarity of Japan's military force as something not necessarily unique but something for which the quest on a world scale has begun.

Our proposal may be seen as idealism, but at the same time we believe it is the direction which is actually being chosen.

However, in the summer of 1994 the Defense Problems Discussion Group, which had been set up as an investigative committee by Prime Minister Hosokawa to consider disarmament proposals, presented its report. The report sketched a future which could scarcely be described as one of disarmament, including (1) an active and constructive security policy, (2) multilateral security policy cooperation centered on the United States, and (3) maintenance and deployment of a highly reliable defense force. Furthermore, in contrast to our proposal, it urged firm maintenance and positive development of the US-Japan Security Treaty, expansion of information exchanges, joint drafting of unit operational plans to make rear support and supply smoother, the conclusion of an agreement on exchange of services, the extension of the 'thanks payments' and the promotion of research on theater missile defense (TMD). As we see it, this report is tied to Cold War thinking and goes against the trend of the times.

Prime Minister Murayama adopted the position that the Self-Defense Forces were constitutional, and the Social Democratic Party of Japan endorsed this view. There is no longer any major political force which holds to the position that the Self-Defense Forces are unconstitutional. The movement for the revision of the text of the constitution may have declined, but what seems likely to emerge hereafter is the argument that a 'normal country' should have a 'normal army,' and that there is no reason why Japan should not have legislation to cope with any emergency, or a crisis control legal system.

As we have already stated, we oppose this direction. It runs counter to the flow of history, and contains the risk of once again plunging the people of Asia into anxiety.

The Social Democratic Party of Japan's recognition of the legitimacy of the Self-Defense Forces must be seen as a big step in the debate at the political level on defense policy. This is because any attempt to raise the organization and structure of the SDF in the Diet has till now been seen to imply a recognition of something which is constitutionally suspect, and so the Diet has not been the body for determination of policy on defense matters.

What is necessary is first of all the publication of the defense facts in the Diet. There are countless secret documents (c. 1.9 million of them in 1991) and other information in the JDA. The 'US-Japan Joint Operations Study,' 'Far Eastern Military Study' and 'Sealane Defense Study' have never been published.

Second is Diet control over defense planning. Defense plans have been decided by cabinet but the Diet has had almost nothing to do with them. It should be obligatory for the detailed contents of defense plans to be reported to the Diet and for the progress of the plans to be reported each year. Till now, reinforcement of equipment has been carried out regardless of changes in the environment.

Third is Diet restraint on defense expenditure. The practice of shifting the financial burden of weapons procurement onto subsequent years invites fiscal rigidification. Auditing of the accounts should be reinforced, and any simple increase in defense expenditure or modernization of weapons checked.

'Defense problems' must not be made into a sanctuary from the Diet as the highest organ of national power. Civilian control or democratic control does not mean restraint of the military by bureaucrats but that the people, and their representatives in the Diet, determine defense policy. We look to the opening of debate on reform of the system in this vein, especially in the Diet's Security Committee.

Finally, we reaffirm once again that the Japanese Constitution is part of a search for a world without war. What the constitution envisages and anticipates is a situation in which armies vanish from individual countries, an international police force is formed and eventually even that becomes unnecessary. The end of the age of world wars has increased the need and the possibility for an effort to realize the ideal of the Japanese Constitution, and we welcome this change. Is it not the immediate task of the Japanese people who possess such a constitution not only to keep up efforts to reduce that military force which is currently possessed and to call on neighboring states to disarm, but also to proceed in the direction of rejecting war, and to exercise persuasion so that not only does the army cease to exist and become a 'special armed force' but also a common defense system without an enemy is constructed?

Notes

1 Koseki Shōichi, Dokkyō University; Maeda Tetsuo, Tokyo International University; Suzuki Yūji, Hōsei University; Takahashi Susumu, Tokyo University; Takayanagi Sakio, Chūō University (d. 1999); Tsuboi Yoshiharu, Waseda University; Wada Haruki, Tokyo University (emeritus); Yamaguchi Jirō, Hokkaido University; and Yamaguchi Sadamu, Osaka City University.
2 'Kyōdō teigen – "Heiwa kihonhō" o tsukurō,' *Sekai*, April 1993, pp. 52–67 (translated by Meredith Patton and edited by Gavan McCormack).
3 'Common security' is the notion originally proposed in a 1982 report to the UN Secretary General by Olaf Palme, in recognition of the fact that in a nuclear age there could not be security for any single state or alliance group; security would have to be for all or for none.
4 '*Tōchi kōi*' refers to the doctrine of 'acts of state.' In 1957, when opponents of US base expansion entered the perimeter of Sunakawa base in Tokyo in protest, they were investigated under the 'Criminal Special Law' but in March 1959 the Tokyo District Court dismissed the case against them, holding that the US-Japan Security Treaty was unconstitutional. In December of the same year, on appeal, that judgement was overthrown by the Supreme Court which ruled that 'matters of high politics which have an extremely grave relationship to Japan's existence, such as the US-Japan Security Treaty, are beyond the scope of the court's judicial investigation.' This view has been cited in subsequent cases, and therefore seems to have constituted a 'doctrine.'
5 'As a sovereign country, naturally Japan possesses a collective self-defense right, but we take the view that the exercise of the self-defense right permitted under Article 9 of the Constitution should not exceed the minimum necessary for the defense of the country (*bōei suru tame hitsuyō saishō gendo no han-i*). The exercise of collective

defense right . . . is not allowed by the Constitution.' (Government statement in the House of Representatives, May 29 1981.)
6 Maeda Tetsuo, *Jieitai wa dōsuru ka*, Tokyo, Iwanami, 1992; and see his article 'Goken jieiryoku e no san jōken', *Seka*i, August 1991.
7 'Ajia Taiheiyō chiiki ampo o kōsō suru' *Sekai*, December 1994, pp.22–40 (translated and edited by Gavan McCormack).
8 Watanabe Osamu, *Seiji kaikaku to kempō kaisei*, Tokyo, Aoki shoten, 1994.
9 Fukase Chūichi, *Sensō hōki to heiwateki seizonken*, Tokyo, Iwanami, 1987; Yamauchi Toshihiro, *Heiwa kempō no riron*, Tokyo, Nihon Hyōronsha, 1992.
10 Because of recognition of the difficulty of the SDF engaging in combat operations under existing domestic laws, the idea of special legislation to cover 'emergency' situations has surfaced from time to time in post-war Japan. In 1965 the existence of a 1963 Defense Plan known as 'Three Arrows' (*Mitsuya kenkyū*) was confirmed. It considered options for an outbreak of hostilities in Korea, and was perfectly clear about the incompatibility of military operations with established laws. When Prime Minister Fukuda in 1978 commissioned the JDA to prepare a study on a 'Crisis Law' and accompanying measures, it became a major issue.

Asahi Shimbun, 'International cooperation and the constitution' (1995)

A path toward a non-military contribution to the world[1]

Asahi Shimbun's *6 Proposals*

1. Enact an International Cooperation Law to upgrade external assistance.
2. Create a Peace Support Corps for taking part in traditional peacekeeping operations.
3. Idealistic Article 9 of the Constitution does not need to be revised.
4. Scale down the SDF into a force exclusively for defending the country.
5. Overcome security arrangements for the Cold War and give emphasis to peace in Asia as a whole.
6. Take the initiative for reforming the UN into a healthier world body.

What is Japan to do to save the human race and this planet? In opening a new chapter in the history of Japan fifty years after our defeat in the war, *Asahi Shimbun* has conducted a company-wide discussion on this question for the past five years. Today, Constitution Day, we present an editorial feature package on the theme of 'International cooperation and the constitution' based on the outcome of the discussion. We hope it will serve as a reference for readers to consider the issue.

Our conclusions can be summarized in two points: first, that the present constitution has not lost its brilliance. We are opposed to its revision, because amending it would do much more harm than good. Second, Japan should make purely non-military contributions to the world community. In cooperating with the rest of the world, we should adopt an activist attitude, even more so than other countries.

Such an attitude could also be characterized as a non-military activist state. Though we are aware that a nation differs from an individual, we aspire to be a nation that is, figuratively speaking, a conscientious objector.

Conscientious objection by individuals is already well-established in the United States, Britain, France and many other developed countries. Germany's Basic Law (in effect its constitution), for example, stipulates that no one shall be forced into military service with weapons against his or her conscience. We suggest that this principle of conscientious objection be applied to our nation.

Those who interpret international cooperation to mean the shedding of one's own blood may criticize our ideas as selfish or cowardly. In fact, conscientious objectors have long been excoriated and persecuted. But to be faithful to a belief, whether for an individual or a nation, under the precept of 'Thou shalt not kill,' that is the only way.

Furthermore, conscientious objection demands considerably strong will and patience. In most countries that accept conscientious objection, conscientious objectors are required to perform alternative service. They are engaged in medical care, or other social welfare services in ways that are sometimes even more demanding than military service. The same would be true for a nation that claims conscientious objection.

We have compiled six proposals as guidelines for a path toward such a non-militarist, activist state – a nation that claims conscientious objection.

In making the accompanying proposals, we have used as a goal for attainment the period around the year 2010. These are certainly turbulent times. *Asahi Shimbun* intends to make unceasing effort to reexamine the proposals, chiefly by editorial writers, in response to changes in the world.

Our first proposal charts in specific terms the course Japan should take at the forefront of non-military international cooperation.

Let us imagine the world of 2010. With the living environment being aggravated as a result of the population explosion, antagonism over the issue of poverty and the gap in wealth among people would have escalated in acrimony. If it is left unattended, regional conflicts can proliferate and the number of refugees could increase dramatically.

To prevent this, remedial measures must be applied now. In particular, an International Cooperation Law should be enacted that expresses the resolve of the Japanese people to spread peace and respect for human rights more widely in the world.

We also advocate qualitative improvement of our official development assistance – foreign aid – and reinforcement of the role of NGOs in tandem as essential elements of such aid.

Our second proposal is creation of a Peace Support Corps. Besides taking preventive steps for the future, what else can be done for people who cannot live as humans because of conflict or natural disaster now?

The Peace Support Corps – an entity separate from the SDF – would respond swiftly with such humanitarian relief and rescue operations in natural disasters.

The Peace Support Corps would also be an active part of UN peacekeeping operations in strictly non-military areas. Although some members of the corps would carry small arms for their own protection, the corps' activities are completely different from those of a regular army because the corps is not a combat force. Nor does it take part in peace-enforcement activities or in multi-lateral forces.

In our third proposal, we express our strong opposition to revision of the present constitution, especially its Article 9, after having clearly stated our position that the constitution does not prohibit possession of self-defense force, based on the right of a nation to defend itself.

Article 9, which renounced war and use of force, is an idealistic norm that embodies the wish of mankind ahead of other nations. The framework that the constitution set up for post-war Japan, especially the ironclad element of not giving precedence to military matters over other matters, is more precious than anything else. That principle must not be sacrificed by revision of the constitution.

What, then, should be the organization for self-defense that is within the scope of the constitution? The criteria and the limits of such an organization are presented in our fourth proposal.

The equipment and organization of such a force are to be strictly limited to defensive defense, and no combat troops would be sent abroad. Because there are strong reservations about the SDF as presently constituted overstepping the bounds of a force for self-defense, a considerable reduction in the SDF should be made, after which its mission, organization and make-up should be completely overhauled.

Given the strategic environment among the countries of the world, the likelihood of Japan being directly invaded is slight at least until early in the next century. Though there is no denying the uncertainties of China and the Korean peninsula, the present SDF, organized in Cold War years and reinforced on the assumption of a Soviet threat, is too large. Phased reduction in personnel by half the present level in the Ground Self-Defense Force, for example, would not put the national security at immediate risk. And if such a reduction encourages arms reduction in neighboring nations, Japan's own security would be enhanced all the more.

Our fifth proposal concerns establishing an organization for peace in Asia and Japan's role in creating it. It is important that Japan and the United States revamp the security arrangements that are oriented towards the Cold War, especially to dismantle or scale back the American military base presence in Japan. The two nations should make a concerted effort to establish an organization that would work for preventive diplomacy and arms control in Asia – similar to the Organization for Security and Cooperation in Europe – by the end of this century.

Last but not least, we would like to propose that Japan stand at the forefront of specific reform of the UN. We suggest that the veto powers for the permanent members of the Security Council be phased out and that discussion of the new permanent seats at the Security Council be made not merely for Japan and Germany but also for three other countries each representing Africa, Asia and Latin America.

Our efforts in these proposals are based upon our assumption that the years after two wars – the Cold War and the Persian Gulf War – will bring still more cataclysmic changes in the world.

For a start, the Soviet bloc disintegrated with the end of the Cold War and the tide of market economics has reached the borders of the socialist nations, old and new, and those in what is referred to as the South. While stagnant societies have revived, the shift to market economies has brought with it wider wealth gaps and a surge in refugees and environmental destruction. As exemplified by the relentless fall of the dollar, the importance of the US economy has diminished and Americans are about to lose their status as the nation of the world's key currency.

If the world thus becomes unstable and the cross-border exchanges in money and goods are stalled, it is Japan, which is heavily dependent on overseas countries, that is hit hardest. It will be necessary for Japan to be more heedful of the fact that its efforts for preventing further deterioration in the economies of the developing world and rectifying its own trade imbalance will be beneficial not merely to the cause of peace in the world but also to its own interests.

The Gulf War, on the other hand, narrowed international cooperation to exclusively military contribution, even though temporarily. Only a few years after the war, however, cases of trouble proliferated that are impervious to mainly military approach. It has become clear that there can be no improvement in the situation unless the root causes of trouble are dealt with.

With the lessened danger of another world war, security arrangements have come to cover wider fields other than the military. Measures for preventing or minimizing damage from natural disasters like earthquakes and man-made disasters like explosions have become even more important.

Despite such obvious changes in the world, some in Japan still clamor for revision of the constitution in a way that would increase the dependence upon military might. We think that such an attitude represents a failure to learn from history and an inability to see the future.

If we are genuinely to protect the constitution and want to be part of a nation that practices conscientious objection – which is directly linked to the spirit of the constitution – the Thou shalt not kill precept must become an article of faith for every one of us. We must be fully prepared for such a task. Without such a will, there is danger that safeguarding the constitution will become a mere slogan.

Because we accepted the constitution that renounced war while leaving the responsibility for the last war ambiguous, is not our awareness about the war still incomplete? Did we not turn a blind eye to harsh realities despite endless conflict in the world and detest being implicated in them?

Or, being intoxicated by postwar prosperity, did not many Japanese fail to pay due attention to the rest of the world and to be considerate to others and extend a helping hand? Were they not too indifferent to the misfortunes of starvation, poverty and violation of human rights that befell others?

We want to call these points into question anew. Fortunately, volunteer activities demonstrated by the young at the time of the Great Hanshin Earthquake give courage to us. When our international cooperation which is freed from condescending attitude of handing out doleouts, our constitution will shine even more brilliantly.

Proposal 1: Enact a law on international cooperation

> *Enact an International Cooperation Law expressing the people's resolve to propagate peace and respect of human rights. In order to eradicate poverty from the face of the earth and prevent environmental pollution, it is necessary to extend outright grants and boldly increase personnel in charge of assistance.*
>
> *Arrangements for provision of assistance are to be radically reformed and an International Cooperation Agency directly responsible to the Prime Minister is to be established. Vigorous NGOs and Official Development Assistance should be nurtured as the heart of Japan's external assistance.*

Japan's Official Development Assistance in 1993 increased to US$11.2 billion, three times as much as a decade earlier, to be larger than the contributions of any other nation for three consecutive years. In part, that was due to the yen's strength. But more important was the fact that the government made specific efforts for making quantitative improvement in aid budget appropriation as the centerpiece of Japan's non-military cooperation with the community of nations.

Now that Japan has become a big power in terms of external assistance, does it occupy 'an honored place in an international society' as the preamble to the Constitution says? Have the people of Japan become confident and proud of living in the community of nations?

Unfortunately, the answer to these questions is no.

The problem lies in the quality of Japan's assistance. Assistance even if it is small, must be one that reaches poor people in the developing world and helps them to stand on their own. Assistance can be put to a good use only if it is backed up by a national effort to send not only money, but people who will roll up their sleeves and test their brains beside those they are helping.

Until now, the question of whether Japan's assistance was really useful to developing nations was a matter of secondary importance to the Japanese government. In the years of rapid economic growth, Japan used its increased aid to other nations as leverage to promote exports and secure resources. After becoming an economic power, Japan was conscious of its world reputation and pressure from the United States, to which the nation was obligated in security and for which it has felt guilt for its strained economic relations. This is not a way to build credibility or esteem, even if Japan were to succeed in pleasing the governments of developing nations.

In response to criticism here and abroad that Japan's overseas assistance is faceless, Japan belatedly adopted an Outline of Official Development Assistance at a Cabinet meeting in 1992. The outline cites humanitarian considerations for the hungry and impoverished as the basic tenet for aid, and asserts that stability and development of such nations are essential for world peace and prosperity. We are in accord with that notion for it accords with the spirit of the Constitution in striving to propagate peace and respect for human rights in the rest of the world.

But why is such a philosophy contained in the government policy outline, but not in legislation? The government contends that if aid discussion is held at the Diet level, the administration could be put into an embarrassing position in conducting diplomacy. Such secretiveness, in which aid and how to give it are the exclusive domain of the administration, has become the key reason for shady relationships between the governments of recipient nations and Japan's trading companies, and has reduced Japan's aid to arbitrary handouts that elude control over their use.

We would first propose that an International Cooperation Law be enacted, incorporating Japan's philosophy in its international cooperation and organizational makeup for external aid and a Peace Support Corps, and requiring that assistance reports be made to the Diet. Such a law would make it clear that the administration is accountable to the Diet for its international cooperation, and such changes will also make it easier for the government to have the understanding and support of the people who pick up the tab.

We also propose that the Upper and Lower Houses of the Diet form permanent International Cooperation Committees and have the government report by region its plans for allocating aid and how it would be used. The International Cooperation Committees of both houses are to hold public hearings from time to time on after-the-fact review of Japan's assistance programs by inviting experts from here and abroad.

Though the Outline of Official Development Assistance stipulates a policy of paying sufficient attention to military spendings and recent developments in regard to weapons of mass destruction in the recipient countries, that principle has become devoid of substance in cases of big powers like China because of the government's short-term diplomatic consideration. If the Diet has more to say about foreign aid, Japan's principle in providing aid would be more persuasive to the receiving nations.

We believe that Japan's provision of assistance should be made more consistent and transparent by creating an International Cooperation Agency through overhaul of the present complex government machinery responsible for foreign aid: to prevent layers of diplomacy practiced by the new agency and the Foreign Ministry the agency should be overseen by the prime minister. Such an agency should be independent of the Foreign Ministry. That is because the government should not handle international cooperation policy but rather deal with it as the question of the highest priority for a country that lives among the community of nations.

The divisions and sections of the Foreign Ministry, the Finance Ministry, the Ministry of International Trade and Industry and the Economic Planning Agency dealing with yen loans and external assistance should be transferred to the new agency. The divisions and sections of other ministries that deal with gratuitous aid should also be merged into the new agency. Such merger will also help slim the government machinery.

The present approach to assistance and the arrangements for foreign aid should also be radically revised. This is because the present approach to yen loans, appropriate for industrial infrastructure-building, especially in East Asia, and the present understaffed situation cannot properly address the new needs of a post-Cold War world.

Priority projects in East Asian countries that should be built by our aid are those that rectify the widening gap between rich and poor resulting from the headlong rush toward market economics, expansion of the urban slums and pollution, and not construction of an industrial infrastructure.

It is also urgent that the living standard be raised for the 1.3 billion poor in West Asia, Africa and other parts of the world who struggle to even attain subsistence livelihood. There is also an urgent need to deal with population explosion, global warming, acid rain and a surge in refugees.

Poverty and environmental problems can better be addressed by grants and assistance that involve people rather than yen loans, because these are not areas in which investment results in profit.

Grants, which include gratuitous aid, technical assistance and contributions to international organizations, account for only a little over 40 percent of its total Official Development Assistance – the lowest level among donor nations. We urge that a target be established to raise the proportion of grants to 80 percent – the average level among donor nations at present – in ten years.

To attain that goal, outright grants must be increased significantly and yen loans gradually reduced. Through such changes West Asian and African nations that now get just a modest part of Japan's foreign aid, would get larger shares, and the proportion allocated for purposes directly related to improving the people's lives such as health and hygiene, education, food self-sufficiency and environmental protection would be raised.

In changing our aid policies, it would be more efficient to establish a new enforcement organization responsible to the International Cooperation Agency by integrating the Overseas Economic Cooperation Fund, which handles yen loans, and the Japan International Cooperation Agency, which is responsible for technical cooperation.

By doing so, duplication of work can be avoided for the choice of the projects to be given assistance, dispatch of investigating teams and dealing with the recipient governments in the developing world. It will also become possible to make comprehensive plans for providing assistance.

The precondition for providing meaningful aid to developing nations to enable them to stand on their own is thorough research into the political, economic and social needs of recipient nations, so as to decide the direction of their future development. We propose establishment of an International Cooperation Research Institute attached to the International Cooperation Agency, with the Institute of Developing Economies forming the core of the new Institute which will be buttressed by absorbing research divisions of the existing aid-providing agencies. It is important that talented people in developing nations should be actively recruited as researchers and their opinions be brought to bear on our aid to such nations.

Such changes in the government machinery should come by the year 2000. In the years before 2000, preparation should be made, and recent accords among the ruling coalition parties regarding integrating the Overseas Economic Cooperation Fund with the Export–Import Bank of Japan and the Institute of Developing Economies with the Japan External Trade Organization – simply a gimmick for appearance's sake – should be scrapped. We cannot condone the mutual backscratching between politicians and bureaucrats, devoid of any sense of policy.

In comparison with large yen loan projects directed mainly to building dams and roads, assistance for eliminating poverty and environmental pollution consumes far more manpower. Though the amount of money involved is small for each case, the amount of paper work involved does not differ much from that required for much larger projects. Larger staff is also needed to advise recipient nations and guide those who will deal with the programs on the ground.

The number of officials now engaged in external assistance posted at government missions abroad and international assistance organizations is just 1,800. That is far fewer than the number from Western countries and all they can do now is to handle budget allocations. We suggest a bold, ten-year program that would vastly increase the staff to 5,000 to improve the quality of aid, rather than just efficiency. Such an increase in staffing should be achieved by moving people from the government agencies and related public corporations who would be otherwise made redundant by the streamlining of the government agencies.

The staff of specialists must also be increased, especially for technicians, medical personnel and teachers, and members of the Japan Overseas Cooperation Volunteers. Although more retired people have applied as volunteers to work in developing nations, it is important to include those who are actively employed in the private sector. Companies would be making a great contribution to the aid program if they adopted voluntary leave policies that would encourage their employees to participate in foreign aid projects while being paid by the companies and enable them to return to their jobs after a specific volunteer period.

Help provided by NGOs can sometimes achieve more than the official development assistance because it is more responsive and more detailed. Such resources outside the government realm which are still tenuous, should be nurtured into robust bodies.

Many NGOs are voluntary organizations without legal protection and financially weak. If they were incorporated, they could more easily solicit contributions and have the benefit of tax breaks. It should be possible for well-organized, even if small, organizations to gain corporate status by relaxing the conditions for *pro bono* corporate bodies.

We take heart in knowing that a wider range of people in local governments, in business foundations and labor organizations are becoming part of the international aid picture. If international cooperation institutions are properly organized and the government and the people work together for the benefit of the world, Japan will be welcomed into the international community with esteem.

Proposal 2: Create a Peace Support Corps

> *A Peace Support Corps is an organ affiliated with the International Cooperation Agency and is to be staffed by about 2,000 members, including part-timers. Its peacekeeping operations are to be confined to conventional ones that abstain from use of force. The corps members are to be sent abroad with the prior approval of the Diet. Its initial work will be limited to transport, logistics, communications and similar duties. The next step is to be taken after ascertaining the success of operations in the initial stage and actual work on peace-keeping operations.*

Although the Cold War has ended, the suffering has not. Helping those who suffer and promoting peace are the most important tasks of the international community. And such efforts are essential components of Japan's international cooperation.

We believe that humanitarian aid to those who are suffering should be accompanied by active participation in UN-led peacekeeping operations.

Troops on peacekeeping missions intervene between parties to a conflict that have agreed to a cease-fire. They patrol and monitor the activities of the warring parties, so that the cease-fire will not be violated until a permanent peace agreement is signed. If there is a cease-fire violation, they investigate it and report their findings to the UN. It is hoped that these activities deter violations and promote negotiated peace.

The UN peacekeeping force was organized to intervene in the 1956 Suez crisis. Dag Hammarskjold, then UN Secretary-General, established the principle of non-use of force – a principle that bars peacekeepers from using arms except in self-defense.

This has long been observed as a basic rule of peacekeeping, together with the principle of consent – allowing troop dispatches only when the warring parties accept their presence – and the principles of neutrality and impartiality, which prohibits peacekeepers from siding with any of the warring parties.

A spate of domestic conflicts since the end of the Cold War led UN Secretary-General Boutros Boutros-Ghali to abandon these principles and introduce a new kind of peacekeeping operation, one for 'peace enforcement.'

This formula of deploying UN troops who are prepared to use force against uncooperative warring parties failed disastrously in Somalia, forcing Boutros-Ghali to revert to peacekeeping rules.

The 'peace support corps,' which we propose to create, would take part in conventional peacekeeping operations, not those of the 'peace enforcement' type.

Why, many people may wonder, is a new organization needed when units of the SDF have already been sent abroad on peacekeeping missions?

Our answer is that we believe units of the SDF, whose duty is limited to the defense of our own territory under the Constitution, should not be sent abroad.

Considering the fact that Japan colonized Korea, waged aggression against

China and sent soldiers in combat boots trampling on countries of Southeast Asia, we believe the SDF should be led with as much restraint as possible.

Certainly, few Asian countries criticized Japan over the dispatch of an SDF contingent to Cambodia, and some Asian leaders say Japan should no longer apologize for its past deeds. But Japan has yet to show remorse and offer a proper apology.

Under these circumstances, we should assume responsibility for history by deeds, not just words, making it clear that no SDF unit shall be sent abroad again.

We believe most people support this view.

Members of the SDF have already been sent abroad several times. But many people, having misgivings about this practice, must nevertheless be resigned to the fact that there is no alternative organization that has the means to send peacekeepers to trouble spots.

The popular sentiment makes politicians hesitant about the dispatch of SDF troops and seeks to impose detailed conditions on troops that are sent.

For example, opposition within the government, for a time, threatened a decision to send SDF troops to Mozambique. It took time for the three ruling parties of the coalition administration to resolve their differences and agree to the dispatch of SDF personnel to help Rwandan refugees.

This shows no doubt that the democratic process is at work. But if it is at the expense of speedy decisions for dispatch, it is not what the people want.

The only way around the dilemma is to form a separate organization apart from the SDF to render international cooperation.

Peacekeeping duties are suited for an organization of experts, not a military body like the SDF.

It has been said that since peacekeeping centers on military duties, it is difficult for a Japanese organization outside the SDF. To be sure, such operations, which entail stepping in to separate warring parties in an area where fighting has just come to an end, has military overtones. But the mission is not to fight. When provoked, the peacekeeping team is supposed to calmly talk the adversarial party into ending hostilities.

Peacekeeping troops sent by Finland at the time of the Yom Kippur War, which represented an Egyptian attempt to win back the Sinai Peninsula, were deployed in the suburbs of Suez. When Israeli troops tried to destroy a UN checkpoint, the Finns blocked it by laying down their arms and forming a human wall.

This was an act true to the spirit of peacekeeping operations.

What the Finns did is entirely different from the duty of soldiers, which is to conquer the enemy with force. Exercises for war, like those of the SDF, are not needed to do something like that. Instead, it is important to study the language and customs of regions in conflict, and learn how to carry out checkpoint inspections without being provocative.

Countries send troops for peacekeeping operations in the absence of expert teams. But the fact remains that an organization of specialists is better suited for the job than troops.

What kind of peace support corps do we have in mind? First of all, let it be clear that the corps would operate on the premise that it would not use force.

The corps would belong to a new International Cooperation Agency, a government agency. It would be in charge of participation in UN peacekeeping operations, humanitarian relief, and disaster relief.

The proposed corps would have a headquarters, under which there would be three units that would be sent abroad – a specialist unit, an administrative unit, and a general unit.

A training center would be established in Japan. The total number of people would be about 2,000, including part-time staff.

The specialist unit would contribute to peacekeeping operations with the skills of its members. It would also provide humanitarian assistance and conduct disaster relief activities.

The elements comprising the unit would be the headquarters in the host country, a medical team, a team of staff for prevention of epidemics and water supply, a communications team and a rescue team.

The rescue team of qualified technicians and aides would work to save lives in disasters and support initial recovery efforts.

A small, rapid-deployment team would be ready to respond within twenty-four hours of being summoned, and would be staffed by full-timers. Some members would also serve full-time in obtaining needed equipment and supplies and in liaison and coordination among other members. But volunteers would be recruited for other jobs.

The part-time recruits would be registered with the corps. They would be required to go through training periodically, so that they could be sent abroad when needed.

The administrative unit would mainly be in charge of peacekeeping operations. It would be composed of a civilian police team and an autonomy team that would provide guidance on election supervision and the like.

Volunteers would be recruited from among police officers and civil servants in general. As with volunteers for the specialist unit they would be registered with the corps and required to go through training periodically to serve abroad in the future.

The general unit would do what peacekeeping operations are supposed to do. It would also handle rescue operations.

Elements of the unit would be the headquarters in the host country, a guard team, a transportation team, a civil engineering team and a UN liaison team.

The members of the general service corps would be full-time staff.

The training center would teach members the principles for them to stand by when they join a peacekeeping operation or provide humanitarian assistance, how to deal with various situations that may arise, and how to protect themselves. It would also instruct them on the state of affairs and customs in the host country and provide linguistic training.

Those engaged in a peacekeeping operation are theoretically immune to attack as they take up their duties only after warring parties have agreed to their presence. Actually, however, there is no absolute guarantee that they would not come under attack from a group that is not controlled by parties to the cease fire agreement, or from a group left out of the accord.

Can anyone send unarmed peacekeepers into such a situation?

Assuming that the protection of the specialist unit and the administrative unit would be left to the UN, we would like to allow the general unit to have a guard team for self-defense.

However, in light of the duties of the general unit, the guard team's arms should be of a light and defensive nature.

Small firearms and non-lethal weapons for peacekeeping should be developed that could temporarily incapacitate assailants.

We believe that a peace support corps with severely restricted equipment, as we have outlined, could participate in the main tasks of peacekeeping falling short of the use of force, such as patrols of the disengagement of forces, and monitoring disarmament.

But peacekeeping operations are still going through a period of trials and errors, which generate distrust and anxiety remaining among the people about participating in them.

Government officials are not necessarily consistent in their explanations about peacekeeping operations. It is still not the time to talk about full participation in them.

The projected peace support corps should start with such tasks as transportation, supplies, communications and road construction

The performance of the corps should be watched for about five years, during which the reality of peacekeeping operations should be determined. Then, a study should be undertaken on what to do next, assuming that a national consensus on such action emerges by that time.

The government would be empowered to send members of the peace support corps on humanitarian aid and disaster relief missions on its own. But in the case of peacekeeping operations, they could be sent only to join conventional operations based on UN resolutions. A decision to send them would require advance approval of the Diet. Depending on developments, the Diet would be able to pass a resolution on their withdrawal halfway and give advice to that effect to the government.

The peace support corps would of course be barred from taking part in a Persian Gulf War-type multinational force.

Members of the corps participating in a peacekeeping operation would be pulled out if any of the attached conditions – the existence of a cease-fire agreement, the consent of warring parties to the presence of peacekeepers from Japan and other countries, and the observance of strict neutrality – were not satisfied. The five existing principles that guide peacekeeping operations, including a provision that members should use their arms only to protect their lives, would be strictly applied to the corps.

We have outlined the proposed peace support corps. This is still a bare-bones proposal. A number of details remain to be worked out, such as the status and pay of corps members and compensation for those killed on duty. There may need to be some changes. What we hope to accomplish in presenting this idea is to provoke debate.

Proposal 3: Do not revise Article 9

> *Article 9 of the constitution, which renounces war and use of force, is an idealistic norm that preemptively undertakes the task facing all mankind. It is now time to consider how it should be put to best use in overhauling the SDF and security arrangements.*
>
> *Article 9 established the framework for not giving preference to military matters in the post-war society. Now that the Cold War is over, revision of the article to give greater emphasis to military matters runs counter to the times and does more harm than good.*

Although the Cold War has ended, the suffering has not. Helping those who suffer and promoting peace are the most important tasks of the international community. And such efforts are essential components of Japan's international cooperation.

Japan's constitution, founded on the three principles of absolute pacifism, the sovereignty of the people and respect for basic human rights, has decisively influenced the nation's postwar history. Had there been the slightest tinge of nationalism, Japan would have been utterly different in freedom, affluence and other aspects.

Japan's constitution was promulgated under the strong weight of the Allied powers when its sovereignty was severely limited during the occupation. No doubt, its constitution is unique in that respect.

However, the will of the people, who had seen enough of the devastation of war and of the militarism that led to war, was reflected in the constitution in its own way in the course of its drafting through Diet discussion. The constitution that resulted was welcomed by the vast majority of the people. Had it not been for the constitution as the overarching guideline for new nation-building, Japan could not have freed itself of a character that marked pre-war Japan.

In particular, Article 9 of the constitution, which renounces war and use of force, is an idealistic provision that embraced the duty of all mankind to seek the path of lasting peace. In an age characterized by military squareoff between East and West, such a proclamation did not seem very realistic. But it has taken on added significance with the end of the Cold War.

What underpins the ideal of Article 9 is a resolve contained in its Preamble to 'preserve our security and existence, trusting in the justice and faith of the peaceloving peoples of the world.'

As weapons have come to have horrifyingly destructive power and as cities and civilization have become sophisticated, a modern state can no longer withstand war or use of force. And, partly as a result of democracy taking root in wider parts of the world, worldwide gains of the concept of human rights and ever deeper mutual economic dependence among nations, the world is entering into an age when a hot war among developed countries is hardly likely.

If a long-range look is taken at the world in post-Cold War years and the future of our planet, now is precisely the time for Article 9 to recover its brilliance.

While we certainly have far to go, the possibility of translating the constitution's ideal into practice is at last upon the horizon.

There have been widely differing interpretations of the overall purpose of Article 9 and the wording of individual provisions. And the most divisive issue in post-war politics has revolved around the question of how the SDF should be understood in the context of the article.

Article 9 was understood as calling for being 'absolutely unarmed' at the time of the promulgation of the constitution. That was in accord with what was uppermost in the minds of the people and the actual condition of being completely disarmed immediately after our defeat in the war. It was supported by the naive popular expectations of the peacekeeping function of the UN. In response to questions in the constitutional assembly in June 1946, then Prime Minister Yoshida Shigeru said: 'As a result of any armament and the right of belligerency not being recognized, we renounced war as a means of exercise of the right of self-defense.'

When the Korean War broke out in 1950, however, the Allied occupation forces compelled the Japanese to organize the Police Reserve Forces, and the US-Japan Security Treaty was signed when the Peace Treaty came into force somewhat later. The government embarked on upgrading defense forces by changing the Police Reserve Forces into the National Security Forces and then into the SDF.

In consequence of the SDF's subsequent modernization and introduction of heavier artillery and other equipment carried out as proof of Japan's being a 'member of the West,' the SDF today ranks as one of the most advanced in the world, especially in quality of its equipment. In view of the government interpretation of the constitution and the ideal of being 'absolutely unarmed' accepted by the people at the time of its promulgation, Article 9 must be said to have gradually been stripped of its spirit against the international background of an aggravating Cold War.

The Japanese, in the meantime, have continued to highly evaluate Article 9 of the constitution. Now that we find ourselves under a completely different situation, what is necessary in ushering in the next century is to reassess Article 9 and give profound thought to applying the provisions of the article to good use in the face of the realities of the SDF and national security policies.

In the context of Article 9 of the constitution, we have serious doubts about the present status of the SDF. How we think of the force for self-defense that is permitted by the constitution will be elaborated in Proposal 4. We do not think that Article 9 rules out the use of force in self-defense. A state is allowed the right of self-defense as a course of last resort in resisting or repelling aggression or use of force by a foreign country. And we do not believe Article 9 went so far as to discard that right.

Asahi Shimbun has long held such views.

On December 16 1953, it said: 'The majority of the people think at their heart that effective force for self-defense is necessary. We are of the same opinion.'

On May 3 1968, it said:

> The constitution does not deny the right of self-defense, which is the basic

right of a state. It also recognizes the minimum force necessary for self-defense. Though such a force must be used against imminent and unjust aggression by a foreign country, such a force should be used strictly within the framework of the provisions of the constitution.

As long as there are countries that have no qualms in the use of force, force for self-defense cannot, regrettably, be ruled out. Unarmed resistance and uprisings alone cannot make people feel secure.

What is important in the interpretation of the constitution is an attitude to flexibly search for its meaning based on the ideals and objectives of its provisions. Too sclerotic an interpretation becomes at times out of step with the times and can undermine the very spirit of the constitution.

The Constitution of the United States has a history of more than 200 years and yet it is kept intact save some revision, including the first ten amendments that were added as the Bill of Rights. It should be remembered that flexible interpretation and precedents in response to changes in American society have served as the lifeblood of the American Constitution.

The constitution is a body of supreme legal codes. But as the principles of government, governmental machinery and rights and obligations of the people are contained in concise and abstract provisions, there is often much room for divergent interpretation. Heated controversy thus arises over the constitutionality of certain policies or pieces of legislation, resulting in bitter political conflict. That is why constitutions are said to be 'political norms' as well as 'legal norms.'

That is neither messy nor unhealthy, however. Controversy should be positively appraised for its role as a safety valve to ensure that Japan's basic policies remain democratic and sound.

In that sense, it would be one-sided to think that Article 9 was 'hollowed out,' or that it has lost its meaning as a norm by being interpreted differently. We think that, objectively speaking, Article 9 has served its role well in guiding the nation and its people for half a century.

During that period, Japan neither sent its troops abroad to kill other peoples nor manufactured weapons for export. Though the SDF have been reinforced, the manner of their operations and their behavior have not been unconstrained. That was because they were constantly subjected to scrutiny in the context of Article 9 of the constitution and to discussion among the people.

Much of the framework for Japan's defense policies – such as the denial of the collective self-defense, prohibitions against sending combat troops abroad, the three non-nuclear principles, denial of the conscription system, banning weapon exports and restraint on defense spending – are results of Article 9 and debate about it.

More important is that the notion of putting much emphasis on military matters has been rejected. Military matters are liable to take precedence over legislation and government's administration over civilian matters on the ground that military matters are 'the basic tasks of a state.' Under Article 9 of the constitution, however, national defense has been treated on the same footing as the government administration in other fields and has not been given preferential treatment.

The fact that the basic framework for not bestowing privileges or giving preferential treatment to military matters has taken root in post-war Japan and that the country does not pose much military threat to neighboring countries clearly owes to the functioning of Article 9.

The SDF are treated as 'military forces' on the international scene. But the SDF units are not ordinary military forces with the same powers and functions as those of other nations.

The SDF is subject to a maze of regulations, such as prior or *ex post facto* approval of the Diet in taking action for defense purposes. According to the government interpretation, exercise of the right of self-defense is contingent upon (1) imminent and unjust aggression against Japan, (2) non-availability of any other means, and (3) use of force to the minimum extent necessary. The SDF can act only on or near Japan's territory, its territorial waters and air space.

Though there is much ambiguity and vagueness in the government's interpretation, the SDF is considerably constrained in its action if those conditions are strictly observed. The SDF can be regarded as not much different from the police and the Maritime Safety Board in that they are subject to many constraints in their action.

Moreover, it is not permitted to limit the rights of the people provided for by the constitution on the pretext of 'an emergency.' And there is neither military tribunal nor legislation authorizing secrecy. It was the pressure of the wide spectrum of the people, who had great faith in Article 9 of the constitution, that has thwarted many attempts to enact laws for dealing with contingencies.

Political action was repeatedly taken, ranging from the contention, made soon after it was promulgated, that the constitution was 'foisted off upon Japan,' to the more recent notion that cast doubt upon it as limiting Japan's ability to make an 'international contribution.' Even more recently, some who once demanded preservation of the constitution now want to revise it purportedly to stop its virtual amendment by farfetched interpretation.

The constitution is not sacrosanct. It is essential that it be examined in the present context. But as far as Article 9 is concerned, what the times require is not that Japan gets free of military constraint but the reverse. Obviously the importance of military power has diminished with the end of the Cold War. The revision of the constitution in such a way as to give greater emphasis to military power clearly runs counter to the trend of the times. We cannot endorse such a move.

It is desirable that defense policy is always open to debate in political processes and a subject of public discussion, as is true in many developed nations. In Japan, Article 9 is the centerpiece of such discussion.

Ultimately, it should be stressed that Article 9 is highly regarded abroad for its ability to check the possibility that Japan could become a country that seeks after its own national interest by sword-rattling. To Asian neighbors, the article is a symbol of what prevents Japan from becoming a dangerous country.

Revision of Article 9 under the present conditions will surely invite wariness and concern in other countries and could trigger an arms race in East Asia. That would hurt, rather than serve, Japan's security interests.

Proposal 4: Changeover of self-defense forces

> *Use of force for self-defense permitted under Article 9 is limited to being within bounds of genuine self-defense. There are strong doubts that the Self-Defense Forces as presently constituted exceed those bounds in both equipment and scale.*
>
> *Plans should be made annually for scaling them back to an organization for protection of the nation's territory with the year 2010 as a goal. Ground Self-Defense Force strength should be halved and Aegis vessels and P-3C anti-submarine patrol planes should be significantly reduced.*

The public approves both Article 9 of the constitution and the existence of the SDF, as has frequently been shown by opinion polls. Most Japanese accept the SDF's existence, even though they put more hope in their relief role in disasters rather than their primary duty in defense and have always been reluctant to support strengthening them.

However, whether the SDF as presently constituted is in accord with the constitution must be examined separately. In a ruling handed down in 1959 by its full bench on the Sunagawa case, in which the constitutionality of the presence of US forces in Japan was challenged, the Supreme Court found that Article 9 of the constitution does not negate the right of self-defense, and said that the government 'can take measures necessary for self-defense in order for this country to maintain its peace and security and fully preserve its existence.' The Supreme Court has not, however, ruled on whether the SDF, in its present form, is constitutional.

The government's official view regarding Article 9 in recent years is that it is legal to 'maintain forces for self-defense to the minimum extent necessary' within the rights inherent in a nation. Even with such interpretation of the constitution, a self-defense organization established on the right to self-defense would be unconstitutional if it oversteps the bound of 'minimum force necessary for self-defense' in scale, equipment, duty or basic action doctrines.

Successive past administrations, however, have strengthened the SDF's combat capability using rationale that can only be described as subterfuge without thoroughly examining these points. By qualifying the minimum with the word 'necessary' they made 'minimum' limit meaningless for practical purposes.

Many wars have been waged in the name of 'protection of interests' or 'self-defense.' If thought is given to that fact, the 'force for self-defense' which will be tolerated under the constitution must be viewed as a limited one which really remains within the bounds of 'self-defense.'

Unlike the government, we think that what is permitted under the Constitution is possession of force that is only sufficient to protect the people and the nation's land from local aggression or use of force that can realistically be assumed.

How much force and what equipment are permitted under the constitution? It is the politicians responsible for civilian control of the SDF, and ultimately the voting public, that set the limits to the force for self-defense. But until now, Diet members have tended to be preoccupied with semantic exegesis over whether or not the SDF's very existence is constitutional. Obviously the Diet has neglected constructive discussion on the SDF's management and their limitation after having defined their proper place in the nation's administrative machinery.

What is force for self-defense permitted by Article 9 of the constitution? We see it this way:

1 The right of self-defense is exercised only in a case of armed attack against the people and their territory. The use of force for self-defense is confined within Japan's territory, territorial waters and air space. This is what is termed 'exclusively defensive defense.'
2 The SDF's equipment and organization must remain within the scale and capability that are appropriate to such objectives. For instance, possession of any weapons that could be used to attack other nations is to be restrained to the utmost.
4 No combat troops will be sent abroad and the right of collective self-defense will not be exercised. Participation in the United Nations peacekeeping operations and any other forms of our international cooperation will be undertaken by a Peace Support Corps, which will be newly created.
5 Great importance will be attached to the SDF's duty of relief activities in natural disasters in order to protect the lives and properties of the people.

Viewed from such perspectives, it is very doubtful that the SDF in its present form is within the boundaries, either in personnel strength or equipment, as set by the constitution.

When Japan's defense-spending is the second largest in the world and the country ranks at the second or the third place in the league table of arms import, is Japan's force for self-defense in its present form a minimum force necessary, even though, admittedly, there may be some problems in making simple comparison of defense spending in dollar terms? In particular, the equipment for the Air and Maritime Self-Defense Forces is the most advanced in the world in both quality or quantity.

In no other nations have F-15 fighters and P-3C anti-submarine patrol aircraft been deployed so densely throughout the land. Such a situation conflicts with the message that the pacifist constitution sends to the rest of the world. That is why Japan is being criticized as a 'contradictory country.'

Moreover, there have been some signs of self-restraint in acquiring weapons for exclusively defensive purposes being eased still further in recent years. Typical of such changes is the development of the FSX, the next generation of fighter support aircraft. And plans are also afoot to procure refuelling aircraft and large transport vessels one after another.

We think that the aggrandized SDF should be reorganized into a smaller force of a National Defense Force or Garrison for Defense of the Japanese Archipelago by the target year of 2010, fifteen years hence. It is time to re-examine the SDF, in terms of both quality and quantity, for reorganizing them into a force dedicated exclusively to the defense of the country.

This is a proposal made not simply from the standpoint of the constitutionality of the SDF.

Some may be worried about possible contingencies. However it has become practically impossible for a hot war to break out between developed countries after the end of the Cold War. Secondly, there is very little likelihood of a regional conflict occurring directly on Japanese soil, even though military build-up in China and uncertainty in the Korean situation are problems besetting the nation. It is precisely the time for Japan to stand at the forefront of a disarmament drive and strive to debunk the perception of armament as something with which to meet threats from others. By doing so, Japan will be inducing neighboring countries to reduce their arms.

The first step toward that end is a large reduction in the Ground Self-Defense Force. As the likelihood of full scale landings on the Japanese land from the north – which were assumed in the Cold War years – has been dramatically reduced, it is not necessary now to have heavy concentration of Ground Self-Defense Force units in the northern part of the country. It is also possible to have smaller divisions.

As it has become even more unrealistic to assume a decisive battle on Japanese soil, a deep cut can be made in the number of large tanks and artillery. The law should also be revised to strike down the SDF's duty of 'dealing with indirect aggression,' which is, in a way, a vestige of the days when law and order in the country were insecure.

Of the equipment of the Maritime Self-Defense Force and the Air Self-Defense Forces, the numbers of Aegis destroyers, P-3C anti-submarine patrol aircraft and AWACS (Airborne Warning and Control System) planes, which have been consistently upgraded for the purpose of dealing with supposed threat from the Soviet Union, should be largely reduced.

To a Japan dependent on import for most of major natural resources, it is, of course, very important to secure the safety of maritime traffic. But that does not justify expanding the scope of the Maritime Self-Defense Force's action. It will be desirable for Japan to sign agreements on safety on the seas with neighboring countries while cooperating with them in their endeavor for security on the seas.

At the same time it will be necessary to upgrade transport capability for more efficiently operating the reduced Self-Defense Force and improving the quality of equipment used exclusively to defend against an enemy landing on our soil. Small, high-powered vessels and various types of helicopters, for instance, will be in greater need. It is also important to have better equipment for fighting natural and chemical disasters.

Such reorganization needs to be phased in on the basis of yearly plans while paying attention to possible changes that might be made in the Japan-US security arrangements.

The first stage (until 2000) The build-up in the defense power, which has been almost consistently carried out since fiscal 1958 on the basis of the Defense Power Build-up Programs, is to be put to an end with the termination of the current Midterm Plan which ends in this fiscal year. The government should launch a National Security Council by the end of 1996 to invite its opinion on how the defense power should be at peacetime in post-Cold War years, what the relationship between the Japan-US security arrangements and the SDF should be and the prospective military technology and defense industry in the years to come, and draw up a blueprint for the National Defense Force by 1998 in line with Article 9 of the constitution.

Force for self-defense is to be reduced for the time being in the order of freezing, reduction in quantity and slowdown in replacement in quality. In carrying out such reduction, a temporary goal for the scaledown should be a return to the level set by the 'Concept of Basic Defense Capability' adopted by the government of Prime Minister Miki Takeo.

The Miki government's plan – which was based on the principles of (1) Japan does not adopt a doctrine of countering external threat with force, (2) the target of improvement in the defense power is force that is necessary in peace time, and (3) the scenario dealing with an invasion should be a limited one – was subsequently turned into meaningless words. But the perception that formed the basis of the plan is still relevant.

The second stage (until 2005) The government should officially pronounce the reorganization of the SDF into a National Defense Corps, legislate the three non-nuclear principles and the three principles of non-export of weapons and begin consultations on security matters with neighboring countries.

The government is to make yearly plans for scaling back the defense power and changing or abolishing equipment, and further press ahead with reduction in arms described for the first stage. In making such plans, the government should avoid entirely depending on officers in uniform. It should take advantage of a consultative body composed of representatives of political parties and specialists in the private sector.

The third stage (until 2010) This is the period for implementing the reduction in arms planned for the second stage and reviewing the plan itself. The troops in the Ground Self-Defense Force should be approximately halved.

Such efforts for phased reorganization of the SDF will be more effective if they are made in parallel with diplomatic activities for ensuring relaxation of tensions in the region and multilateral security.

Proposal 5: Pull away from Cold-War security arrangements

> *Multilateral talks and consultations should be repeatedly held and a target should be set for forming an organization in Asia, similar to the Organization for Security and Cooperation in Europe, for preventive diplomacy and arms control. The emphasis in the new organization is to deal with new threats such as arms buildup and disputes over resources and economic issues.*

One of the most remarkable changes since the end of the Cold War has been the emergence of prospering East Asian nations. A decade ago who could have taken seriously a prediction that the combined economic scale of China plus Hong Kong and Taiwan, South Korea and Southeast Asian nations would approach that of the United States in 2010? What were once theaters of Japan's aggression have become strategic plant sites and markets that drive the global economy.

How are we, living in an insular country on the eastern tip of Asia, to face such changes?

First, we should deepen mutual dependence with neighboring countries, and extend a helping hand to their development. Our doing so will contribute to peace in the region by entrenching democracy in those countries and stabilizing their external policies.

It is also important to contribute to creation of a stable security environment. For nothing is more important than peace to economic and social development of these countries.

The days are long gone when the only thing we had to do was to simply scream – along with the United States – about a Soviet threat. How can we establish a lasting peace and prosperity in East Asia in the new age? Japan's diplomatic capability will be put to a more pointed test than ever.

We think that the tasks facing us are threefold as described below.

The first is to put into practice our resolve to never again pose a military threat to other countries – through our own disarmament and participation in peace-keeping operations – and continue to strive to dispel concerns about us on the part of our neighbors. That is the starting point for Japan's taking part in East Asian politics.

The second is to enhance confidence among nations by frequent multilateral talks and consultations for preventing conflict; it is hoped that the results of such talks will lead to formation by the end of this century of a body similar to the Organization for Security and Cooperation in Europe dedicated to maintenance of peace, reduction in armaments and cooperation in security matters.

The third is to press ahead with reexamination of the Japan-US security arrangements at the same time. That means we make efforts for reshuffling the arrangements – made primarily for containing the Soviet Union – into those that will contribute to peace in Asia, while keeping in mind the course that Japan should take as a peace-loving nation.

Hope and anxiety coexist in this region. Though the danger of imminent clashes is reduced, there are still roots of conflicts.

North Korea's isolationist foreign policies and its military-oriented economy are causes for serious concern. China's squabbling with the Philippines and other nations over the Spratly Islands is entangled by possible existence of oil resources. Relations between China and Taiwan are also delicate.

Countries in Southeast Asia are very wary of future China. They fear that China, a big power without any doubt, may eventually embark on a strong-arm diplomatic policy on the strength of its military power.

It was for that reason that these countries welcomed the policy of the United States government to maintain its 100,000-strong force in the East Asia and Pacific region for the next ten years.

Not a few are also afraid Japan may become a militarily big power in counter to China if China poses a military threat. Against such a background, Southeast Asian countries are hurriedly importing state-of-the-art weapons for modernizing their armaments.

What is most effective in severing the chain reaction that heightens mistrust and tension is for the countries in the region to build up a framework for nipping the causes of disputes in the bud and protecting peace in cooperation with other countries outside the region.

An experiment is already under way for directing the momentum for nascent economic integration toward that direction: the ASEAN Regional Forum. The forum is the first arena for multilateral talks on peace in the region involving nearly all the interested parties.

To resolve the issue of suspected nuclear development by North Korea, the Korean Energy Development Organization was established, and the new organization has the support of China as well. That is another new attempt at regional security. And it is also expected that the Asia-Pacific Economic Cooperation Forum will have increased political weight in coming years.

To take steps toward a security system, talks and consultation have to be conducted on a variety of subjects at many different levels.

For instance, pollution of the air in China and other environmental problems are to be discussed among neighboring countries. If the mobility of labor increases in the region and talks are held on labor markets and working conditions, such talks will also be useful to prevent gaps in the levels of economic development from turning into strains among nations. Cooperation for space development and greater exchanges of students and other people will also contribute to building confidence.

Japan has started talks with China and Russia over security matters. Japan should also try to realize a six-nation consultation by Japan, the United States, China, South Korea, Russia and North Korea on the subject. Such consultations will be meaningful in creating a favorable atmosphere for solution of the territorial dispute between Japan and Russia. Japan can also contribute to mediation in the dispute over the Spratlys and preparing the ground for international cooperation in matters concerned with the safety of maritime traffic and relief in disasters.

Hopefully the series of those efforts will lead to systematization of confidence-building measures. Making overtures to these countries for such purposes is an important role for Japan.

There is another unavoidable task: reducing the threat of nuclear weapons. Joining hands with Southeast Asian countries and other non-nuclear powers, Japan should have talks with the United States, China and Russia over non-use of nuclear weapons and regulation of their deployment while giving support to the denuclearization of the Korean peninsula. That will be the first step toward establishment of a nuclear-free zone in the future. Most probably, that is in accord with the wish of the majority of the nations and is also a way for extricating Japan itself from America's nuclear umbrella.

Conventional military alliances do not work against new threats that arise from such issues as natural resources, territories, refugees and environmental destruction. As East Asia is a grouping of diverse countries, the climate was not favorable to creation of arrangements to take the place of military alliances. The major players here are still bilateral alliances led by the United States and organized in Cold War years.

In particular, work is under way in the American administration for 'redefining' the US-Japan Security Treaty – which was, along with the North Atlantic Treaty Organization in Europe, a bastion for the West for nearly half a century – to have the alliance take over the function of maintaining peace in the region.

Japan should ponder, however, whether the security arrangements between Japan and the United States as they are will contribute to peace in Asia in the long run.

From a historical standpoint, there is no doubt that those arrangements helped stabilize the relations between Japan and the United States and formed a basis for Japan's economic development – which is termed as miraculous – with the United States as its trading partner. It is an undeniable fact that some people in Asian countries and the United States think that without the Japan-US security arrangements Japan would not have abided by its pacifist Constitution and would have become a military power.

But it should not be overlooked that such arrangements also contain contradictions. It is claimed that Japan did not require more than light weapons precisely because of its security arrangements with the United States. But did not the American pressure for Japan's arms build-up aggrandize Japan's Self-Defense Forces and thereby fuel the neighboring countries' sense of being threatened by Japan?

Action taken by American troops in Japan beyond the limit of the Far East, for practical purposes if not in theory, set by the security treaty and ambiguity in the nature of 'prior consultation' (which is to be conducted when the American troops make important changes in their deployment of equipment in Japan and when they are engaged in combat operations from their Japanese bases) have harmed healthy relations between Japan and the United States. Massive amounts spent on supporting the stationing of the American troops in Japan attests to the fact that the security arrangements between the two countries have changed, in practice, into those of mutual obligations and benefits instead of one-sided favor.

The security arrangements have also had immeasurable 'negative utility' in giving military consideration out of all proportion to the United States and having thus hindered Japan's own diplomacy in relation to Asian nations.

The security arrangements between Japan and the United States may have been an unavoidable choice for Japan to return to the community of nations under the wing of the United States and achieve development soon after our defeat in the war. In the light of the ideal of the Constitution, however, Japan's participation in a military alliance, which could implicate Japan into America's wars, was a transitional and exceptional choice.

As long as there are no credible regional security arrangements and many countries in the region pin hope on deployment of American troops as deterrent to conflicts and also on Japan's assistance, however, it is necessary to take an incremental approach to changes in the Japan-US security arrangements. That is because we fear that instability arising as a result of abrupt change can stem the tide of rapprochement.

But some problems demand immediate attention. The first is a reduction or dismantling of the American military bases in Okinawa, which burden inhabitants in the prefecture, and solution of the noise problem around bases elsewhere in Japan. It is necessary to review the Japan-US agreement on the status of the American troops in Japan, which is much more indulgent to the American troops in their manoeuvres and use of facilities than similar arrangements in the countries of the North Atlantic Treaty Organization.

A fresh look should also be taken at the management of the security arrangements between the two countries based on the Cold War assumptions, such as planning joint operations. Those are part of the work for eliminating 'negative utility.'

The second is to discuss the deployment of American forces and their preparedness at the ASEAN Regional Forum and other multilateral meetings. Talks at such conference tables will not only enhance the deterrent effects on conflicts but also prevent American military action from becoming counterproductive.

The only way possible for the regional security arrangements in the years ahead is unceasing effort to be made by the countries in the region for preventing conflicts and build on such effort to develop them into a comprehensive collective security system which is capable of taking sanctions and conducting peacekeeping operations, even though such a process may be time-consuming.

Japan's close relations with the United States will continue to be the most important asset to Japan. And the importance to the world community of cooperation between Japan and the United States, two economic powerhouses in the world, for helping the growth of the world economy and providing assistance to developing countries will never diminish.

But there is little doubt that in the next century the world's political and security order centered around the United States will be gradually weakened and its military presence in the region will begin to decline. To try to construct a full-fledged regional security system, carried out with American cooperation, is to prepare for that.

Proposal 6: Leading reform of the United Nations

> *Broaden powers of the General Assembly in the interest of democratizing the United Nations and phasing out the veto power to make the Security Council a fairer body.*
>
> *Establish a strong socio-economic Security Council to give greatest priority to keeping disputes from growing.*
>
> *Scrap the passivist perception of the United Nations and take the lead in reforming the world body to achieve a better world. What is important for a non-nuclear Japan that makes no military contribution is not that it has a permanent seat on the Security Council, but what it does after getting it.*

Japan's postwar diplomatic policies have been based on the two major principles of 'Japan-US relations as the corner-stone of diplomacy' and 'United Nations-centered diplomacy.' If the former was a very realistic policy of establishing the nation's security by an alliance with the United States, the latter was an expression of Japan's intention to strive to realize the ideals of the United Nations Charter, which Japan recognized was resonant with the spirit of the constitution, as Japan envisioned an ideal future international community centered on the United Nations.

The United Nations, which was formed as a result of the soul-searching over two world wars, wanted above all to spare future generations from the scourge of war and obliged all member nations by the Charter to peacefully settle international disputes and refrain from the use or threat of force.

The United Nations aspired to be a body for collective security, by which the member nations act together to take sanctions against violators and take coercive measures by force when necessary. But the proper United Nations force for ensuring peace through the world body has not yet come into being.

Responding to such an ideal of the United Nations Charter, Japan's Constitution proclaimed renouncing war and the threat or use of force as a means for settling international disputes.

Soon after its founding, however, the United Nations sailed into the rough waters of the Cold War and has not lived up to expectations in the half-century of its existence. Still, liberation of colonies and independence for about eighty nations since then would have been unimaginable without the United Nations. And it was the United Nations that has sought to end racial and sexual discrimination and enhanced the awareness of the states and peoples about such problems as population explosion and environmental destruction.

Nor should it be forgotten that the United Nations offered a precious arena to medium and small countries for pleading their positions out of a desire to prevent international politics from being driven by the selfish interests of big powers.

Fifty years after the end of the last war, however, the world is very different from the time of the foundation of the United Nations. Discrepancy between what the world expects of the United Nations and the actual United Nations has become much too great.

The United Nations, which started with fifty-one victors in the Second World War as its charter members, has evolved into a universal international organization with 185 members. As it evolved, however, strains in the composition of the major United Nations organizations such as the Security Council and the Economic and Social Council and imbalance in the powers of those organizations have become so conspicuous that they can no longer be tolerated.

Japan, a 'former enemy' according to the Charter, makes financial contributions to the world body second largest among member nations. Japan is also expected to provide 15.65 percent of all contributions – about equal to the combined contributions of four permanent members of the Security Council excepting the United States – in 1997. The fact that permanent seats for Japan and Germany at the Security Council are talked about in connection with reform of the United Nations is symbolic of the changes that have taken place in the last half century.

The character of the problems that threaten 'international peace and security' referred to in the Charter has also clearly changed. Regional conflicts and ethnic disputes have proliferated while people are freed from the nightmare of a nuclear show-down between the United States and the Soviet Union.

In place of ideological confrontation, poverty, environmental destruction and various gaps in societies have come to be perceived as major problems confronting the world. Shift of emphasis from military-oriented security to human-centered security for stopping the spread of conflict has been gaining ground.

The 1994 version of the Report on Human Development prepared by the United Nations Development Program notes that one fifth of the population in poor countries suffer from starvation and a quarter do not have basic necessities while large quantities of food are thrown away and needless weapons are produced abundantly in rich countries.

Nor does the problem end there. In a borderless age, national boundaries no longer have the same meaning. Regions are being integrated. Nations are no longer the exclusive players in international politics, and problems facing mankind cannot be addressed properly without joining forces with nongovernmental organizations and regional bodies.

It is obvious that the United Nations lags behind such changes in the times. The world body is confronted with an urgent need for radically reexamining its organizational makeup and priorities in its activities.

From such a viewpoint, we propose that Japan stand at the forefront of reform of the United Nations. It is hoped that the proposal will serve as a guideline for Japan, a big power half a century after the end of the war, in adopting future-oriented political and diplomatic policies.

The major targets of the reform are: (1) to strengthen the power of the General Assembly for the sake of democratization of the United Nations, (2) to phase out veto powers to make the Security Council a fairer and more transparent organization,

(3) to create an Economic and Social Security Council to meet the requirements of the times, (4) to clearly define peacekeeping operations in the Charter.

The starting point for the reform of the United Nations is to part with a passive perception of the United Nations. The United Nations is a laboratory for human beings to bring the reality in the world closer to its ideals. What is important is the ability to have visions about the manner of our participation in the world body in light of the world as it should be and the course that Japan should take and to act on such visions.

Some in Japan advocate revising its constitution to make more active 'international contribution' under a reinvigorated United Nations. However, we should neither unquestioningly accept the United Nations as it is nor impetuously change its basic policies. Japan should take the lead in the reform of the United Nations while making serious efforts toward international contribution that is appropriate to Japan.

Strengthening the power of the General Assembly for democratization of the United Nations   The lifeblood of the United Nations is the member nations' confidence in it. It is important that rules and principles are fairly applied regardless of the size and strength of the member nations. That is why democratization comes at the top of our objectives.

The countries in 'the South' are increasingly concerned that the United Nations has tended to be driven by major countries. The power of the General Assembly should be strengthened so that the voices of the developing countries are better reflected in United Nations activities.

The resolutions adopted by the General Assembly are not binding at present. And Article 12 of the Charter stipulates that without the Security Council's explicit request, the General Assembly shall not make any recommendation on matters related to peace and security if the Security Council is performing its duties in such matters.

Because the Security Council is very powerful, it is not healthy that the United Nations lacks in institutional arrangements for examining the relevance of the decisions and other action of the Security Council. The Charter should be revised to enable the General Assembly to always keep track of the Security Council and oversee it. It should also be made possible for the General Assembly to make recommendation on peace and security from perspectives that are different from those of the council.

Phasing out veto power for a fairer Security Council   The reform of the Security Council, the focal point in the overhaul of the United Nations, should be made with the greatest emphasis placed on securing greater transparency in discussion at the council and thereby ensuring fairness.

The veto power should be abolished. In the first phase, which is to be put into effect by the end of this century, change is to be made in the veto power in such a way that it is effective only when two or three permanent council members concur and secondly, it is abolished outright by the target year of 2005.

Japan and Germany are regarded as important candidates for new permanent members of the Security Council. But any reform worth its name would call for inviting three other countries, each representing Africa, Asia and Latin America, as new permanent members. Moreover, nonpermanent members should be increased by about five seats so that smaller countries and those in the South are better represented.

In the second phase of reform the Security Council should be entirely overhauled by around 2010.

The five permanent members of the Security Council are all nuclear powers and major suppliers of weapons. Export of weapons by these countries accounted for 86 percent of the total arms trade in the world in 1993. While the danger of proliferation of nuclear arms and modern weapons to developing countries is more and more serious, the root cause of the danger is traced to the five countries that assume greatest responsibility for maintaining peace and security in the world.

A breakthrough will be found by changing the Security Council so that it can make an honest effort at nuclear disarmament and regulation of transfer of conventional weapons.

Japan, unique in its three non-nuclear principles, refusing to export weapons and not making military contribution to the world community, should stand at the forefront of reform of the United Nations. And if it is so requested, Japan should become a permanent member of the council. What is important is not that Japan has a permanent seat on the Security Council but what it does after getting it.

Defining peacekeeping operations in the Charter   Peacekeeping operations are not formally defined in the Charter and the peacekeeping efforts are described as action based on 'Chapter 6 and half' because they are in between Chapter 6, which provides for pacific settlement of disputes and Chapter 7, which stipulates sanctions and use of military power.

The conventional peacekeeping operations were based on principles of (1) consent of the parties to the dispute, (2) nonparticipation by permanent members of the Security Council and parties to the dispute, and (3) not taking military action. Departing from the tradition after the end of the Cold War, however, the United Nations attempted to impose peace through force. But the failure in Somalia put the prestige of the United Nations at risk and Secretary-General Boutros Boutros-Ghali expressed his intention to return to traditional peacekeeping efforts. It is desirable to clearly define peacekeeping in the chapter so that it will not overstep the mark in future.

Japan should actively take part in such operations through its nonmilitary organization.

Chapter 6 of the Charter should more clearly define the course of action for peace, such as a guideline on mediation.

Creation of an Economic and Social Security Council   To thwart growth of disputes, emphasis in UN activities should be placed on such problems as poverty, human rights and the environment. But the present Economic and Social Council is not powerful enough for that. Many specialized organizations have branched out of the United Nations in these fields and their functions partly duplicate. But under the present circumstance, the Economic and Social Council cannot properly make comprehensive plans and control or adjust specialized agencies.

An Economic and Social Council should be established in these fields with power commensurate with the power of the Security Council in peace and security. Special attention should be paid to joining forces with non-governmental organizations and the role of the non-governmental organizations should be clearly defined in the Charter.

These are only some of the tasks in reforming the United Nations. But every one of them will put Japan to a test in regard to its basic policies and its diplomatic and political capability. It is hoped that Japan, while promoting reform of the United Nations and disarmament in the countries of the world, will be a country that takes steps forward without losing sight of the day when the United Nations will have a credible United Nations Police Force.

EDITORIAL[2]

Nonmilitary activism is Japan's best contribution

> *As we see it, the Self-Defense Forces are constitutional as 'an organization that devotes itself exclusively to defending the country' and should not be thoughtlessly used for other purposes.*

(This is a follow-up to the editorial package on international contribution and the Constitution that appeared on May 3.)

Recently, another argument for (constitutional) revision has emerged. That is to say there is a growing number of advocates of revising Article 9, saying it is a matter of urgency that Japan possess a self-defense military force to cooperate with the United Nations.

From the standpoint that Japan attaches first priority to the United Nations, those people maintain that Japan cannot justify not sending armed forces to cooperate with UN peacekeeping or police forces. They maintain that since Japan cannot perform international duties with the SDF that are not allowed to be deployed overseas, it should possess an army that can freely be dispatched overseas

These statements seem to be an explanation of the circumstances of the constitution and politics in recent years. In fact, the observations were made more than thirty years ago, in September 1962. They are the words of Ryū Shintarō, then chief editorial writer of *Asahi Shimbun*, who was asked to speak at a central public hearing of the government Commission on the constitution.

Article 9 as a bar to contribution

Isn't Article 9 of the constitution obstructing Japan's international contribution?

It is still fresh in our memory that the Persian Gulf crisis and war that started with the Iraqi invasion of Kuwait in August 1990 and the subsequent post-war settlement triggered such an argument, giving rise to a major political current in Japan.

As is clear from Ryu's statements, however, the debate linking the constitution and international contribution is not particularly new, but is part of a recurring surge in the movement for constitutional revision.

In thinking about Japan's course in the twenty-first century, how should we tackle this new yet old issue? The editorial special 'International Cooperation and the Constitution' that we published on May 3 was an attempt to respond to the question from several angles.

Ryu, who termed the ideal outlined by the Constitution 'a World Federation,' devoted himself to advocating that cause. In the public hearing, Ryu said: 'The ban on overseas dispatch underlies the fundamental rule of the SDF today, and I also think it represents the pride and honor to signify its peaceful nature.' He thus stressed the importance of nonmilitary cooperation and opposed the revision of Article 9.

A world federation that denies national sovereignty and aims at a community of mankind is a dream as far from reality now as it was then. But now that the Cold War has ended and a bedrock for building world peace has begun to surface, it would be against the current of the times to choose a path that will lead further away from the ideal. We are advocating the concept of a 'non-militarist, activist state,' which is clearly different from the current that advocates a military contribution under national sovereignty. Once again, we believe our direction fits into the framework for 'global history' of the future.

We received many letters by mail and facsimile from readers who responded to our editorial package. Most of the messages were of understanding and support, which encouraged us tremendously. But we also received strong opposing opinions and views questioning our proposals. We wish to respond to some of them and offer supplementary observations.

First, we heard from readers who expressed criticism and doubts from the viewpoint of security policies concerning our proposal to scale down the SDF into forces exclusively for defending the country. They questioned: 'Is that really safe? Isn't it the responsibility of the government to prepare the country for unexpected situations, considering the trends in China and the Korean peninsula?'

A multitude of uncertainties

It is true that Japan is surrounded by uncertain factors – China's military build-up, North Korea's suspected nuclear development programs, improvement of its missile technology and revival of nationalism in Russia. They need to be watched carefully.

Yet, from an objective viewpoint, it is unlikely that these countries have the motives or factors that could trigger them to attack Japan. While confrontations and tension may arise, it is unrealistic to think that they could lead to military aggression.

If we stress 'threats' and keep pushing the idea 'to prepare oneself for unexpected situations,' the argument could escalate endlessly to a point that would advocate Japan arming itself with nuclear weapons, eventually becoming a major nuclear power. Only when we implement policies that take a new look at today's SDF from its roots which grew out of Cold War military thinking, can we break away from the vicious cycle in which military build-up promotes further military build-up.

Second, in response to our proposal for the establishment of a 'Peace Support Corps' to participate in UN peacekeeping operations as well as humanitarian and disaster relief missions, we received critical opinions from readers who said such an organization would be the same as having a second SDF, and asked why those missions could not be undertaken by the current SDF.

As we see it, the SDF is constitutional as 'an organization that devotes itself exclusively to defending the country' and should not be thoughtlessly used for other purposes. Members of the SDF did not join thinking that they would be assigned to such missions outside Japan.

The general unit may engage in activities in areas classified as 'military divisions' in peacekeeping operations. But in conventional peacekeeping operations in which the Peace Support Corps will take part will not use weapons except for self-defense. Therefore, there is no need for military exercises that use all sorts of weapons and equipment, including tanks and planes.

Even if the corps is told to join multinational forces as in the Persian Gulf war, since it does not have the capability, there are limits to what activities it can take part in. While the corps members will carry small firearms, it is not 'a second SDF.'

How constitutional is the SDF?

Finally, we wish to refer to the criticism that the degree of self-defense capability permitted is vague and the boundary of constitutionality of the SDF is unclear.

Whether something is constitutional or not, be it the SDF or other matters, is an expression of a certain political view. Thus, the boundary is usually unclear for anyone because it has more than one side.

Of course, if the Supreme Court presents a standard of constitutionality and makes a clear ruling based on the standard, the decision could provide us with a tentative conclusion. But it is possible, as well as meaningful, to demand a reversal of the ruling. In other words, what is significant is the presence of constitutional debate among the people and that their opinions are reflected in court rulings and policy formation.

In Japan, the issue of constitutionality tends to be replaced by fruitless confrontation between proponents and opponents on a given issue. Assertions that it is unrealistic not to say the SDF are constitutional also dominate, despite the fact that if the nation possesses a self-defense capability that exceeds 'the necessary minimum' it is unconstitutional even by government interpretation.

Recently, Tokyo Governor Aoshima Yukio offered his opinion in the Tokyo Metropolitan Assembly that the SDF are unconstitutional. In response, members of the Liberal-Democratic Party and the New Frontier Party (Shinshintō) attacked him, asking, 'Isn't it selfish to ask them for help in disasters while saying they're unconstitutional?'

The reaction is a childish argument that ignores the fact that actual administrative and social systems are functioning on the basis of individual laws. It is sad that debate concerning the constitution, which is a guiding principle of a nation, is used as a mere tool of harassment in an assembly.

Let us discuss the constitution not superficially but looking squarely at reality. We published the editorial special with such an idea in mind, seeking a way to make the constitution useful in international cooperation. We intend to revive the issue from time to time and to continue to study it.

(*Asahi Shimbun*, May 22 1995)

Notes

1 Editorial, *Asahi Evening News*, May 3 1995.
2 *Asahi Evening News*, May 28 1995.

Ozawa Ichirō, 'A proposal for reforming the Japanese Constitution' (1999)

Breaking a post-war Japanese taboo, a current Japanese politician rewrites its provisions

Ozawa Ichirō, President of the Liberal Party of Japan, translation by Julia Parton

The Japanese Constitution was adopted by the House of Representatives (Lower House) plenary session on August 24 1946. It was promulgated on November 3, and came into effect on May 3 the following year. It is also widely known that MacArthur, the Supreme Commander of the Allied Forces, proposed the draft of the constitution to the government. Today, over half a century later, it remains without a single amendment.

> This Constitution shall be the supreme law of the nation and no law, ordinance, imperial rescript or other act of government, or part thereof, contrary to the provisions hereof, shall have legal force or validity.

This is the provision of Article 98 of the Japanese Constitution which establishes the constitution as 'the supreme law' amongst all other laws. A constitution represents the rules that a nation decides upon in order to protect the lives, property and rights of the people, enabling them to live in peace. Although it is natural for these rules to change with time, our constitution has not been revised for over fifty years. There have been no additions to reflect the changing values of each new era, and we as a nation have become attached to a fossil. Despite this, there are many people who talk about the current constitution as if it were almost perfect.

At the risk of being misunderstood, it seems abnormal to me that a constitution imposed by the occupation authorities continues to function after Japan has become an independent nation. In civil law, it is a self-evident truth that a contract is invalid when imposed while under imprisonment or through coercion. Despite this, when discussion turns to the constitution, the spirit of the law is ignored through arguments which posit that 'although the constitution was introduced during the Occupation, it was debated in the Diet and established after following correct procedure.'

In 1946, Japan was under military occupation. It was not an environment where Japanese people were able to express themselves freely. A constitution which is decided under abnormal conditions is invalid under international law.

162 *Japan's contested constitution*

This is a principle enshrined in the Hague Convention of 1907; and even in the Potsdam Declaration, which Japan accepted after the war, there is a clause which states that the form of Japanese sovereignty 'should follow the freely expressed will' of the Japanese people.

Looking at the constitutions of other countries, it is written in the constitution of the Republic of France, for example, 'No amendment procedure shall be commenced or continued where the integrity of the territory is jeopardized.'[1] It is stated in the constitution (the 'Basic Law') of the Federal Republic of Germany, the former West Germany, that 'this Basic Law, which is valid for the entire German people following the achievement of the unity and freedom of Germany, shall cease to be in force on the day on which a constitution adopted by a free decision of the German people comes into force.'[2]

For a long time in Japan, people have hesitated about even discussing revision of the constitution. If politicians like me asserted the need for reform, they were labelled as 'right-wing reactionaries' by those who are grateful for our 'peace constitution.' Of course, I do not believe that all of the constitution is wrong simply because it was established during the Occupation. On the contrary, I regard it quite highly. When I was at school, I wanted to be a lawyer, and often pored over the constitution. However, what exactly is 'peace'? What exactly is 'the constitution'? Is it not time to reconsider what these words mean?

The constitution established under the Occupation is invalid

To state my conclusion first, Japan should have used the opportunity, presented when it was internationally recognized as an independent country with the conclusion of the San Francisco Peace Treaty in 1951, to announce that the constitution established under the Occupation was invalid, that it was returning to the Imperial Constitution, and that it would then establish a new constitution. Of course, no problem would be posed if the newly established constitution were 'the Japanese Constitution.'

This is not an original idea of my own. In fact the question of whether the constitution was invalid as a document established under the Occupation was a common topic of discussion. This opinion was typical of the Kyoto School, including the scholars Sasaki Sōichi and Ōishi Yoshio.

A rather unique mentality developed in our country under the so-called '1955 system,' where Japan strove to achieve high-speed economic growth under the background of Soviet–US confrontation. Named 'constitutional protectionism,' it presented itself as a firmly held belief, but rather represents an understanding that the status quo should not be breached. An irresponsible way of thinking permeated deeply throughout Japanese society, where people told themselves that the current system was fine, and there was no need to think about such difficult matters. A particularly Japanese idea dominated that, 'We must defend the constitution, therefore we cannot debate it.' The constitution became immutable, with the ruling Liberal-Democratic Party suspending its call for the establishment of an 'independent constitution' which was included in its party platform at the time, and the main opposition Socialist Party continuing to defend the 'Peace Constitution.' The insights of the scholars of Kyoto University, including Sasaki and Ōishi, also came to be forgotten.

As we approach the beginning of the twenty-first century, there are few who could deny that Japan is entering into a period of great change. It is impossible for Japan to respond to these domestic and international changes while maintaining the system of Japanese 'collusionism.' Surely there is not a single citizen who wants to go back to the isolation of the Edo period, and therefore then the only path open to us is to change the people's consciousness to bring it in line with the rest of the world. In order to achieve this goal, it is necessary to reconsider whether the imperfections embedded in the constitution, which is at the root of our legal system, can be neglected. Through discussion of constitutional reform, the potential exists to break through the blockade we are confronting.

I will soon have spent over thirty years as a politician, and have resolved it is time to speak out against Japan's post-war taboos. It was decided recently in the Diet to establish a committee to investigate reform of the constitution. Although this committee is in the ambiguous position of having no right to make any proposals, it can be considered a step forward given the situation up until now. Here I would like to present my own thoughts on constitutional reform as honestly and openly as I can, and encourage people to make a reasoned judgement of my proposals.

Let me start by pointing out that I am not a specialist in law so, from a legal perspective, there are probably many examples of inappropriate wording and unpolished phrasing. It should therefore be understood that these proposals simply represent my opinions with regard to the constitution.

Simplifying expression

The Japanese Constitution, which came into effect in 1947, starts with a preamble of only 600 characters.

> We, the Japanese people, acting through our duly elected representatives in the National Diet, determined that we shall secure for ourselves and our posterity the fruits of peaceful cooperation with all nations and the blessings of liberty throughout this land, and resolved that never again shall we be visited with the horrors of war through the action of government, do proclaim that sovereign power resides with the people and do firmly establish this constitution.

Firstly, it should be pointed out that constitutional interpretation cannot use historical context as basis for a decision. In interpreting the law, the motives of its writers should not be included, but it should be interpreted as much as possible according to its provisions. For example, the circumstances at the time the constitution was established meant that the American Occupation forces wanted to prevent Japan from having the ability to fight another war. They thought that the Japanese were a fanatical race who regarded the Americans and the British as barbarians. This policy changed with the consolidation of the Cold War structure between the US and the USSR, but one of the fundamental principles of interpreting law is that such historical circumstances should not be included in the interpretation of a constitution.

The basic principles of the Japanese Constitution are written in the preamble: the principles of pacifism; respect for fundamental human rights; sovereignty of the people; and, what I would like to emphasize, the principle of international cooperation. There is no need to change these four principles, in my opinion.

I have used modern, simplified Chinese characters here, but the actual constitution is written using pre-war characters, which makes it difficult to read. I do not, however, intend to touch upon this, or other stylistic problems. Rather, I would prefer to concentrate on the content of the constitution. Having said that, it is preferable that the constitution be expressed in the simplest terms possible. Moreover, I am in basic agreement with the argument that the preamble of the constitution should also elaborate the unique characteristics of the Japanese, which stem from our traditions and culture.

Furthermore, abstract principles, which should be recorded in the Preamble, are contained in the various articles, causing confusion in the courts. For example, Article 25, which states that: 'All people shall have the right to maintain the minimum standards of wholesome and cultured living,' should really be in the preamble of the constitution, whereas principles such as international cooperation should be included in the body.

The Emperor is the head of the Japanese State

The articles related to the 'Emperor' are recorded in Chapter 1 (Articles 1–8). The following is the first article of the first chapter of the Japanese Constitution:

> The Emperor shall be the symbol of the State and the unity of the people, deriving his position from the will of the people with whom resides sovereign power.

In other words, those who think that the constitution is simply a 'peace constitution,' as the post-war left wing claim, are mistakenly swept along by the principles recorded in the preamble. The Japanese Constitution is based on the principle of a constitutional monarchy. The fact that the emperor is in the very first provision should make this clear.

The claim of Miyazawa Toshiyoshi, former professor at the University of Tokyo, and others, that 'the Prime Minister is the head of state,' is wrong. Miyazawa's argument regards the Japanese Constitution to be republican in character, in comparison to the Japanese Imperial Constitution. However in Article 6, for example, it is the emperor who appoints the Prime Minister and the Chief Judge of the Supreme Court, in the name of, or as a representative of, the people. Moreover, the emperor acts as head of state in foreign affairs, and is treated as such abroad. These facts should remove any doubt that the emperor is the head of state. Some want it to be clearly stated that the emperor is the head of state, but the emperor is already the head of state according to the current constitution. I often studied Miyazawa's theory while a student, but it appears to me to follow the argument employed by the post-war left wing, and which has continued through post-war society to the present day.

Following the order of the constitution, let us move on to Chapter 2: 'the renunciation of war' (Article 9).

Right of self-defense

1   Aspiring sincerely to an international peace based on justice and order, the Japanese people forever renounce war as a sovereign right of the nation and the threat or use of force as means of settling international disputes.
2   In order to accomplish the aim of the preceding paragraph, land, sea, and air forces, as well as other war potential, will never be maintained. The right of belligerency of the state will not be recognised.

The contents of Article 9 have been the most debated topic in post-war Japan. This is the principle that we should limit the exercising of a sovereign right, that is to say, the right to self-defense, whether it be individual or collective defense. To put it plainly, we will not use force to counterattack unless we come under direct attack. The subheading for Article 9 should be 'Exercising the right of self-defense,' rather than 'Renouncing war potential,' or 'Denying the right of war.'

Self-defense can be likened to the legitimate right of defense every individual enjoys. This type of right is properly recognized as a 'natural right,' and cannot be denied by any law, including, of course, the constitution as the supreme law, or international treaties. In countries that have a criminal law system with the power of enforcement, the legitimate right to defense and emergency refuge are recognized. In international society, which does not have a unified legal order with the power of enforcement, it is a natural right of a state as a matter of course. A constitution cannot exist if a state's legitimate right of defense is not recognized. Accordingly, Article 9 should be changed thus:

(Right of self-defense)
1   Aspiring sincerely to an international peace based on justice and order, the Japanese people forever renounce war as a sovereign right of the nation and the threat or use of force as means of settling international disputes.

166 *Japan's contested constitution*

2   In order to accomplish the aim of the preceding paragraph, land, sea, and air forces, as well as other war potential, will never be maintained. The right of belligerency of the state will not be recognised.
3   The regulation in paragraph 2 does not prevent the maintenance of military power for the purpose of exercising Japan's right of self-defense against military attack by a third country.

(Ozawa proposal)

Article 9 starts with the words: 'aspiring sincerely to an international peace based on justice and order.' Moreover, it is stated in the Preamble that 'we desire to occupy an honored place in an international society striving for the preservation of peace, and the banishment of tyranny and slavery, oppression and intolerance for all time from the earth,' which is an expression of Japan's positive role in the creation of peace. However, how should Japan actually support justice and order in international society?

I believe that the only way for Japan to participate in peacekeeping activities is through the United Nations, to which the nations of the world belong, and which is the only global organization for peace. It is desirable that 'peaceful cooperation with all nations,' as recorded in the Preamble, should also be specifically referred to in the body of the constitution. Thus, following on from Article 9 in Chapter 2, a new article should be created, which would make clear the principle of 'peaceful cooperation with all nations,' for which the constitution aims.

(International Peace)
   In order to maintain, and restore, international peace and safety from threats to, the collapse of, or aggressive actions against, peace, the Japanese people shall contribute positively to world peace, through various means including taking the lead in participating in international peacekeeping activities, and supplying troops.

(Ozawa proposal)

The spirit of this article is the same as Chapter 7 of the United Nations' Charter[3] and, moreover, has the same tenor as the statement released when Japan joined the UN.

Having approved the UN Charter upon joining, it is inconsistent to say that 'participation in UN-recognized peacekeeping activities is not allowed according to the domestic constitution.' As I said earlier, the principle of 'peaceful cooperation with all nations' runs right through the Preamble of the constitution. If we explicitly express the notion of pacifism in the new era based on this principle, we can avert the fears and misunderstandings of neighboring countries that Japan is gradually becoming a military power. It is written in the current Preamble to the constitution that 'we desire to occupy an honored place in . . . international society.' We must make every effort in order to occupy that honored place. Simply providing money is no longer enough.

Creating a 'UN standing army'

Japan maintains the Self-Defense Forces (SDF) as a minimum military force in order to repel a direct military attack. In addition, as a member of the United Nations and in cooperating with peacekeeping activities as a member of the UN, Japan is able to participate in planning for the creation of a 'UN standing army,' disarmament, and the abolition of nuclear weapons, and can incorporate such aims into law (the Basic Security Law).

In order to maintain peace and survive as we approach the next century, Japan must align itself further with international society. There is no other way to do this than to participate actively in all activities led by the UN. For this reason, I believe that Japan should take the lead in proposing a plan for a UN standing army. The development of weapons and technology has meant that the traditional theory of the sovereign state no longer holds water. It is no longer possible to defend national peace solely through individual or collective self-defense. The only way to maintain order is through the concept of collective security, in other words, policing power on a global scale. The SDF will end its historical mission, and will be scaled down. Instead, Japan should provide both human assistance and financial power to a UN standing army.

At the time of the Meiji Restoration, the Imperial Court did not possess any military power. It had no police, or authority, so an Imperial Guard was created centred on the Satsuma and Chōshū clans. Today's UN is in a similar position to the Imperial Court after the Meiji Restoration. Because it does not have its own military strength, when an incident occurs, it calls upon its members to form a multi-lateral force to be used in peacekeeping operations. As a result, there are times when swift action cannot be taken in response to emergencies, due to the concerns or circumstances of individual countries, which often leads to ineffective interventions. I believe, therefore, that we should take a step forward by creating a standing army for the UN rather than continuing in the present vein. Japan could not exist without international cooperation, so it is Japan that should actively call for the establishment of a standing army. While the US may not support this idea, we should work to persuade them of its merits. Japan should also actively advocate the establishment of a standing army to all countries that have the necessary economic and military power, and should be seen taking the lead in realizing this goal.

When discussing collective security centered on the UN, national interest is of course also involved. At the time of the Gulf War, there were those who claimed that America's motive was the protection of a major oil supply. Certainly, there is some truth in saying that America sent troops to protect its own interests. It is pointless, however, to criticize America in such a simplistic way.

It is a problem of globalization. There are some amongst those who rail against this trend who criticise globalization as 'internationalization based on Anglo-Saxon principles.' Such an assessment, however, offers us no solutions, as the world functions according to these rules. Instead, we must respond to and overcome the challenges we are presented with. Breaking off our alliance with

America would be like Japan going into isolation. If we could assure ourselves that such a course would bring true happiness, then I think that this is one way of living and one philosophy. However, aiming to enjoy increasing material wealth while at the same time complaining about globalization is nothing but Japanese 'self-indulgence.'

In conclusion, active contribution by Japan in order to restore and maintain international peace and security is completely different in character from the 'war as a sovereign right of the nation' mentioned in Article 9 of the constitution.

In other words, by contributing to UN activities based on the UN Charter in order to secure everlasting world peace, including through the provision of troops, Japan is ultimately protecting its own peace and security.

Indeed, this is the very starting point of 'cooperation with international society,' which the Japanese Constitution strives to attain.

Enlightenment of public welfare

The 'Rights and duties of the people' are laid out in Articles 10–40 in Chapter 3 of the current constitution.

I have pointed out that one of the faults with the Japanese Constitution is that its abstract language makes it difficult to understand, and this tendency is clearly visible in Chapter 3. The phrase 'public welfare' is particularly noticeable. It appears in Articles 12 and 23, and is also frequently used in Articles 22 and 29. The word 'public' is over-used to the point of abuse, yet the meaning of the phrase 'public welfare' is not defined anywhere in the constitution. Constitutional debate thus falls into the trap of semantics.

Article 12 states that

> the freedoms and rights guaranteed to the people by this constitution shall be maintained by the constant endeavor of the people, who shall refrain from any abuse of these freedoms and rights and shall always be responsible for utilizing them for public welfare.

The 'respect . . . [of] individuals,' as stated in Article 13, is only 'to the extent that it does not interfere with the public welfare.' The basic principle of Article 1 of the Civil Code is that 'private rights conform to public welfare,' and it is written that one has an obligation to exercise one's rights and perform one's duties sincerely and in good faith. In contrast to this, in the Constitution, the rules of 'public welfare' are not explicit and, because they are buried in the text, they are abstract and undefined. My proposal for reform of both of these articles provides that 'public welfare' be stipulated in Article 12, and the importance of endeavor by the people to protect their liberty and rights be recorded in Article 13. Articles 12 and 13 therefore, should be revised as follows. As a result, the use of the phrase 'public welfare' will be unnecessary in the other articles.

(Public welfare)
    The fundamental human rights guaranteed to the people by this Constitution shall respect public welfare and public order. Matters regarding public welfare and order shall be stipulated in law.
(Ozawa proposal)

(The right to pursue happiness)
    The right to life, liberty, and the pursuit of happiness guaranteed to the people by this constitution shall be maintained by the constant endeavour of the people. The people shall refrain from any abuse of these freedoms and rights.
(Ozawa proposal)

    The concept of public welfare is not understood in Japan, making it impossible to enact laws limiting the rights of the individual. In order for the Japanese to become truly independent, it is necessary to make it clear that the freedom of the individual will be limited at times.

    The government also holds some responsibility. The Telecommunications Interception Bill (often referred to as the 'wire-tapping law'), for example, is essential for the maintenance of public safety, including national defense. This fact has been kept from the public, and the government has tried to pass the bill through misrepresentation by saying it is important for investigation purposes. Similarly, creating a citizens' register is not only for tax purposes. Surely this issue should be discussed in terms of the importance of a registration system for crisis management in emergencies and security contingencies.

    Japanese politics is misinterpreting its mission. Surely we should be gaining the clear understanding of the people regarding the concept of public welfare, and then proposing a concrete system of crisis management. Then it would be possible to enlighten the public of the disadvantage it is in danger of being placed by organized crime. Of course, abuse of this right by the authorities would also have an adverse effect on the public, so a heavy punishment for such abuses should also be stipulated.

    In Chapter 3 there are also many articles that can be considered common sense, and so should not be written in the constitution. Leaving in articles which are no longer relevant to the times can be the cause of judicial problems.

    There are some instances where the values specified in the constitution are not in accord with the Japanese traditional culture. The Shinto rite of worshipping one's ancestors is very different from the idea of religion in the West. The 'Tamagushiryō Decision' of the Supreme Court against Ehime Prefecture, which declared that making donations to purchase *tamagushi* was against the Constitution based on the religious freedom of Article 20, would not strike the Japanese (who believe in many gods) as anti-constitutional.[4] Perhaps it would be better to impose restrictions on religious freedom only in order to suppress the development of state-sponsored religious fascism.

    Moreover, we should introduce new human rights, such as 'environmental rights,' or 'the right to know.'

Upper House elections are unnecessary

The next chapter is problematic.

Chapter 4, 'The Diet' (Articles 41–64), should be completely revised. It is written in Article 42 that: 'The Diet shall consist of two Houses, namely the House of Representatives and the House of Councillors.' In other words, Japan has a bicameral system. It is my feeling, however, that this system is not working. Both the House of Representatives and the House of Councillors have approximately the same amount of power, and both are chosen through elections, meaning that the party structure inevitably extends into the House of Councillors. The division of functions with the House of Representatives, which is the aim of the bicameral system, is breaking down.

Although the House of Representatives is superior to the House of Councillors in the passing of budgets, treaties, and the appointment of the prime minister, if the Upper House votes against any bill, it requires a special vote in the House of Representatives, which must obtain a majority of two-thirds of the members present in order to become law. In all other aspects, the two houses are completely equal, leading to criticism of the Upper House as a carbon copy. The current political situation clearly shows that it is impossible to exercise strong leadership even after securing a majority in the Lower House. Because both houses are effectively equal, the opinion expressed by the people in general elections is also poorly reflected in politics. The selection of representatives by the people in elections should be restricted to the House of Representatives, and the House of Councillors should be given the function of serving as a check on the Lower House.

I envisage the House of Councillors being like the British 'powerless House of Lords.' In the UK, 659 Members of Parliament are chosen by direct election – approximately one member for every 100,000 people. In the House of Lords, there are approximately 1,300 members. Real power lies with the House of Commons (Lower House) however, so that in a sense the British system can be understood as a unicameral system.

If Japan were to adopt a system which was in essence unicameral like the British and others, then the 500 members of the House of Representatives would represent approximately one Diet member per 250,000 constituents. In terms of population, therefore, it would be reasonable for there to be more than double the number of existing Diet members. However given that the Japanese system has two houses which are equivalent in power and play similar roles, people criticize the system as wasteful, and call instead for a reduction in the number of Diet members.

Therefore, my solution would be to change the system so that membership of the House of Councillors becomes an honorary position which is not decided through election, but is bestowed on those who have admirable achievements or distinguished careers, from a broad cross-section of society. To be elected to office means representing the interests of certain groups in one form or another. The advantage to having Upper House members consisting of people with honorary posts is that any personal interests would be eliminated, allowing them to make fair and neutral decisions. If the House of Councillors rejects a bill that has been passed by the House of Representatives, it should be returned to the Lower House, where a simple majority would ensure its passage. The real significance of a bicameral system will be realized through an Upper House which is unburdened by vested interests, and functions as a checking mechanism.

When I say the House of Councillors should be like the House of Lords however, I do not mean that it should be a hereditary system. If the honor is limited to one generation, then the abuses of a hereditary system will not materialize. Instead, decorations and titles could be awarded liberally. Article 14 states that while peers and peerage shall not be recognized, honors and awards should. Furthermore, the financial burden on the state would be drastically reduced.

For example, decorations should be awarded to those members of the House of Representatives who have served for twenty-five years, and they should become lifetime members of the House of Councillors. Mrs Thatcher, the former British Prime Minister, became a baroness and moved to the House of Lords. I, for one, would be delighted to move to the House of Councillors. Being awarded such an honor, and not having to fight another election, I suspect that everyone would jump at the chance to move to the Upper House. There would be no need to push for benefits to be provided for the local constituency, and members could give their opinions from a national perspective. For this reason they would do it happily, rather than in order to increase their pensions, and it would also lead to a more youthful House of Representatives.

Revisions to Chapter 4, 'The Diet,' should be as follows.

Firstly, paragraph 1 of Article 43, 'Both Houses shall consist of elected members, representative of all the people,' should be changed to:

> Both Houses shall consist of elected members, representative of all the people. The number of the members of each House, and matters concerning elections, shall be fixed by law.
>
> (Ozawa proposal)

Next, Article 46 would become:

> The Emperor shall appoint members of the House of Councillors as designated by the House of Representatives. The term of office shall be for life.
>
> (Ozawa proposal)

(Note: the appointment of members of the House of Councillors will be added to the Emperor's responsibilities in matters of state.)

In addition, paragraph 2 of Article 59 would change as follows:

> A bill, which is passed by the House of Representatives, and upon which the House of Councillors makes a decision different from that of the House of Representatives, shall become law if passed a second time by the House of Representatives.
>
> (Ozawa proposal)

There are other problem areas in Article 4 that should be revised and adjusted after being debated, and it should be adequate to remove passages other than those which have an institutional effect on the Diet or the structure of the cabinet. In the same way that the lack of a written constitution does not cause problems in the UK, a functioning set of laws applied properly should be adequate.

Do not allow Cabinet measures which are above the law

Chapter 5 concerns 'the Cabinet' (Articles 65–75). Since I have made substantial changes to the role of the House of Councillors in Chapter 4, the following paragraph of Article 67 will also need to be changed: 'The Prime Minister shall be designated from among the members of the Diet by a resolution of the Diet.'

> The Prime Minister shall be designated from among the members of the House of Representatives by a resolution of the House of Representatives.
> (Ozawa proposal)

Unlike America, which has an independent administration, Japan has a Cabinet system where the Prime Minister is selected from the majority party in the Diet.

As it is stated in Article 66 that, 'The Cabinet shall, in the exercise of executive power, be collectively responsible to the Diet,' the Prime Minister appoints the ministers of state to form a Cabinet, and according to the principle of 'unanimity of the Cabinet,' acts as a unified body within the Diet. In other words, in a parliamentary Cabinet system, the Diet and the Cabinet are not positioned in opposition to one other. Rather, it is the ruling party and opposition parties that oppose one another. The majority of the Japanese, however, mistakenly believe that Cabinet is superior, and even the ruling party thinks that the Diet and the Cabinet are in opposition to one another. Also, by separating the government and the ruling party, they are able to further avoid any political responsibility.

The most serious issue concerning the question of the Cabinet is the clear establishment of Cabinet powers during a state of emergency. Not only the LDP, but also other parties and bureaucracies have no understanding of what to do if a state of emergency occurs. Their solution, therefore is to resort to measures that are above the law.

This is of grave concern. It is a denial of democracy, and the argument of dictatorship. Acting above the law is to assert that the ruler is the state. Democracy should mean protecting the promises that were agreed to by all, but this becomes a farce when the solution is to act above the law. Clear rules must be established in preparation for a state of emergency. Democracy must always be carried out according to the due process of law.

This not only applies to wars, but also to natural disasters. If any lesson is to be learned from the Kobe earthquake, it is the importance of crisis management.

Therefore, as one of the powers of the Cabinet, a provision should be created to grant it greater authority during a state of emergency.

(State of emergency)
> In the case where a state of emergency has arisen which has the potential to have an important influence on the nation or the lives of the people, the Cabinet shall declare a state of emergency. Matters concerning states of emergency shall be fixed by law.
>
> (Ozawa proposal)

The issue of reporting to the House of Representatives (the Diet) was discussed during the debate over the 'Guidelines' bills but, because Japan has a parliamentary Cabinet system whereby the party that occupies a majority forms the Cabinet, fundamentally there should be no question of difference in the will of the Cabinet and the Diet. Further, it may perhaps be better for the emperor to make the declaration of a state of emergency as one of his constitutional functions.

Finally, concerning the Cabinet system, I would like to point out that arguments for public elections for the Prime Minister are mistaken. The public election of the Prime Minister would mean the abolition of the emperor system. You cannot build up an argument for public elections, while supporting the emperor system.

One of the emperor's constitutional functions is the attestation of the appointment and dismissal of ministers of state. The speaker of the House of Representatives, however, does not need to be attested by the emperor, nor does the emperor attest Diet members. This is because Diet members are chosen directly by the people, who are the sovereign power. The will of the people as sovereign is final and, at the same time, absolute. That is why there is no need for the attestation of the emperor in the name of the people. The public election of the Prime Minister would mean that the people would be voting directly for the country's highest position of responsibility. The elected Prime Minister would certainly be the head of state, or, in other words, the President, and in these circumstances, it would be impossible to have in place an emperor. Therefore, apart from taking the abolition of the emperor system as a prerequisite, the public election of the Prime Minister is not tenable as a system.

Establishing a Constitutional Court

In the next three chapters: Chapter 6, the 'Judiciary' (Articles 76–82), Chapter 7, 'Finance' (Articles 83–91) and Chapter 8, 'Local Self-government' (Articles 92–95), I shall limit myself to pointing out the significant problems.

The biggest problem with the judicial system is that the courts progress extremely slowly. Rather than the Constitution, the laws governing procedure firstly need to be reformed. The Japanese judicial system may already be fatigued to breaking point. Courts could be sped up through the rationalization of the legal system.

The other thing that I would like to propose is the creation of a Constitutional Court. I would like to establish a court for dealing only with constitutional lawsuits.

> The whole judicial power is vested in a Constitutional Court, a Supreme Court, and in such inferior courts as are established by law.
>
> (Ozawa proposal)

As I have already stated, the Japanese Constitution contains many abstract phrases, resulting in the courts having to deal with a large number of ridiculous constitutional lawsuits, some of which may take ten or twenty years for a decision to be reached. Under normal circumstances, the court should dismiss these cases, but they are approaching constitutional issues in a negative way due to the backlog in civil and criminal cases. Even if one accepts that each issue has its own set of circumstances, courts often avoid coming to a clear decision. They should provide a rational decision, whatever their conclusion might be.

Judicial power is the stronghold of the Constitution. We should establish a Constitutional Court, like that of Germany, France and Italy, and entrust it with the role of determining the constitutionality of any law, order, regulation or official act, and amend Article 81.

> The Constitutional Court is the court of last resort with power to determine the constitutionality of any law, order, regulation or official act.
>
> (Ozawa proposal)

Constitutional Court judges should not be chosen in the same way as other judges, but should be appointed by the Diet or by the Cabinet from former judges or intellectual circles.

Chapter 7, which concerns finance, is said not to have as many problem areas as other chapters. However, it is often said that the country's finances are on the verge of collapse. Annual budgets (Article 86) and the reporting of the state of national finances (Article 91) are subjects which should become issues for discussion in the future.

Article 89 has become a focus of constitutional debate recently, with 'private school subsidies,' based on the Private Schools Promotion Subsidy Law, at issue.

> No public money or other property shall be expended or appropriated for the use, benefit or maintenance of any religious institution or association, or for any charitable, educational or benevolent enterprises not under the control of public authority.

Reading this article, it is clear that private school subsidies are against the constitution. Given that the first section, which concerns religious institutions and associations, also overlaps with Article 20 about freedom of religion, I think that Article 89 should be revised as soon as possible.

Regarding 'local self-government,' as I wrote in my book, *Blueprint for a New Japan*, a 'Law on the Fundamental Principles of Local Government' should be established, and the unipolarization of Tokyo reversed.[5] Many local authorities are suffering from financial collapse in the same way as the state. We should revise Article 94, which deals with the right of local public entities to 'manage their property, affairs and administration and to enact their own regulations within law.'

Be resolute, Japanese!

So far, I have discussed my proposal for reform of the constitution, but finally we come to a bottleneck. Chapter 9, 'Amendments,' contains only Article 96. Without revising this, arguments for reform have little power of persuasion. Article 96 might as well say, 'this constitution cannot be revised.'

1   Amendments to this constitution shall be initiated by the Diet, through a concurring vote of two-thirds or more of all the members of each House and shall thereupon be submitted to the people for ratification, which shall require the affirmative vote of a majority of all votes cast thereon, at a special referendum or at such election as the Diet shall specify.
2   Amendments when so ratified shall immediately be promulgated by the Emperor in the name of the people, as an integral part of this constitution.

Two-thirds of all the members is an insurmountable barrier. As the term of office of the House of Councillors is six years, even if a party gains an overwhelming majority in the House of Representatives, a two-thirds majority is unattainable. Perhaps it might be possible to revise this in order to allow constitutional amendments through the approval of one-half of members.

According to most recent public opinion polls, the majority of the people of Japan are in favor of reforming the constitution. Even then, two-thirds of the Diet remains an insurmountable barrier to change. The Liberal Party is therefore proposing to establish the legal basis for carrying out referenda in order to revise the constitution. This law provides for the establishment of referendum dates, the provision of information to the electorate, the form of the vote, expenses, penal regulations, and so on. National referendum campaigns are, as a principle, free. The aim is to provoke debate. We must not give up, even if we cannot amend the constitution.

For example, can the national referendum not be held before the Diet vote? The constitution is for the people. In order to change a constitution which no longer suits the times, the will of the people as sovereign should be respected first.

We also have the option of returning to the constitutional debate of the Kyoto school. That is to say, to put it to the vote whether to declare the current constitution invalid in the Diet, and to create a new constitution instead.

The Japanese are a cautious people, and so find it difficult to make resolute decisions to change the current situation. Despite this there is the fear that, should a 'Taepodong' missile be fired at Japan, for example, the Japanese people would end up acting in an extreme way. Media commentary would heat up, and, without perhaps going as far as calling the Americans and the British barbarians of the pre-war era, headlines such as 'Strike North Korea Immediately!' may spring up. This would be little more than history repeating itself.

Therefore, I ask people to consider calmly what I have said. Each person should come to their own careful considered conclusion, not just follow what Ozawa Ichirō has said.

Notes

1 Taken from <www.france.diplomatie.fr/france/instit/constit/titre16.gb.html> Title XVI, Article 89, Paragraph 4. The English translation was prepared under the joint responsibility of the Press, Information and Communication Directorate of the Ministry of Foreign Affairs and the European Affairs Department of the National Assembly.
2 Taken from <www.jura.uni-sb.de/law/GG/gg14.htm> Article 146.
3 Chapter 7 of the Charter of the United Nations is headed: 'Action with respect to threats to the peace, breaches of the peace, and acts of aggression.' Taken from <www.un.org/aboutun/charter/chapter7.htm>.
4 In the Ehime Tamagushiryō Decision of April 2 1997, concerning donations made for the purchase of sprigs of sacred trees to be given as offerings at Yasukuni Shrine, or other national shrines, the Supreme Court ruled that public donations count as religious activity, which is prohibited in the constitution, and thus are unconstitutional. The Supreme Court ordered the then governor of Ehime Prefecture to return 166,000 yen to the Prefecture. This was the first time that the Supreme Court issued a ruling of unconstitutionality, and led to renewed debate over official visits to Yasukuni Shrine.
5 Ichirō Ozawa, *Blueprint for a New Japan*, Tokyo, Kodansha International, 1994, pp. 78, 160.

Part 3
Constitution texts

The Constitution of the Empire of Japan (Meiji Constitution, 1889)[1]

Imperial Oath sworn in the sanctuary in the Imperial Palace

We, the Successor to the prosperous Throne of Our Predecessors, do humbly and solemnly swear to the Imperial Founder of Our House and to Our other Imperial Ancestors that, in pursuance of a great policy co-extensive with the Heavens and with the Earth, We shall maintain and secure from decline the ancient form of government.

In consideration of the progressive tendency of the course of human affairs and in parallel with the advance of civilization, We deem it expedient, in order to give clearness and distinctness to the instructions bequeathed by the Imperial Founder of Our House and by Our other Imperial Ancestors, to establish fundamental laws formulated into express provisions of law, so that, on the one hand, Our Imperial posterity may possess an express guide for the course they are to follow, and that, on the other, Our subjects shall thereby be enabled to enjoy a wider range of action in giving Us their support, and that the observance of Our laws shall continue to the remotest ages of time. We will thereby to give greater firmness to the stability of Our country and to promote the welfare of all the people within the boundaries of Our dominions; and We now establish the Imperial House Law and the Constitution. These Laws come to only an exposition of grand precepts for the conduct of the government, bequeathed by the Imperial Founder of Our House and by Our other Imperial Ancestors. That we have been so fortunate in Our reign, in keeping with the tendency of the times, as to accomplish this work, We owe to the glorious Spirits of the Imperial Founder of Our House and of Our other Imperial Ancestors.

We now reverently make Our prayer to Them and to Our Illustrious Father, and implore the help of Their Sacred Spirits, and make to Them solemn oath never at this time nor in the future to fail to be an example to our subjects in the observance of the Laws hereby established.

May the heavenly Spirits witness this Our solemn Oath.

Imperial rescript on the promulgation of the Constitution

Whereas We make it the joy and glory of Our heart to behold the prosperity of Our country, and the welfare of Our subjects, We do hereby, in virtue of the

Supreme power We inherit from Our Imperial Ancestors, promulgate the present immutable fundamental law, for the sake of Our present subjects and their descendants.

The Imperial Founder of Our House and Our other Imperial ancestors, by the help and support of the forefathers of Our subjects, laid the foundation of Our Empire upon a basis, which is to last forever. That this brilliant achievement embellishes the annals of Our country, is due to the glorious virtues of Our Sacred Imperial ancestors, and to the loyalty and bravery of Our subjects, their love of their country and their public spirit. Considering that Our subjects are the descendants of the loyal and good subjects of Our Imperial Ancestors, We doubt not but that Our subjects will be guided by Our views, and will sympathize with all Our endeavors, and that, harmoniously cooperating together, they will share with Us Our hope of making manifest the glory of Our country, both at home and abroad, and of securing forever the stability of the work bequeathed to Us by Our Imperial Ancestors.

Preamble

Having, by virtue of the glories of Our Ancestors, ascended the throne of a lineal succession unbroken for ages eternal; desiring to promote the welfare of, and to give development to the moral and intellectual faculties of Our beloved subjects, the very same that have been favored with the benevolent care and affectionate vigilance of Our Ancestors; and hoping to maintain the prosperity of the State, in concert with Our people and with their support, We hereby promulgate, in pursuance of Our Imperial Rescript of the twelfth day of the tenth month of the fouteenth year of Meiji, a fundamental law of the State, to exhibit the principles, by which We are guided in Our conduct, and to point out to what Our descendants and Our subjects and their descendants are forever to conform.

The right of sovereignty of the State, We have inherited from Our Ancestors, and We shall bequeath them to Our descendants. Neither We nor they shall in the future fail to wield them, in accordance with the provisions of the Constitution hereby granted.

We now declare to respect and protect the security of the rights and of the property of Our people, and to secure to them the complete enjoyment of the same, within the extent of the provisions of the present Constitution and of the law.

The Imperial Diet shall first be convoked for the twenty-third year of Meiji and the time of its opening shall be the date, when the present Constitution comes into force.

When in the future it may become necessary to amend any of the provisions of the present Constitution, We or Our successors shall assume the initiative right, and submit a project for the same to the Imperial Diet. The Imperial Diet shall pass its vote upon it, according to the conditions imposed by the present Constitution, and in no otherwise shall Our descendants or Our subjects be permitted to attempt any alteration thereof.

Our Ministers of State, on Our behalf, shall be held responsible for the carrying out of the present Constitution, and Our present and future subjects shall forever assume the duty of allegiance to the present Constitution.

Chapter 1 The Emperor

Article 1
The Empire of Japan shall be reigned over and governed by a line of Emperors unbroken for ages eternal.

Article 2.
The Imperial Throne shall be succeeded to by Imperial male descendants, according to the provisions of the Imperial House Law.

Article 3
The Emperor is sacred and inviolable.

Article 4
The Emperor is the head of the Empire, combining in Himself the rights of sovereignty, and exercises them, according to the provisions of the present Constitution.

Article 5
The Emperor exercises the legislative power with the consent of the Imperial Diet.

Article 6
The Emperor gives sanction to laws, and orders them to be promulgated and executed.

Article 7
The Emperor convokes the Imperial Diet, opens, closes, and prorogues it, and dissolves the House of Representatives.

Article 8
The Emperor, in consequence of an urgent necessity to maintain public safety or to avert public calamities, issues, when the Imperial Diet is not sitting, Imperial ordinances in the place of law.

Such Imperial Ordinances are to be laid before the Imperial Diet at its next session, and when the Diet does not approve the said Ordinances, the Government shall declare them to be invalid for the future.

Article 9
The Emperor issues or causes to be issued, the Ordinances necessary for the carrying out of the laws, or for the maintenance of the public peace and order, and for the promotion of the welfare of the subjects. But no Ordinance shall in any way alter any of the existing laws.

Article 10
The Emperor determines the organization of the different branches of the administration, and salaries of all civil and military officers, and appoints and dismisses

the same. Exceptions especially provided for in the present Constitution or in other laws, shall be in accordance with the respective provisions (bearing thereon).

Article 11
The Emperor has the supreme command of the Army and Navy.

Article 12
The Emperor determines the organization and peace standing of the Army and Navy.

Article 13
The Emperor declares war, makes peace, and concludes treaties.

Article 14
The Emperor declares a state of siege.
The conditions and effects of a state of siege shall be determined by law.

Article 15
The Emperor confers titles of nobility, rank, orders and other marks of honor.

Article 16
The Emperor orders amnesty, pardon, commutation of punishments and rehabilitation.

Article 17
(1) A Regency shall be instituted in conformity with the provisions of the Imperial House Law.
(2) The Regent shall exercise the powers appertaining to the Emperor in His name.

Chapter 2 Rights and duties of subjects

Article 18
The conditions necessary for being a Japanese subject shall be determined by law.

Article 19
Japanese subjects may, according to qualifications determined in laws or ordinances, be appointed to civil or military or any other public offices equally.

Article 20
Japanese subjects are amenable to service in the Army or Navy, according to the provisions of law.

Article 21
Japanese subjects are amenable to the duty of paying taxes, according to the provisions of law.

Article 22
Japanese subjects shall have the liberty of abode and of changing the same within the limits of the law.

Article 23
No Japanese subject shall be arrested, detained, tried or punished, unless according to law.

Article 24
No Japanese subject shall be deprived of his right of being tried by the judges determined by law.

Article 25
Except in the cases provided for in the law, the house of no Japanese subject shall be entered or searched without his consent.

Article 26
Except in the cases mentioned in the law, the secrecy of the letters of every Japanese subject shall remain inviolate.

Article 27
The right of property of every Japanese subject shall remain inviolate. Measures necessary to be taken for the public benefit shall be any provided for by law.

Article 28
Japanese subjects shall, within limits not prejudicial to peace and order, and not antagonistic to their duties as subjects, enjoy freedom of religious belief.

Article 29
Japanese subjects shall, within the limits of law, enjoy the liberty of speech, writing, publication, public meetings and associations.

Article 30
Japanese subjects may present petitions, by observing the proper forms of respect, and by complying with the rules specially provided for the same.

Article 31
The provisions contained in the present Chapter shall not affect the exercises of the powers appertaining to the Emperor, in times of war or in cases of a national emergency.

Article 32
Each and every one of the provisions contained in the preceding Articles of the present Chapter, that are not in conflict with the laws or the rules and discipline of the Army and Navy, shall apply to the officers and men of the Army and of the Navy.

Chapter 3 The Imperial Diet

Article 33
The Imperial Diet shall consist of two Houses, a House of Peers and a House of Representatives.

Article 34
The House of Peers shall, in accordance with the ordinance concerning the House of Peers, be composed of the members of the Imperial Family, of the orders of nobility, and of those who have been nominated thereto by the Emperor.

Article 35
The House of Representatives shall be composed of members elected by the people, according to the provisions of the law of Election.

Article 36
No one can at one and the same time be a Member of both Houses.

Article 37
Every law requires the consent of the Imperial Diet.

Article 38
Both Houses shall vote upon projects of law submitted to it by the Government, and may respectively initiate projects of law.

Article 39
A Bill, which has been rejected by either the one or the other of the two Houses, shall not be brought in again during the same session.

Article 40
Both Houses can make representations to the Government, as to laws or upon any other subject. When, however, such representations are not accepted, they cannot be made a second time during the same session.

Article 41
The Imperial Diet shall be convoked every year.

Article 42
A session of the Imperial Diet shall last during three months. In case of necessity, the duration of a session may be prolonged by the Imperial Order.

Article 43
(1) When urgent necessity arises, an extraordinary session may be convoked in addition to the ordinary one.
(2) The duration of an extraordinary session shall be determined by Imperial Order.

Article 44
(1) The opening, closing, prolongation of session and prorogation of the Imperial Diet, shall be effected simultaneously for both Houses.
(2) In case the House of Representatives has been ordered to dissolve, the House of Peers shall at the same time be prorogued.

Article 45
When the House of Representatives has been ordered to dissolve, Members shall be caused by Imperial Order to be newly elected, and the new House shall be convoked within five months from the day of dissolution.

Article 46
No debate can be opened and no vote can be taken in either House of the Imperial Diet, unless not less than one-third of the whole number of Members thereof is present.

Article 47
Votes shall be taken in both Houses by absolute majority. In the case of a tie vote, the President shall have the casting vote.

Article 48
The deliberations of both Houses shall be held in public. The deliberations may, however, upon demand of the Government or by resolution of the House, be held in secret sitting.

Article 49
Both Houses of the Imperial Diet may respectively present addresses to the Emperor.

Article 50
Both Houses may receive petitions presented by subjects.

Article 51
Both Houses may enact, besides what is provided for in the present Constitution and in the Law of the Houses, rules necessary for the management of their internal affairs.

Article 52
No Member of either House shall be held responsible outside the respective Houses, for any opinion uttered or for any vote given in the House. When, however, a Member himself has given publicity to his opinions by public speech, by documents in print or in writing, or by any other similar means, he shall, in the matter, be amenable to the general law.

Article 53
The Members of both Houses shall, during the session, be free from arrest, unless with the consent of the House, except in cases of flagrant delicts, or of offenses connected with a state of internal commotion or with a foreign trouble.

Article 54
The Ministers of State and the Delegates of the Government may, at any time, take seats and speak in either House.

Chapter 4 The Ministers of State and the Privy Council

Article 55
The respective Ministers of State shall give their advice to the Emperor, and be responsible for it.

All Laws, Imperial Ordinances, and Imperial Rescripts of whatever kind, that relate to the affairs of the state, require the countersignature of a Minister of State.

Article 56
The Privy Councillors shall, in accordance with the provisions for the organization of the Privy Council, deliberate upon important matters of State when they have been consulted by the Emperor.

Chapter 5 The Judicature

Article 57
The Judicature shall be exercised by the Courts of Law according to law, in the name of the Emperor.
  The organization of the Courts of Law shall be determined by law.

Article 58
The judges shall be appointed from among those, who possess proper qualifications according to law.
  No judge shall be deprived of his position, unless by way of criminal sentence or disciplinary punishment.
  Rules for disciplinary punishment shall be determined by law.

Article 59
Trials and judgments of a Court shall be conducted publicly. When, however, there exists any fear, that such publicity may be prejudicial to peace and order, or to the maintenance of public morality, the public trial may be suspended by provisions of law or by the decision of the Court of Law.

Article 60
All matters that fall within the competency of a special Court, shall be specially provided for by law.

Article 61
No suit at law, which relates to rights alleged to have been infringed by the illegal measures of the administrative authorities, and which shall come within the competency of the Court of Administrative Litigation specially established by law, shall be taken cognizance of by Court of Law.

Chapter 6 Finance

Article 62
The imposition of a new tax or the modification of the rates (of an existing one) shall be determined by law. However, all such administrative fees or other revenue having the nature of compensation shall not fall within the category of the above clause.
  The raising of national loans and the contracting of other liabilities to the charge of the National Treasury, except those that are provided in the Budget, shall require the consent of the Imperial Diet.

Article 63
The taxes levied at present shall, in so far as they are not remodelled by a new law, be collected according to the old system.

Article 64
The expenditure and revenue of the State require the consent of the Imperial Diet by means of an annual Budget.

Any and all expenditures overpassing the appropriations set forth in the Titles and Paragraphs of the Budget, or that are not provided for in the Budget, shall subsequently require the approbation of the Imperial Diet.

Article 65
The Budget shall be first laid before the House of Representatives.

Article 66
The expenditures of the Imperial House shall be defrayed every year out of the National Treasury, according to the present fixed amount for the same, and shall not require the consent thereto of the Imperial Diet, except in case an increase thereof is found necessary.

Article 67
Those already fixed expenditures based by the Constitution upon the powers appertaining to the Emperor, and such expenditures as may have arisen by the effect of law, or that appertain to the legal obligations of the Government, shall be neither rejected nor reduced by the Imperial Diet, without the concurrence of the Government.

Article 68
In order to meet special requirements, the Government may ask the consent of the Imperial Diet to a certain amount as a Continuing Expenditure Fund, for a previously fixed number of years.

Article 69
In order to supply deficiencies, which are unavoidable, in the Budget, and to meet requirements unprovided for in the same, a Reserve Fund shall be provided in the Budget.

Article 70
When the Imperial Diet cannot be convoked, owing to the external or internal condition of the country, in case of urgent need for the maintenance of public safety, the Government may take all necessary financial measures, by means of an Imperial Ordinance.

In the case mentioned in the preceding clause, the matter shall be submitted to the Imperial Diet at its next session, and its approbation shall be obtained thereto.

Article 71
When the Imperial Diet has not voted on the Budget, or when the Budget has not been brought into actual existence, the Government shall carry out the Budget of the preceding year.

188 *Japan's contested constitution*

Article 72

The final account of the expenditures and revenues of the State shall be verified and confirmed by the Board of Audit, and it shall be submitted by the Government to the Imperial Diet, together with the report of verification of the said board.

The organization and competency of the Board of Audit shall be determined by law separately.

Chapter 7 Supplementary rules

Article 73

When it has become necessary in future to amend the provisions of the present Constitution, a project to the effect shall be submitted to the Imperial Diet by Imperial Order.

In the above case, neither House can open the debate, unless not less than two-thirds of the whole number of Members are present, and no amendment can be passed, unless a majority of not less than two-thirds of the Members present is obtained.

Article 74

No modification of the Imperial House Law shall be required to be submitted to the deliberation of the Imperial Diet.

No provision of the present Constitution can be modified by the Imperial House Law.

Article 75

No modification can be introduced into the Constitution, or into the Imperial House Law, during the time of a Regency.

Article 76

Existing legal enactments, such as laws, regulations, Ordinances, or by whatever names they may be called, shall, so far as they do not conflict with the present Constitution, continue in force.

All existing contracts or orders, that entail obligations upon the Government, and that are connected with expenditure, shall come within the scope of Article 67.

Note

1   The text here is the semi-official translation, which appeared in H. Ito, *Commentaries on the Constitution of the Empire of Japan*, trans. M. Ito, 1889.

The Constitution of Japan (1947)

Preamble

We, the Japanese people, acting through our duly elected representatives in the National Diet, determined that we shall secure for ourselves and our posterity the fruits of peaceful cooperation with all nations and the blessings of liberty throughout this land, and resolved that never again shall we be visited with the horrors of war through the action of government, do proclaim that sovereign power resides with the people and do firmly establish this constitution. Government is a sacred trust of the people, the authority for which is derived from the people, the powers of which are exercised by the representatives of the people, and the benefits of which are enjoyed by the people. This is a universal principle of mankind upon which this constitution is founded. We reject and revoke all constitutions, laws ordinances, and rescripts in conflict herewith.

    We, the Japanese people, desire peace for all time and are deeply conscious of the high ideals controlling human relationship and we have determined to preserve our security and existence, trusting in the justice and faith of the peace-loving peoples of the world. We desire to occupy an honored place in an international society striving for the preservation of peace, and the banishment of tyranny and slavery, oppression and intolerance for all time from the earth. We recognize that all peoples of the world have the right to live in peace, free from fear and want.

    We believe that no nation is responsible to itself alone, but that laws of political morality are universal; and that obedience to such laws is incumbent upon all nations who would sustain their own sovereignty and justify their sovereign relationship with other nations. We, the Japanese people, pledge our national honor to accomplish these high ideals and purposes with all our resources.

Chapter 1 The Emperor

Article 1
The Emperor shall be the symbol of the State and the unity of the people, deriving his position from the will of the people with whom resides sovereign power.

Article 2
The Imperial Throne shall be dynastic and succeeded to in accordance with the Imperial House Law passed by the Diet.

Article 3
The advice and approval of the Cabinet shall be required for all acts of the Emperor in matters of state, and the Cabinet shall be responsible therefor.

Article 4
(1) The Emperor shall perform only such acts in matters of state as are provided for in this Constitution and he shall not have powers related to government.
(2) The Emperor may delegate the performance of his acts in matters of state as may be provided for by law.

Article 5
When, in accordance with the Imperial House Law, a Regency is established, the Regent shall perform his acts in matters of state in the Emperor's name. In this case, paragraph one of the preceding Article will be applicable.

Article 6
(1) The Emperor shall appoint the Prime Minister as designated by the Diet.
(2) The Emperor shall appoint the Chief Judge of the Supreme Court as designated by the Cabinet.

Article 7
The Emperor shall, with the advice and approval of the Cabinet, perform the following acts in matters of state on behalf of the people:
(1) Promulgation of amendments of the constitution, laws, cabinet orders and treaties.
(2) Convocation of the Diet.
(3) Dissolution of the House of Representatives.
(4) Proclamation of general election of members of the Diet.
(5) Attestation of the appointment and dismissal of Ministers of State and other officials as provided for by law, and of full powers and credentials of Ambassadors and Ministers.
(6) Attestation of general and special amnesty, commutation of punishment, reprieve, and restoration of rights.
(7) Awarding of honors.
(8) Attestation of instruments of ratification and other diplomatic documents as provided for by law.
(9) Receiving foreign ambassadors and ministers.
(10) Performance of ceremonial functions.

Article 8
No property can be given to, or received by, the Imperial House, nor can any gifts be made therefrom, without the authorization of the Diet.

Chapter 2 Renunciation of War

Article 9
(1) Aspiring sincerely to an international peace based on justice and order, the Japanese people forever renounce war as a sovereign right of the nation and the threat or use of force as means of settling international disputes.
(2) In order to accomplish the aim of the preceding paragraph, land, sea, and air forces, as well as other war potential, will never be maintained. The right of belligerency of the state will not be recognized.

Chapter 3 Rights and Duties of the People

Article 10
The conditions necessary for being a Japanese national shall be determined by law.

Article 11
The people shall not be prevented from enjoying any of the fundamental human rights. These fundamental human rights guaranteed to the people by this Constitution shall be conferred upon the people of this and future generations as eternal and inviolate rights.

Article 12
The freedoms and rights guaranteed to the people by this Constitution shall be maintained by the constant endeavor of the people, who shall refrain from any abuse of these freedoms and rights and shall always be responsible for utilizing them for the public welfare.

Article 13
All of the people shall be respected as individuals. Their right to life, liberty, and the pursuit of happiness shall, to the extent that it does not interfere with the public welfare, be the supreme consideration in legislation and in other governmental affairs.

Article 14
(1) All of the people are equal under the law and there shall be no discrimination in political, economic or social relations because of race, creed, sex, social status or family origin.
(2) Peers and peerage shall not be recognized.
(3) No privilege shall accompany any award of honor, decoration or any distinction, nor shall any such award be valid beyond the lifetime of the individual who now holds or hereafter may receive it.

Article 15
(1) The people have the inalienable right to choose their public officials and to dismiss them.
(2) All public officials are servants of the whole community and not of any group thereof.

(3) Universal adult suffrage is guaranteed with regard to the election of public officials.
(4) In all elections, secrecy of the ballot shall not be violated. A voter shall not be answerable, publicly or privately, for the choice he has made.

Article 16
Every person shall have the right of peaceful petition for the redress of damage, for the removal of public officials, for the enactment, repeal or amendment of laws, ordinances or regulations and for other matters; nor shall any person be in any way discriminated against for sponsoring such a petition.

Article 17
Every person may sue for redress as provided by law from the State or a public entity, in case he has suffered damage through illegal act of any public official.

Article 18
No person shall be held in bondage of any kind. Involuntary servitude, except as punishment for crime, is prohibited.

Article 19
Freedom of thought and conscience shall not be violated.

Article 20
(1) Freedom of religion is guaranteed to all. No religious organization shall receive any privileges from the State, nor exercise any political authority.
(2) No person shall be compelled to take part in any religious acts, celebration, rite or practice.
(3) The State and its organs shall refrain from religious education or any other religious activity.

Article 21
(1) Freedom of assembly and association as well as speech, press and all other forms of expression are guaranteed.
(2) No censorship shall be maintained, nor shall the secrecy of any means of communication be violated.

Article 22
(1) Every person shall have freedom to choose and change his residence and to choose his occupation to the extent that it does not interfere with the public welfare.
(2) Freedom of all persons to move to a foreign country and to divest themselves of their nationality shall be inviolate.

Article 23
Academic freedom is guaranteed.

Article 24
(1) Marriage shall be based only on the mutual consent of both sexes and it shall be maintained through mutual cooperation with the equal rights of husband and wife as a basis.

(2) With regard to choice of spouse, property rights, inheritance, choice of domicile, divorce and other matters pertaining to marriage and the family, laws shall be enacted from the standpoint of individual dignity and the essential equality of the sexes.

Article 25
(1) All people shall have the right to maintain the minimum standards of wholesome and cultured living.
(2) In all spheres of life, the State shall use its endeavors for the promotion and extension of social welfare and security, and of public health.

Article 26
(1) All people shall have the right to receive an equal education correspondent to their ability, as provided for by law.
(2) All people shall be obligated to have all boys and girls under their protection receive ordinary education as provided for by law. Such compulsory education shall be free.

Article 27
(1) All people shall have the right and the obligation to work.
(2) Standards for wages, hours, rest and other working conditions shall be fixed by law.
(3) Children shall not be exploited.

Article 28
The right of workers to organize and to bargain and act collectively is guaranteed.

Article 29
(1) The right to own or to hold property is inviolable.
(2) Property rights shall be defined by law, in conformity with the public welfare.
(3) Private property may be taken for public use upon just compensation therefor.

Article 30
The people shall be liable to taxation as provided for by law.

Article 31
No person shall be deprived of life or liberty, nor shall any other criminal penalty be imposed, except according to procedure established by law.

Article 32
No person shall be denied the right of access to the courts.

Article 33
No person shall be apprehended except upon warrant issued by a competent judicial officer which specifies the offense with which the person is charged, unless he is apprehended, the offense being committed.

Article 34
No person shall be arrested or detained without being at once informed of the

charges against him or without the immediate privilege of counsel; nor shall he be detained without adequate cause; and upon demand of any person such cause must be immediately shown in open court in his presence and the presence of his counsel.

Article 35
(1) The right of all persons to be secure in their homes, papers and effects against entries, searches and seizures shall not be impaired except upon warrant issued for adequate cause and particularly describing the place to be searched and things to be seized, or except as provided by Article 33.
(2) Each search or seizure shall be made upon separate warrant issued by a competent judicial officer.

Article 36
The infliction of torture by any public officer and cruel punishments are absolutely forbidden.

Article 37
(1) In all criminal cases the accused shall enjoy the right to a speedy and public trial by an impartial tribunal.
(2) He shall be permitted full opportunity to examine all witnesses, and he shall have the right of compulsory process for obtaining witnesses on his behalf at public expense.
(3) At all times the accused shall have the assistance of competent counsel who shall, if the accused is unable to secure the same by his own efforts, be assigned to his use by the State.

Article 38
(1) No person shall be compelled to testify against himself.
(2) Confession made under compulsion, torture or threat, or after prolonged arrest or detention shall not be admitted in evidence.
(3) No person shall be convicted or punished in cases where the only proof against him is his own confession.

Article 39
No person shall be held criminally liable for an act which was lawful at the time it was committed, or of which he had been acquitted, nor shall he be placed in double jeopardy.

Article 40
Any person may, in case he is acquitted after he has been arrested or detained, sue the State for redress as provided for by law.

Chapter 4 The Diet

Article 41
The Diet shall be the highest organ of the state power, and shall be the sole law-making organ of the State.

Article 42
The Diet shall consist of two Houses, namely the House of Representatives and the House of Councillors.

Article 43
(1) Both Houses shall consist of elected members, representative of all the people.
(2) The number of the members of each House shall be fixed by law.

Article 44
The qualifications of members of both Houses and their electors shall be fixed by law. However, there shall be no discrimination because of race, creed, sex, social status, family origin, education, property or income.

Article 45
The term of office of members of the House of Representatives shall be four years. However, the term shall be terminated before the full term is up in case the House of Representatives is dissolved.

Article 46
The term of office of members of the House of Councillors shall be six years, and election for half the members shall take place every three years.

Article 47
Electoral districts, method of voting and other matters pertaining to the method of election of members of both Houses shall be fixed by law.

Article 48
No person shall be permitted to be a member of both Houses simultaneously.

Article 49
Members of both Houses shall receive appropriate annual payment from the national treasury in accordance with law.

Article 50
Except in cases as provided for by law, members of both Houses shall be exempt from apprehension while the Diet is in session, and any members apprehended before the opening of the session shall be freed during the term of the session upon demand of the House.

Article 51
Members of both Houses shall not be held liable outside the House for speeches, debates or votes cast inside the House.

Article 52
An ordinary session of the Diet shall be convoked once per year.

Article 53
The Cabinet may determine to convoke extraordinary sessions of the Diet. When a quarter or more of the total members of either House makes the demand, the Cabinet must determine on such convocation.

Article 54

(1) When the House of Representatives is dissolved, there must be a general election of members of the House of Representatives within forty (40) days from the date of dissolution, and the Diet must be convoked within thirty (30) days from the date of the election.

(2) When the House of Representatives is dissolved, the House of Councillors is closed at the same time. However, the Cabinet may, in time of national emergency, convoke the House of Councillors in emergency session.

(3) Measures taken at such session as mentioned in the proviso of the preceding paragraph shall be provisional and shall become null and void unless agreed to by the House of Representatives within a period of ten (10) days after the opening of the next session of the Diet.

Article 55

Each House shall judge disputes related to qualifications of its members. However, in order to deny a seat to any member, it is necessary to pass a resolution by a majority of two-thirds or more of the members present.

Article 56

(1) Business cannot be transacted in either House unless one-third or more of total membership is present.

(2) All matters shall be decided, in each House, by a majority of those present, except as elsewhere provided for in the Constitution, and in case of a tie, the presiding officer shall decide the issue.

Article 57

(1) Deliberation in each House shall be public. However, a secret meeting may be held where a majority of two-thirds or more of those members present passes a resolution therefor.

(2) Each House shall keep a record of proceedings. This record shall be published and given general circulation, excepting such parts of proceedings of secret session as may be deemed to require secrecy.

(3) Upon demand of one-fifth or more of the members present, votes of the members on any matter shall be recorded in the minutes.

Article 58

(1) Each House shall select its own president and other officials.

(2) Each House shall establish its rules pertaining to meetings, proceedings and internal discipline, and may punish members for disorderly conduct. However, in order to expel a member, a majority of two-thirds or more of those members present must pass a resolution thereon.

Article 59

(1) A bill becomes a law on passage by both Houses, except as otherwise provided for by the Constitution.

(2) A bill, which is passed by the House of Representatives, and upon which the House of Councillors makes a decision different from that of the House of

Representatives, becomes a law when passed a second time by the House of Representatives by a majority of two-thirds or more of the members present.
(3) The provision of the preceding paragraph does not preclude the House of Representatives from calling for the meeting of a joint committee of both Houses, provided for by law.
(4) Failure by the House of Councillors to take final action within sixty (60) days after receipt of a bill passed by the House of Representatives, time in recess excepted, may be determined by the House of Representatives to constitute a rejection of the said bill by the House of Councillors.

Article 60
(1) The budget must first be submitted to the House of Representatives.
(2) Upon consideration of the budget, when the House of Councillors makes a decision different from that of the House of Representatives, and when no agreement can be reached even through a joint committee of both Houses, provided for by law, or in the case of failure by the House of Councillors to take final action within thirty (30) days, the period of recess excluded, after the receipt of the budget passed by the House of Representatives, the decision of the House of Representatives shall be the decision of the Diet.

Article 61
The second paragraph of the preceding Article applies also to the Diet approval required for the conclusion of treaties.

Article 62:
Each House may conduct investigations in relation to government, and may demand the presence and testimony of witnesses, and the production of records.

Article 63
The Prime Minister and other Ministers of State may, at any time, appear in either House for the purpose of speaking on bills, regardless of whether they are members of the House or not. They must appear when their presence is required in order to give answers or explanations.

Article 64
(1) The Diet shall set up an impeachment court from among the members of both Houses for the purposes of trying those judges against whom removal proceedings have been instituted.
(2) Matters relating to impeachment shall be provided for by law.

Chapter 5 The Cabinet

Article 65
Executive power shall be vested in the Cabinet.

Article 66
(1) The Cabinet shall consist of the Prime Minister, who shall be its head, and other Ministers of State, as provided for by law.

(2) The Prime Minister and other Ministers of State must be civilians.
(3) The Cabinet shall, in the exercise of executive power, be collectively responsible to the Diet.

Article 67
(1) The Prime Minister shall be designated from among the members of the Diet by a resolution of the Diet. This designation shall precede all other business.
(2) If the House of Representatives and the House of Councillors disagree and if no agreement can be reached even through a joint committee of both Houses, provided for by law, or the House of Councillors fails to make designation within ten (10) days, exclusive of the period of recess, after the House of Representatives has made designation, the decision of the House of Representatives shall be the decision of the Diet.

Article 68
(1) The Prime Minister shall appoint the Ministers of State. However, a majority of their number must be chosen from among the members of the Diet.
(2) The Prime Minister may remove the Ministers of State as he chooses.

Article 69
If the House of Representatives passes a non-confidence resolution, or rejects a confidence resolution, the Cabinet shall resign en masse, unless the House of Representatives is dissolved within ten (10) days.

Article 70
When there is a vacancy in the post of Prime Minister, or upon the first convocation of the Diet after a general election of members of the House of Representatives, the Cabinet shall resign en masse.

Article 71
In the cases mentioned in the two preceding Articles, the Cabinet shall continue its functions until the time when a new Prime Minister is appointed.

Article 72
The Prime Minister, representing the Cabinet, submits bills, reports on general national affairs and foreign relations to the Diet and exercises control and supervision over various administrative branches.

Article 73
The Cabinet shall, in addition to other general administrative functions, perform the following functions:

1   Administer the law faithfully; conduct affairs of state.
2   Manage foreign affairs.
3   Conclude treaties. However, it shall obtain prior or, depending on circumstances, subsequent approval of the Diet.
4   Administer the civil service, in accordance with standards established by law.
5   Prepare the budget, and present it to the Diet.

6   Enact cabinet orders in order to execute the provisions of this Constitution and of the law. However, it cannot include penal provisions in such cabinet orders unless authorized by such law.
7   Decide on general amnesty, special amnesty, commutation of punishment, reprieve, and restoration of rights.

Article 74
All laws and cabinet orders shall be signed by the competent Minister of State and countersigned by the Prime Minister.

Article 75
The Ministers of State shall not, during their tenure of office, be subject to legal action without the consent of the Prime Minister. However, the right to take that action is not impaired hereby.

Chapter 6 Judiciary

Article 76
(1) The whole judicial power is vested in a Supreme Court and in such inferior courts as are established by law.
(2) No extraordinary tribunal shall be established, nor shall any organ or agency of the Executive be given final judicial power.
(3) All judges shall be independent in the exercise of their conscience and shall be bound only by this Constitution and the laws.

Article 77
(1) The Supreme Court is vested with the rule-making power under which it determines the rules of procedure and of practice, and of matters relating to attorneys, the internal discipline of the courts and the administration of judicial affairs.
(2) Public procurators shall be subject to the rule-making power of the Supreme Court.
(3) The Supreme Court may delegate the power to make rules for inferior courts to such courts.

Article 78
Judges shall not be removed except by public impeachment unless judicially declared mentally or physically incompetent to perform official duties. No disciplinary action against judges shall be administered by any executive organ or agency.

Article 79
(1) The Supreme Court shall consist of a Chief Judge and such number of judges as may be determined by law; all such judges excepting the Chief Judge shall be appointed by the Cabinet.
(2) The appointment of the judges of the Supreme Court shall be reviewed by the people at the first general election of members of the House of Representatives

following their appointment, and shall be reviewed again at the first general election of members of the House of Representatives after a lapse of ten (10) years, and in the same manner thereafter.

(3) In cases mentioned in the foregoing paragraph, when the majority of the voters favors the dismissal of a judge, he shall be dismissed.

(4) Matters pertaining to review shall be prescribed by law.

(5) The judges of the Supreme Court shall be retired upon the attainment of the age as fixed by law.

(6) All such judges shall receive, at regular stated intervals, adequate compensation which shall not be decreased during their terms of office.

Article 80

(1) The judges of the inferior courts shall be appointed by the Cabinet from a list of persons nominated by the Supreme Court. All such judges shall hold office for a term of ten (10) years with privilege of reappointment, provided that they shall be retired upon the attainment of the age as fixed by law.

(2) The judges of the inferior courts shall receive, at regular stated intervals, adequate compensation which shall not be decreased during their terms of office.

Article 81

The Supreme Court is the court of last resort with power to determine the constitutionality of any law, order, regulation or official act.

Article 82

(1) Trials shall be conducted and judgement declared publicly.

(2) Where a court unanimously determines publicity to be dangerous to public order or morals, a trial may be conducted privately, but trials of political offenses, offenses involving the press or cases wherein the rights of people as guaranteed in Chapter 3 of this Constitution are in question shall always be conducted publicly.

Chapter 7 Finance

Article 83

The power to administer national finances shall be exercised as the Diet shall determine.

Article 84

No new taxes shall be imposed or existing ones modified except by law or under such conditions as law may prescribe.

Article 85

No money shall be expended, nor shall the State obligate itself, except as authorized by the Diet.

Article 86

The Cabinet shall prepare and submit to the Diet for its consideration and decision a budget for each fiscal year.

Article 87
(1) In order to provide for unforeseen deficiencies in the budget, a reserve fund may be authorized by the Diet to be expended upon the responsibility of the Cabinet.
(2) The Cabinet must get subsequent approval of the Diet for all payments from the reserve fund.

Article 88
All property of the Imperial Household shall belong to the State. All expenses of the Imperial Household shall be appropriated by the Diet in the budget.

Article 89
No public money or other property shall be expended or appropriated for the use, benefit or maintenance of any religious institution or association, or for any charitable, educational or benevolent enterprises not under the control of public authority.

Article 90
(1) Final accounts of the expenditures and revenues of the State shall be audited annually by a Board of Audit and submitted by the Diet, together with the statement of audit, during the fiscal year immediately following the period covered.
(2) The organization and competency of the Board of Audit shall be determined by law.

Article 91
At regular intervals and at least annually the Cabinet shall report to the Diet and the people on the state of national finances.

Chapter 8 Local self-government

Article 92
Regulations concerning organization and operations of local public entities shall be fixed by law in accordance with the principle of local autonomy.

Article 93
(1) The local public entities shall establish assemblies as their deliberative organs, in accordance with law.
(2) The chief executive officers of all local public entities, the members of their assemblies, and such other local officials as may be determined by law shall be elected by direct popular vote within their several communities.

Article 94
Local public entities shall have the right to manage their property, affairs and administration and to enact their own regulations within law.

Article 95
A special law, applicable only to one local public entity, cannot be enacted by the Diet without the consent of the majority of the voters of the local public entity concerned, obtained in accordance with law.

Chapter 9 Amendments

Article 96

1) Amendments to this constitution shall be initiated by the Diet, through a concurring vote of two-thirds or more of all the members of each House and shall thereupon be submitted to the people for ratification, which shall require the affirmative vote of a majority of all votes cast thereon, at a special referendum or at such election as the Diet shall specify.

2) Amendments when so ratified shall immediately be promulgated by the Emperor in the name of the people, as an integral part of this constitution.

Chapter 10 Supreme law

Article 97

The fundamental human rights by this constitution guaranteed to the people of Japan are fruits of the age-old struggle of man to be free; they have survived the many exacting tests for durability and are conferred upon this and future generations in trust, to be held for all time inviolate.

Article 98

(1) This constitution shall be the supreme law of the nation and no law, ordinance, imperial rescript or other act of government, or part thereof, contrary to the provisions hereof, shall have legal force or validity.

(2) The treaties concluded by Japan and established laws of nations shall be faithfully observed.

Article 99

The Emperor or the Regent as well as Ministers of State, members of the Diet, judges, and all other public officials have the obligation to respect and uphold this constitution.

Chapter 11 Supplementary provisions

Article 100

(1) This constitution shall be enforced as from the day when the period of six months will have elapsed counting from the day of its promulgation.

(2) The enactment of laws necessary for the enforcement of this constitution, the election of members of the House of Councillors and the procedure for the convocation of the Diet and other preparatory procedures necessary for the enforcement of this constitution may be executed before the day prescribed in the preceding paragraph.

Article 101

If the House of Councillors is not constituted before the effective date of this constitution, the House of Representatives shall function as the Diet until such time as the House of Councillors shall be constituted.

Article 102
The term of office for half the members of the House of Councillors serving in the first term under this constitution shall be three years. Members falling under this category shall be determined in accordance with law.

Article 103
The Ministers of State, members of the House of Representatives, and judges in office on the effective date of this constitution, and all other public officials who occupy positions corresponding to such positions as are recognized by this constitution shall not forfeit their positions automatically on account of the enforcement of this constitution unless otherwise specified by law. When, however, successors are elected or appointed under the provisions of this constitution, they shall forfeit their positions as a matter of course.

The Constitution of Japan, November 3 1946

I rejoice that the foundation for the construction of a new Japan has been laid according to the will of the Japanese people, and hereby sanction and promulgate the amendments of the Imperial Japanese Constitution effected following the consultation with the Privy Council and the decision of the Imperial Diet made in accordance with Article 73 of the said Constitution.

Signed:

HIROHITO, Seal of the Emperor, This third day of the eleventh month of the twenty-first year of Showa (November 3 1946).

Countersigned:

Prime Minister and concurrently
   Minister for Foreign Affairs
  YOSHIDA Shigeru,
Minister of State
  Baron SHIDEHARA Kijuro,
Minister of Justice
  KIMURA Tokutaro,
Minister for Home Affairs
  OMURA Seiichi,
Minister of Education
  TANAKA Kotaro,
Minister of Agriculture and Forestry
  WADA Hiroo,
Minister of State
  SAITO Takao,
Minister of Communication
  HITOTSUMATSU Sadayoshi,

Minister of Commerce and Industry
  HOSHIJIMA Jiro,
Minister of Welfare
  KAWAI Yoshinari,
Minister of State
  UEHARA Etsujiro,
Minister of Transportation
  HIRATSUKA Tsunejiro,
Minister of Finance
  ISHIBASHI Tanzan,
Minister of State
  KANAMORI Tokujiro,
Minister of State
  ZEN Keinosuke.

Index

AEGIS defense systems 121
Africa 131, 135, 156
aid *see* humanitarian issues
Ainu 18
Air Self-Defense Force (ASDF) 14, 146–7
Alien Registration Act 22
amendments *see* constitutional reform
Amnesty International 22
Ampo see US-Japan Security Treaty
antimilitarism *see* pacifism
Aoshima, Y. 160
armaments, conventional 112, 118, 142, 146–7, 150, 175; arms trade 156; *see also* nuclear armaments
Article 9 (1947) 8, 59, 91, 94, 165–6, 192; debate on 4, 41, 42, 86–90, 92–3, 110, 158; implementation of 10, 13–17; 102–9, 143; positive effects of 21–2, 101, 143–4; reassessment of 31–4, 86; revision of 34, 36, 38–40, 59–60, 87, 95–6, 111, 165–6; support for 14, 101, 130–31, 141–4
Asahi Shimbun 12, 32, 40–1, 129–60; proposal 38, 129–60: Article 9 141–4, 157–8; editorial 157–60; humanitarian aid 133–7; main points 129–30; Peace Support Corps 137–40; reform of UN 153–7; response to 158; security arrangements 148–52, 158–9; Self-Defence Forces 145–8, 157–60
ASEAN 124, 151–2
ASEAN Maritime Police 125
Ashida, H. 87, 104
Asia-Pacific, maritime issues 125; relations 120–1, 144, 145, 149, 151; security 124–5, 131
Asia Pacific Human Rights Information Center 23
ASEAN Regional Forum (ARF) 120, 124, 150

Asia-Pacific Economic Cooperation Forum (APEC) 150
Asia-Pacific regional security 108–16
Asia-Pacific Security and Economic Cooperation Conference (CSCA) 124
Assembly for the Establishment of a Sovereign Constitution 14
Atsugi 123
Australia 22, 119–20, 124

Basic Defense Capability, concept of 148
Basic Law on Agriculture (1961) 37–8
Basic Law on Education (1947) 37
Basic Peace Law 38, 41, 93–108, 110–11, 121, 125
Basic Security Law 167
Berlin Wall 3
Blair, T. 40
Blueprint for a New Japan 174
Bosnia 115
Boutros-Ghali, B. 136, 156
Bush, G. 99

Cabinet 171–2; Articles relating to 75–8, 197–9
Cambodia 32–3, 111, 115, 120, 138
Camp Zama 123
Canada 124
censorship 19, 29; Articles relating to 62; *see also* 'chrysanthemum taboo'
Central Intelligence Agency (CIA) 13, 99
centralization of power 20, 25–6
Chief Justice of the Constitutional Court 58
China 6, 22, 44, 105, 117, 120–1, 124–5, 131, 138, 148–51, 158, 164
Choshu clan 167
'chrysanthemum taboo' 12, 35
CIA *see* Central Intelligence Agency
civil rights 19–20, 25, 168–9; Articles

relating to 60–8, 182–3, 191–4; suppression of 11, 18, 24–6, 44
Clark, C. J. 124
Clinton, Bill 124
coastguard 112–13
Cold War 13–15 *passim*, 22, 40, 100, 131, 153, 156; post- 3–4, 29–34, 38, 85, 92, 99, 108, 110, 114–25, 164, 124, 131–2, 137, 141, 144, 147, 148–52, 158
Columbia 87
Common Security Conference for Asia (CSCA) 125
Common Security Conference for Europe (CSCE) 114–15, 120, 124–5
communism 8, 12, 19, 30
compensation 100, 102
Comprehensive Security Council 37
confession, forced 19–20; Articles relating to 66
conscientious objection 129–30, 132
conscription 22, 89, 95, 100, 114–5, 143
conservatism 20, 34–5, 42, 104
Constitution Day 38
Constitution of Japan (1947), Articles
  Amendments (Article 96): 9, 43, 84–5, 175, 202
  Cabinet (Articles 65–75): *Article 65*: 74, 197; *Article 66*: 21, 74, 87, 97, 172, 197–8; *Article 67*: 75, 198, (proposed change to 172); *Articles 68–9*: 75, 198; *Article 70–2*: 76, 198; *Article 73*: 77, 198–9; *Articles 74*: 77, 199; *Articles 75*: 77–8, 199
  Diet (Articles 41–74): *Article 41*: 20, 68, 194; *Article 42*: 68, 170, 195; *Article 43*: 68, 195, (proposed change to 170); *Articles 44–5*: 68, 195; *Article 46*: 69, 195, (proposed change to 170); *Article 47*: 69, 195; *Articles 48–51*: 69, 195; *Articles 52–4*: 70, 196; *Article 55*: 70–1, 196; *Articles 56–8*: 71, 196; *Article 59*: 9, 72, 196–7, (proposed change to 170); *Articles 60*: 72–3, 197; *Articles 61–2*: 73, 197; *Article 63*: 73–4, 197; *Article 64*: 74, 197
  Emperor (Articles 1–8): *Article 1*: 5–7, 57, 164, 189; revision of 35; *Articles 2–3*: 7, 35, 57, 190; *Article 4*: 6–7, 35, 57, 172, 190; *Article 5*: 7, 35, 57, 190; *Article 6*: 7, 35, 58, 165, 190; *Article 7*: 7, 35, 58, 87, 190; *Article 8*: 7, 35, 59, 88, 190
  finance (Articles 83–91): *Articles 83–5*: 82, 200; *Article 86*: 82, 174, 200; *Article 87*: 82, 201; *Article 88*: 83, 201; *Article 89*: 83, 174, 201; *Article 90*: 83, 201; *Article 91*: 83, 174, 201
  Judiciary (Articles 76–82): *Articles 76*: 78, 80, 199; *Article 77–8*: 81, 199; *Article 79*: 79–80, 199–200; *Article 80*: 80, 200; *Article 81*: 78, 200, (proposed change to 174); *Article 82*: 81, 200
  local self-government (Articles 92–5): *Article 92*: 20, 83–4, 201; *Article 93*: 20, 84, 201; *Article 94*: 20, 84, 175, 201; *Article 95*: 20, 25, 84, 201
  renunciation of war (Article 9): *see* Article 9
  rights and duties of the people (Articles 10–40): *Article 10*: 56, 191; *Article 11*: 60, 191; *Article 12*: 9, 22, 168, 191; *Article 13*: 25, 61, 88, 168, 191; *Article 14*: 9, 61, 90, 171, 191; *Article 15*: 67, 191–2; *Article 16*: 20, 61, 67, 192; *Article 17*: 67–8, 192; *Article 18*: 20, 61, 89, 192; *Article 19*: 8, 11, 19, 62, 192; *Article 20*: 6, 9–10, 19, 62, 168, 174, 192; *Article 21*: 9, 19, 62, 192; *Article 22*: 9, 63, 64, 168, 192; *Article 23*: 19, 63, 168, 192; *Article 24*: 5, 9, 63, 192–3; *Article 25*: 25, 63, 164, 193; *Article 26*: 29, 64, 193; *Article 27*: 64, 193; *Article 28*: 19, 64, 193; *Article 29*: 25, 64, 168, 193; *Articles 30–3*: 64, 193; *Article 34*: 65, 193–4; *Article 35*: 65–6, 194; *Article 36*: 20, 66, 194; *Article 37*: 66, 194; *Article 38*: 19, 66, 194; *Articles 39*: 66–7, 194; *Articles 40*: 67, 194
  supplementary provisions (Articles 100–3): *Articles 100–1*: 202; *Articles 102–3*: 203
  Supreme law (Articles 97–9): *Article 97*: 6, 19, 60–1, 85, 202; *Article 98*: 60, 85, 91, 161, 202; *Article 99*: 9, 85, 202
Constitution of Japan (1947), Allied forces draft of 3, 6; Imperial Rescript to 5; origins 3, 5; Preamble 3, 32, 39, 55–6, 90, 94, 163, 166, 189; promulgation of 4, 161; proposed revision of 54–176; role of Emperor in 5; satire of 26–7; and UN Charter 166; validity of 161–3

Constitution of Japan – the right answers 26–9
Constitution of the Empire of Japan (1889) 4–5, 6, 18, 39, 41; Articles: *Articles 1–9*: 181; *Article 10*: 181–2; *Articles 11–22*: 182; *Articles 23–33*: 183; *Articles 34–45*: 184; *Articles 46–55*: 185; *Article 56*: 185–6; *Article 57–63*: 186; *Articles 64–71*: 187; *Article 72*: 187–8; *Article 73–6*: 188; the Diet 183–5; the Emperor 181–2; finance 186–8; Imperial Oath 178; Imperial rescript to 178; Judicature 186; Ministers and Privy Council 185–6; Preamble 180–1; rights and duties of subjects 182–3; supplementary rules 188
Constitution Song 15
constitution, definitions of 4, 103
Constitutional Lawyers' Society 111
Constitutional Reform Committee 106
constitutional reform: amendments 175, Articles relating to 84–5; movements 14–15; proposals: *Asahi Shimbun* 129–60, Ozawa 162–76, *Sekai* 92–128, *Yomiuri Shimbun* 55–91
Constitutional Research Councils 3, 8, 36, 43
constitutional rights 7, 19; restriction of 19, 26; *see also* legal issues
Convention on the Elimination of All Forms of Discrimination Against Women 22
Costa Rica Constitution (1948) 8, 17
crime, organized 169; *see also* violence, war crimes
Criminal Special Law 122
crisis/disasters 36–7, 132, 147, 159–60, 172; management 169, 172–3; *see also* humanitarian issues

Date, A. 16
Defense Agency 88; *see also* Japan Defense Agency
defense issues 33, 34, 37, 40, 59, 60, 87–90, 92–128, 131, 140, 146–8 *passim*, 165–7; national security 86, 88, 142–3, 167–8, 169, 175–6; Articles relating to 59; regional security 108–27, 149–50, 158–9; *see also* militarism, Self-Defense Forces
Defense Power Build-up Programs 147–8
Defense Problems Discussion Group 126
demilitarization 121–5, 131, 147–8

democracy 12, 13, 18, 40, 43, 98, 99, 125, 141, 149; Articles relating to 66–8; and armies 115; *see also* Cabinet, Diet
Democratic Party of Japan 43
Diet, Imperial 183–5; National; 3–5 *passim*, 144, 146, 172–5; Articles relating to 55, 57, 68–78, 82–5, 183–5, 194–7; and constitutional reform 9, 15, 109, 175; and defense issues 96–7, 125–6, 143; democracy 13; legislation 17, 21, 25–6, 35, 43, 133, 136, 139, 140; proposed reform of 37, 40, 169–71; satirized 27; *see also* House of Councillors, House of Representatives
Dietman's Association for Establishment of an Autonomous Constitution 14
disarmament 125–6, 166; nuclear 17, 38, 87, 93–5 *passim*, 98–9, 150–51; problems with 101–2; of SDF 113, 147–9 *passim*
discrimination 18, 42, 153
Dower, J. 6, 16

East Asia 23, 105, 107, 135, 1444, 149–51; *see also* Asia-Pacific, Southeast Asia
Eastern Europe 3
economic factors 25, 33, 39, 90, 96, 103, 141, 151, 152; financial aid 133–5, 166; international 96, 99–101, 132, 149–50; wealth divide 96, 130, 132, 135, 154; *see also* finance
Economic Planning Agency 134
Edo period 163
education 11, 19, 26, 35, 44, 174; Articles relating to 63
Egypt 138
elections 173
Emperor of Japan 5, 36, 40, 100; Articles relating to 57–9, 164, 181–2, 189–90; decline in support for 21; divine status of 5, 164–5, 173; Heisei 10; as 'puppet' ruler 7; religious role 5–6, 10; satirical treatment of 27; support for 34–6 *passim*; as war criminal 6–7, 12; *see also* Hirohito, 'symbolic emperor' system
Endō, O. 109
environmental issues 25, 36–8 *passim*, 59–60, 131, 135–6, 150, 153
equal rights 42, 56; Articles relating to 61, 63; *see also* discrimination

ethnic issues 18; conflicts 101, 108; *see also* discrimination, equal rights
European Union (EU) 114–15
European Conventional Force Reduction treaty (CFE) 120
Evans, G. 124
Export–Import Bank of Japan 136

Far Eastern Military Study 126
fascism 43, 169; *see also* nationalism
Ferris University 12
feudalism 5, 9, 18
finance 92, 174–5; Articles relating to 82–3, 186–8, 200–1; defense expenditure 119, 126
Finland 138
First World War 98, 113
France 8, 100, 129, 174; constitution of 162
Fukase, C. 110, 112

G8 Summit (2000) 24
Garrison for Defense of the Japanese Archipelago 146
Gengohō 10
Germany 5, 7, 10, 33, 99–100, 107, 119, 129, 131, 174; constitution of 162
Ghaly plan 111
globalization 167–8; *see also* international issues
Goken supporters (Constitutionalists) 4
gokenron 93
Golan Heights 33
Green Helmets 114
Ground Self-Defense Force (GSDF) 14, 38, 147–8
Guam 118
Gulf War 3–4, 22, 24–5, 29, 31–2, 103, 115, 118, 131, 140, 158–9, 167

Hague Convention (1907) 162
Haiti 115
Hammarskjold, D. 137
Hanshin Earthquake, Great 132; *see also* Kobe earthquake
Harbinger Party (*Sakigake*) 88, 109
Hasegawa, M. 41
Hata Tsutomū coalition government 13
Hatoyama, I. 43
Heisei emperor 10
Hinomaru flag 10, 30, 35, 44
Hiratsuka, T. 203
Hirohito 7, 10, 23–4, 100, 203; death of 12; *see also* Emperor of Japan

Hiroshima 23
Hitler, A. 100
Hitotsubashi University 110, 112
Hokkaido 18
Hokusei Gakuen University 110
Honduras 33
Hong Kong 149
Hosokawa, M. 13, 20, 31, 109, 126
Hoshijima, J. 203
House of Councillors 58, 68, 70–3, 170–71, 175
House of Representatives 58, 68, 70–5, 113, 161, 170–1, 173, 175
House of Representatives' Constitution Research Council 42
House of Representatives' Special Committee on the Bill for Revision of the Japanese Constitution 88
human rights 6, 9, 18–20, 22–3, 24, 34, 36, 37, 41, 141, 169; abuse 18, 19–20; Articles relating to 6, 19, 60–1, 85, 202
humanitarian issues 36, 38, 91, 98, 154, 159–60; aid 133–8, 166; *see also* human rights, relief organizations

Ienaga, S. 19
Imawano, K. 12
Imperial Court 167
Imperial House Law (1947) 5–6, 27–8, 57–9
Imperial Japanese Army 23, 105
Imperial Rescript on Education (1889) 19, 41
Imperial Throne, the 27, 57
imperialism 40–1, 102; symbols of 10; *see also* Emperor of Japan
imprisonment 19–20; Articles relating to 65–6
Inaba, O. 15
Inchon 13
information, freedom of 98; illegal gathering of 105; *see also* censorship
Inoki, M. 88
Institute of Developing Economics 135–6
International Christian University 110
International Cooperation Agency 134–5, 139
International Cooperation Law 38, 41, 134–5
International Cooperation Research Institute 135
International Covenant on Civil and Political Rights 22

International Covenant on Economic, Social and Cultural Rights 22
International Covenant on Human Rights 20
international issues 7, 13–14, 16–17, 21–2, 29–33, 37, 38, 40, 59–60, 90–1, 95–6, 99, 132–6, 149–50, 166; *see also* United Nations, US-Japan Security Treaty
International Relief Force 38, 98
Iraq 115, 158
Ise Shrine 6
Ishibashi, M. 29
Ishibashi, T. 41, 203
Italy 5, 10, 86, 174
Iwakuni 123
Iwanami Publishing Company 37–8; *see also Sekai*

Japan Communist Party (JCP) 13–14, 26, 109; see also communism
Japan Defense Agency (JDA) 33, 113, 118–19, 126; *see also* Defense Agency
Japan External Trade Organization 136
Japan International Cooperation Agency 135
Japan International Volunteers (JVC) 22
Japan Maritime Safety Board 125
Japan Overseas Cooperation Volunteers 136
judiciary: appointment of 58; Articles relating to 78–81, 186–8, 199–200; conservatism of 20; legal challenges against government 11, 16, 19; proposed reform of 172–4; *see also* Supreme Court

Kaiken (Constitutional Revisionists) 4
Kaishaku Kaiken 4
Kanamori, T. 203
Kawai, Y. 203
Kellogg-Briand Pact (1928) 8
Kempō 17
KGB 99
Kigensetsu 10
Kimigayo anthem 10–12, 30, 35, 44
Kimura, H. 113
Kimura, T. 203
Kishi, N. 13–15, 17, 19, 21–2, 30, 32–3
Kitakyushu City Department of Education 11
Kitakyushu 11–12
Kobe earthquake 37, 172; *see also* Hanshin earthquake

Kokutai 34
Komeitō 109
Korea 6, 13–14, 18, 24, 118–19, 123–5, 131, 137, 147, 151, 158; *see also* North Korea, South Korea
Korean Energy Development Organization 149
Korean War 13–14, 113, 117, 122, 142; *see also* South Korea
Korea-United Nations Status Agreement 122
Koseki, S. 6
Kunihiro, M. 43
Kuwait 158
Kyoto 35, 162
Kyoto University 163

labor movements 19; Articles relating to 64
Land Expropriation Law 122
Land Use Special Measures Law 122
Latin America 131, 152
Law on International Cooperation 133–6
legal issues 94, 98, 134, 169, 172–5; Articles relating to rights 60–8; Articles relating to trials 81; Constitutional Court 173–5; *see also* Diet, judiciary, protests
Liberal View of History Study Group 35
Liberal-Democratic Party (LDP) 9, 12–13, 15, 18–20, 29–30, 34, 37, 39, 88, 101, 104, 107–9, 160, 163, 172, 175
local government 20, 25, 42, 174; Articles relating to 83–4, 201
Lower House of Representatives 3

MacArthur, D. 3, 5, 7, 9, 13, 23, 161
Maeda, T. 103
Mainichi Daily News 12
Malacca Straits 106, 125
Maritime Safety Board 144
Maritime Self-Defense Force (MSDF) 14, 22, 32, 144–5
McNelly, T. 8
media 11, 12, 21, 36–9, 42, 175
Meiji Constitution *see* Constitution of the Empire of Japan
Meiji emperor 6
Meiji Gakuin University 12
Meiji state system 9, 34, 165
Miki, T. 148
militarism 13–15, 21–2, 29–34, 38–41 *passim*, 95, 141; of China 149–50;

support for 33; *see also* military bases, US-Japan Security Treaty
military bases 17, 35, 100, 122–3, 131, 152; effect on local area 25; *see also* Okinawa
military, intervention 115, 117; superpowers 99, 102; Japanese *see* Self-Defense Forces; *see also* conscription
Militia, the 113
Minimum Defensive Force 94, 97–8, 105–7, 111–14
Minister of Justice 15
Ministry for Peace and Disarmament 38, 97–8
Ministry of Education 10–11, 19
Ministry of Finance (MOF) 134
Ministry of Foreign Affairs (MOFA) 22, 134
Ministry of International Trade and Industry (MITI) 134
Ministry of the Navy 113
Ministry of Transport 113
Misawa 123
Miyazawa, K. 15
Miyazawa, T. 164–5
Mori, Y. 13
Mozambique 33, 138
Murayama, T. 43, 126

Nakagawa, Y. 34
Naganuma Case, the 16
Nagasaki 12, 23
Nago City 24–5
Nagoya University 41–2
Nakasone, Y. 14–15, 17, 19, 43, 125
National Anthem and Flag Law 10, 24, 28–9, 30, 43, 44
National Defense Army 34
National Defense Corps 148
National Defense Force 148
National Foundation Day 10
National Guard 94, 98
National Safety Force 113
National Security Council 148
nationalism 34–6, 39, 43; *see also* fascism
Nazism 100
neutrality 21, 102
New Frontier Party (*Shinshintō*) 160
New Liberal Club 13
Nippon Kaigi (Nippon Conference) 35
Nippon no ibuki (Breath of Japan) 35
Nishimura, S. 33
Nixon, R. 14

non-governmental organizations (NGOs) *see* relief organizations
Norota, H. 33
North Atlantic Treaty Organization (NATO) 100, 108, 114, 119, 150–2
North East Asian Peace Conference 124
North Korea 32–3, 105, 119–20, 123–4, 149–50, 158
nuclear armaments 14, 16–17, 23, 33, 59, 87, 96, 99, 150, 156, 157; environmental effects of tests 25; *see also* disarmament, US-Japan Security Treaty
nuclear war, threat of 30–1, 87, 99; *see also* Cold War

Obuchi, K. 33–4, 43
Official Development Assistance (ODA) 100, 116, 134
Oishi, Y. 162–3
Okinawa 5, 17, 23–6, 42, 118, 123, 152; Battle of 23
Okudaira, Y. 110
Omura, S. 203
Open Skies Treaty 120
Organization for Security and Cooperation in Europe 131, 149
Orwell, G. 43
Ota, M. 25
Outline Educational Directives 11
Overseas Development Assistance Charter (ODA) 22, 116
Overseas Economic Cooperation Fund 135–6
Ozaki, Y. 41
Ozawa, I. 40, 41, 43, 104, 166, 169, 171–5; proposal 39–40, 161–75: creation of Constitutional Court 173–5; creation of UN standing army 168–9; elections 174; public welfare 168–9; right of self defense 165–6; special powers of Cabinet 172–3; status of Emperor 164–5; validity of Constitution 161–3

Pacific-Asia Resource Center (PARC) 22–3
pacifism, state 3, 5, 8, 13–17, 21–2, 30, 35, 36–7, 38, 40–3 *passim*, 86, 90, 149, 166; 'war' 16; *see also* Article 9, Basic Peace Law, Peace Support Corps
Palestine 115
Paris Anti-War Treaty (1928) 86

Peace Issues Discussion Group 21
Peace Keeping Bill (1992) 32
Peace Support Corps 38, 130, 134, 137–40, 146, 159
peacekeeping 166; *see also* Peace Support Corps, Self-Defense Forces, United Nations
Peace Treaty *see* San Francisco Peace Treaty
Philippines 86–7, 118, 149
Police Duties Implementation Law 112
police force 19, 104, 112–13 *passim*; international 127, 142
Police Reserve Forces 142
Polidor K. K. 12
Political Reform and Constitutional Revision 110
Potsdam Treaty 8, 162
Private Schools Promotion Subsidy Law 174
Privy Council, Articles relating to 185–6
property rights 18, 25–6; Articles relating to 64–5 *passim*, 83
protests, against government 11, 21, 22, 25

Refugee Convention 22
Regional Contingency Law (1999) 31, 43
Reischauer, E. O. 7
relief organizations 22, 105, 116, 130, 136; *see also* Overseas Development Assistance, Peace Support Corps, United Nations
religion 5–6, 10, 169, 174; Articles relating to freedom of 62; protest against enforcement of 11–12, 28–9
Report on Japanese Defense Problems 124
RIMPAC (Rim of the Pacific) 119, 121
Ronken 4
Rwanda 33, 138
Ryu, S. 157–8

Saitō, T. 203
San Francisco Peace Treaty 7, 23–4, 91, 117, 162
Sarin attack on Tokyo subway 37
Sasaki, S. 162–3
Sasebo 118
Satsuma clan 167
Science and Technology Agency 43
Sealane Defense Operational Research 121
Sealane Defense Study 125
Second World War 23, 38, 99–100, 102, 154
Secrets Protection Law 119

security *see* defense issues
Security Treaty *see* US-Japan Security Treaty
Sekai 40–1; proposal 37–8, 92–128: Basic Peace Law 92–108; conscription 95; disarmament 95, 97, 98; international issues 99–108; Minimum Defensive Force 105–7, 111–14; regional security 108–27; response to 109–10; Self-Defence Force 100–105 *passim*, 106–26; US-Japan Security Treaty 117–21
Self-Defense Forces (SDF) 167; civilian control of 87–8; constitutionality of 14, 29, 36, 37, 86–8, 92–4, 101–6, 108–12, 145–6, 159–60; expansion of 15–17, 43, 111, 113–4, 119, 142, 151; origins 14, 100, 159; as National Security Forces 142; as peacekeepers 22, 31–3, 36, 111, 116, 137–8, 157, 159; proposed reform 38, 41, 98, 121–6, 131, 142–8; regulations governing 144, 158; support for 14
Shidehara, K. 5, 203
Shinto high-priest 6
Shinto ritual 10, 11, 169
Showa emperor *see* Emperor of Japan, Hirohito
Sinai Peninsula 138
Sino-Japanese War (1894–5) 100
'Smash the Security Treaty' 26
Social Democratic Party of Japan (SDPJ) 13–14, 21, 29–30, 85, 86, 87, 108, 109, 110, 126
socialism 98; *see also* communism
Socialist Party 21, 85, 87; *see also* Social Democratic Party of Japan
Society for the Making of New School Textbooks in History 35
Sōken (creative constitutionalists) 4, 29
Somalia 111, 115, 137, 156
Song Festival for Constitutional Revision 15
Songs for National Independence 15
South China Seas 125
South Korea 21, 105, 119–20, 124, 149–50; *see also* Korea
Southeast Asia 138, 148, 151
sovereignty 4; popular 3, 5, 20, 24, 34, 36, 37, 40, 56, 173; imperial 4; national 158, 167
Soviet Union 3, 13, 99, 101–2, 105, 117–21, 123–5, 131, 148, 150–51, 154, 158, 162, 164

Special Civil Law 122
Suez Crisis 137
Sunagawa case 145
Supreme Court 19–20, 25, 145, 159, 165; Articles relating to 78, 79–81
supreme law 3, 91, Articles relating to 60, 85, 202
surveillance 29, 43, 169; Articles relating to 62; *see also* information
'symbolic emperor' system 3, 5–7, 9–13, 21, 24, 42, 173

Taiwan 118, 149
Takarazuka acting and dance troupe 15
Tamagushiryō decision 169
Tanaka, M. 43
Tanaka, S. 109
Tariff Special Law 122
taxation, Articles relating to 65, 81
Telecommunications Interception Bill 167
Thatcher, M. 171
Three Sacred Treasures 6
Tōjo, H. 100
Tokyo 15, 23–4, 26, 123, 174
Tokyo Metropolitan Assembly 160
Tokyo University 164
Torishima 25
torture, Articles relating to 66; *see also* imprisonment
Treaty for the Renunciation of War (1928) 86
Treaty of Non-Agression (1928) 106

Ueda, K. 109
Uehara, K. 109, 203
United Kingdom 14, 42–3, 129, 164; House of Commons 170; House of Lords 170–1
United Nations (UN) 168; Agreement Regarding the Status of Forces in Japan 122; Charter 33, 91, 95–6, 106, 153–4, 166, 168; Commission on Human Rights 22; security issues 91, 101, 106–7, 109, 120; Development Program Report on Human Development 154; Economic and Social Council 154, 157; Economic and Social Security Council 155–7; financial contributions to 33, 154; General Assembly 154–5; membership of 34, 39, 153; military intervention 116, 122; peacekeeping operations 22, 32, 39, 91, 98, 111, 137, 139–40, 142, 146, 156, 159, 166–7; Police Force 157; proposed reform of 96, 130, 131, 153–7, 167–8; Security Council (UNSC) 33, 37, 39, 44, 93, 122, 131, 154–7; support for 21; veto power 155
United States of America (US) 129, 154, 162, 164, 168; Bill of Rights 143; Cold War 39, 99–102, 105; Constitution 143; drafting of Japanese Constitution 6–8; economy 132; military presence in Japan 12, 17, 22–6, 38, 117–22, 131–2, 152; opposition to 24–6; 26–9, 30–1, 35, 110; perception of Japan 7, 164; police 113; political involvement in Asia-Pacific 12–13, 15, 124, 149–52; preferential treatment of 119, 122, 126, 151–2; support for 150; and United Nations 33, 122; *see also* Central Intelligence Agency, Gulf War, US-Japan Security Treaty, Vietnam
US-Japan Defense Cooperation Guidelines 118
US-Japan Joint Operations Study 126
US-Japan Security Treaty (*Ampo*) 40, 92–3; support for 36–7; constitutionality of 15–16, 40; demilitarization of 123–5; implementation 117–20; opposition to 16, 21–2, 26–9, 30–1; origins 14, 142; revision of 17, 108, 120–21, 124–5, 148, 149 151–2
US-Philippines Treaty 120, 124
US-Republic of China (Taiwan) Treaty 120
US-Republic of Korea Mutual Defense Treaty 119, 120, 124

Vietnam 13, 22, 24, 117
violence: by right-wing groups 12; crimes by US military personnel 25; *see also* torture, war crimes

Wada, H. 203
war crimes 6–7, 13, 100
warfare, conventional 104; nuclear *see* nuclear war; *see also* Cold War, Second World War
Warsaw Pact 108, 119
Washington 7
Watanabe, O. 110
Western European Union (WEU) 114
Woo, R. T. 124

X Day 12

Yamaguchi, J. 44
Yamahana, S. 29
Yamauchi, T. 112
Yamazaki, T. 19
Yasukuni Shrine 105
Yokosuka 118
Yokota 123
Yom Kippur War 138
Yomiuri Constitution Study Council (1992) 88
Yomiuri Shimbun 32, 38, 40–1; proposal 36–7, 55–91: amendments 84–4; Article 9 86–7, 89–90; Cabinet 74–8; civil rights 61–4; Diet 68–74, 74–8; the emperor 57–9; finance 82–3; human rights 60–1; international cooperation 59–60, 90–1; judiciary 78–81; legal rights 64–8; local government 83–4; national security 59; pacifism 86–7; Preamble 55–6; self defense 87–8; sovereign power 56
Yoshida, S. 8, 15, 30, 100–1, 106, 113, 142, 203
Yugoslavia 103

Zaire 33, 111, 116